SKETCHBOOK
SAILOR

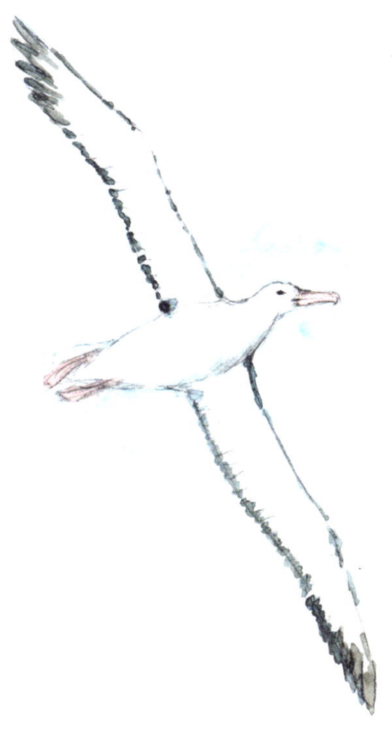

Published in 2020 by Golden Duck (UK) Ltd.
Sokens, Green Street, Pleshey, near Chelmsford,
Essex, CM3 1HT
golden-duck.co.uk

Written by Claudia Myatt

Illustrated by Claudia Myatt

Typeset by Bertie Wheen

Printed by Biddles Books Ltd.
biddles.co.uk

ISBN 978-1-899262-44-1

Also from Claudia Myatt
from Golden Duck Publishing

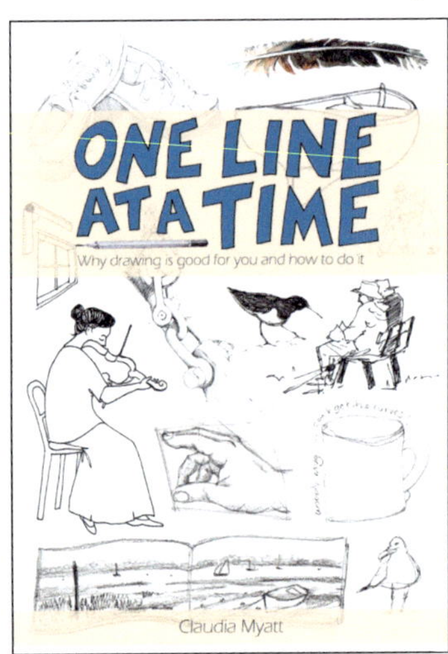

There's a world of difference between saying 'I want to' and 'I will'
(Bernard Moitessier)

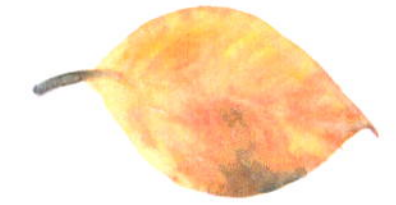

TECLA CREW LIST

GALAPAGOS TO EASTER ISLAND

2007 nautical miles, 13 days

Captain: Gijs Sluik   Netherlands
Mate: Krista Swedberg USA
Bosun: Will Armstrong   Tasmania
Crew: Nico Remkes   Netherlands

Voyage crew

Claudia Myatt   UK
George McLeod   UK (Scotland)
Annette Seifert   New Zealand
Marty Brash   New Zealand
Theo Winkel   Netherlands
Chris Forrest   UK
Alison Stephens   UK
Robert Richardson   Eire
Carter Barker   USA
Chris Barker   USA
Michelle Holian   Australia

EASTER ISLAND TO FALKLANDS

3700 nautical miles, 27 days

Captain: Jet Sluik   Netherlands
Mate: Krista Swedberg USA
Bosun: Will Armstrong   Tasmania
Crew: Enki

Voyage crew:

Claudia Myatt   UK
Siyu Chen   USA
Russ Melin   USA
David Wood   USA
Paul   Australia
Kate Garner   UK
Melanie Port   UK
Dennis Stratmann   Germany
Kersten   Germany

CONTENTS

I returned from my voyaging in January 2020, when reports were starting to appear on the news of a dangerous new virus in China. By February Covid-19 was spreading worldwide and on 23rd March, to reduce the rate of infection, the UK was put into lockdown. All unnecessary travel, work and human contact was banned. The sudden closing down of ordinary life was shocking at first. We had no way of knowing whether the supermarkets would be able to provide enough food, or how we would manage financially. It was like running into a brick wall, trying to come to terms with this strange new world in which we were unable even to meet our friends.

During the uneasy early days of that strange time I was able to gather my notes and sketchbooks together and write this book. As the year went on the pandemic showed no signs of ending. Restrictions were eased in the summer, then tightened again as infection numbers varied. At the time of going to press, November 2020, we have become accustomed to this 'new normal' and have hopes that next year and the possibility of a vaccine will enable restrictions to be lifted.

March, 2020

We're facing a period of isolation for at least a month, probably more. There's nowhere to go except my own small space and the view won't change. Nothing to do but sleep, eat, read, get a bit of exercise each day, prepare to be anxious and at times uncomfortable, knowing that when it's over our views about the world will have changed. Don't look too far ahead, just take it one day at a time.....

I'm writing this during the coronavirus pandemic, the first week of lockdown as we face the unfamiliar and struggle to find a new routine. Those first sentences also reflected my feelings as I set off on a sailing ship voyage down the Pacific Ocean, south to the Southern Ocean and around Cape Horn. There's no contest - I would rather do that again, with all its challenges and discomforts, than go through this uncertain time, in spite of the fact that I'm charting these new and alarming waters of isolation in the warm cabin of the little ship that I live on, safely tethered to the shore.

The word 'isolation' was thrilling when I set off on my travels. Cities hold no appeal for me. I was hungry for the wide open spaces and the thought of several weeks at sea on a small boat out of sight of land, with nothing to see but the sea, was both exciting and daunting. Challenges that we've chosen ourselves (and paid for!) are a whole lot easier to deal with than the sort the world throws at us.

The rebellious side of 60

In 2018 I was 62, the age where you start thinking: 'If not now - when?'. I'm not brave, not particularly fit and although I love the idea of travel and new experiences, each year seemed to bring a gradual loss of confidence. This was annoying; I wanted a wholehearted participation in my life and the precious time that is left. It was in this dangerous state of mind that I read an email from Classic

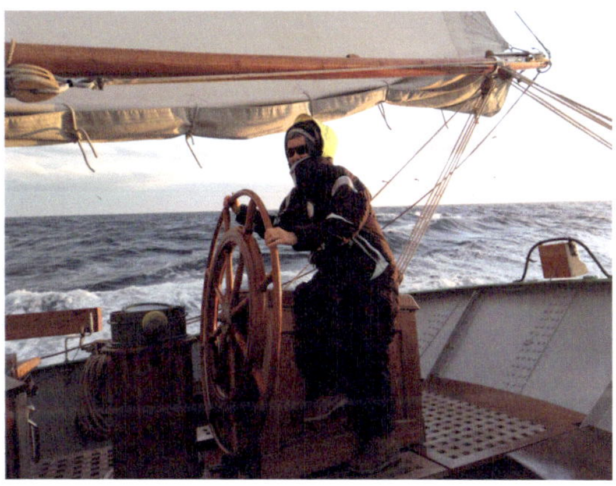

Picture by George Macleod

Sailing, the travel agency for traditional boats, telling me about an opportunity in November 2019 to sail from Galapagos to Easter Island on *Tecla*, a Dutch sailing ship.

I've sailed on many traditional boats, but never far from shore, and have always wondered what it would be like making a long ocean passage. And I have always been fascinated by islands; I've lived on several, travelled to over 40 of them, and both Galapagos and Easter Island were on my wish list.

It was a long way to go, though, for three weeks, a lot of long haul flying. I looked at where *Tecla* was going after Easter Island. Oh dear, she was going to the Falklands, another name on my island wish list and a more straightforward flight home. It was a long voyage from Easter Island to Falkland, over three weeks at sea, and there were two good reasons not to do it. Firstly, I was about to blow almost all of my rainy day savings. Secondly, we would have to sail around Cape Horn. Even landlubbers have heard of Cape Horn, dreaded by sailors for centuries, the inhospitable stretch of water between the tip of South America and Antarctica where wind and wave travel unhindered round the globe.

Modern navigation aids and weather forecasting have now made the passage safer, and indeed it can be done on a cruise ship, but it's still a big deal for small boat sailors. Could I cope with big waves, strong winds, being cold, wet and thrown around for a couple of weeks? Perhaps it was time I found out. Rainy day savings? I decided it was pouring, and booked the trip.

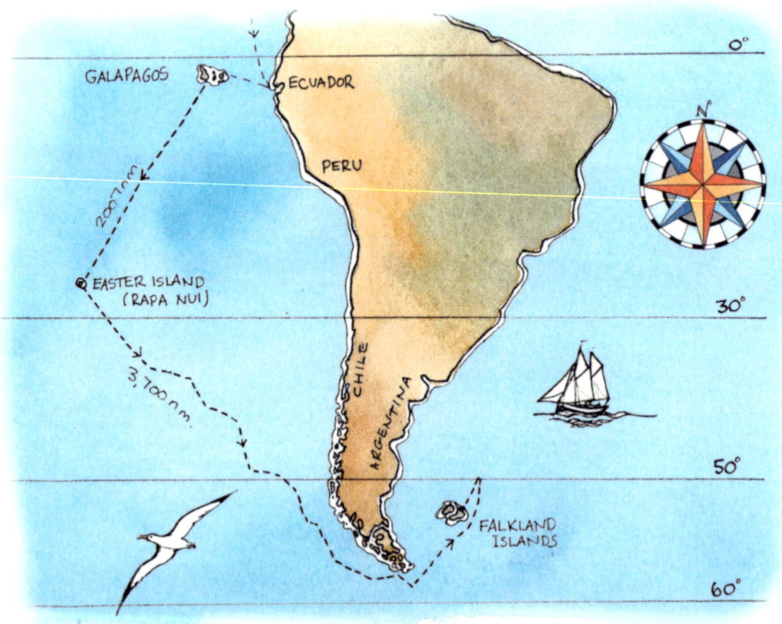

A little ship

Tecla is 28m on deck and weighs 120 tons. Built of steel in 1915 as a herring drifter she is strong, well equipped, well run and has been round the world once already. She is owned and sailed by a Dutch family - brother and sister team Gijs and Jet Sluik take turns to lead the boat with a professional crew of three and up to 12 paying 'voyage crew' on each trip.

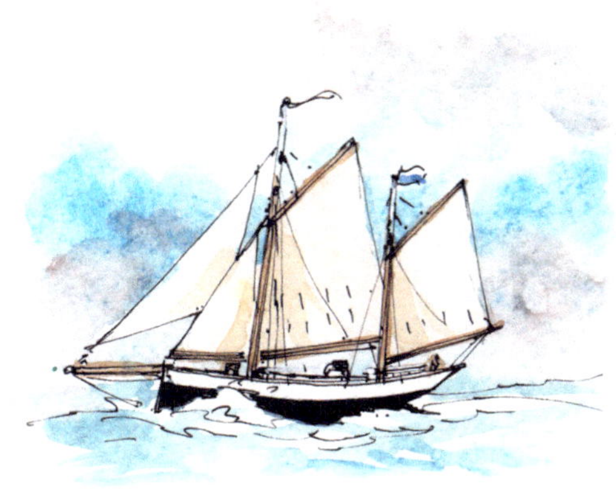

Tecla spent many years chartering in European waters, particularly the Hebrides, but both Gijs and Jet have a love of more adventurous sailing, particularly if icebergs are involved somewhere along the way.

Her 2019 cruise, two years in the planning, has been the most ambitious yet as it effectively amounted to a circumnavigation of the Americas. From Holland she headed north to Shetlands, Faroes, Iceland, Greenland, through the Northwest Passage to the Bering Straits, down the Pacific coast of Alaska, Canada and then to Galapagos. After Falklands her route took her to Antarctica, South Georgia and Cape Town where she was delayed in quarantine before heading back up the Atlantic home to the Netherlands.

What, no camera?

Early on in my planning stage I made a decision to take no camera with me. I used my phone for the few photos and videos that I did take, but I think that in general, because taking photos has never been easier, we over-use them. I have noticed on my travels that for many, taking a photo has become a reflex action, an automatic response to a new experience or place. I wonder whether we are becoming de-sensitised to photos so that they have less and less impact? And are we losing the ability to convey our experiences in words and sketches - tools that early explorers had to use with as much skill as they could manage, whether or not they considered themselves artists or writers?

Making thoughts visible

Photographs show you what's there; a sketchbook can offer a more personal viewpoint. A sketch should be able to express what you felt about what you saw, what grabbed, inspired, amused and impressed you. I wanted to see if I could resist the habit of reaching for the camera at every new place, be content to try and deepen my appreciation by recording it in my own way using the language of words and sketches. Or perhaps not record it at all - sometimes it's quite liberating to be simply in the moment, without the need to post a photo on social media and say 'look at me! look where I am! look at this!'

You are probably now thinking, 'Well that's all very well if you can draw, but I can't.' I believe that if you'd like to learn to draw, then you can. I recommend it. Your drawings don't have to be perfect - even a bad sketch will have made you look at something with total attention and concentration. Most of us were fortunate enough to be taught to write and we use words freely in our diaries without worrying about how 'good' our writing is.

Most of us weren't taught how to draw but it's never too late to learn the language of line if you're happy to put in a bit of enjoyable effort and learn a few skills. You can already 'read' pictures, but you've not been taught the alphabet to 'write' pictures. I wasn't a natural, I had to learn how. I'm still learning.

I wonder if the over-use of photos has made us a little bit lazy with words, too? Are we losing our powers of description? I'm not sure, it's just a thought. Maybe I spend too much time studying the notes and log books of maritime explorers, who had only words and illustrations to describe things that they had never seen before.

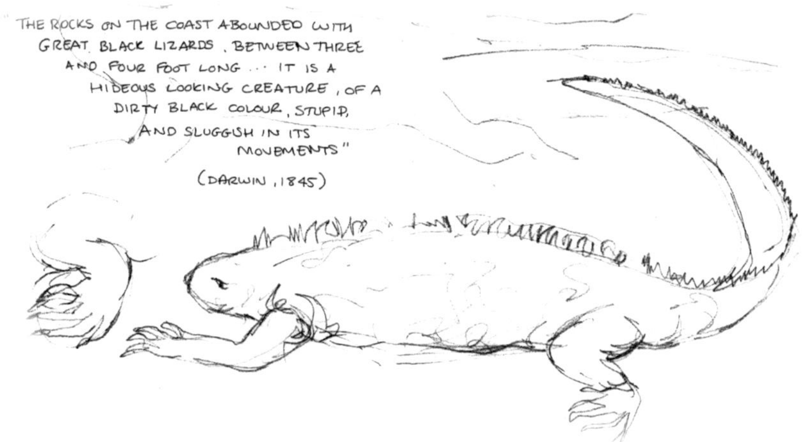

The journey begins...

6th November 2019, three flights:
Heathrow to Bogota, Bogata to Quito,
Quito to Galapagos, arriving at
Puerto Ayora on Santa Cruz in the
afternoon of 7th November.

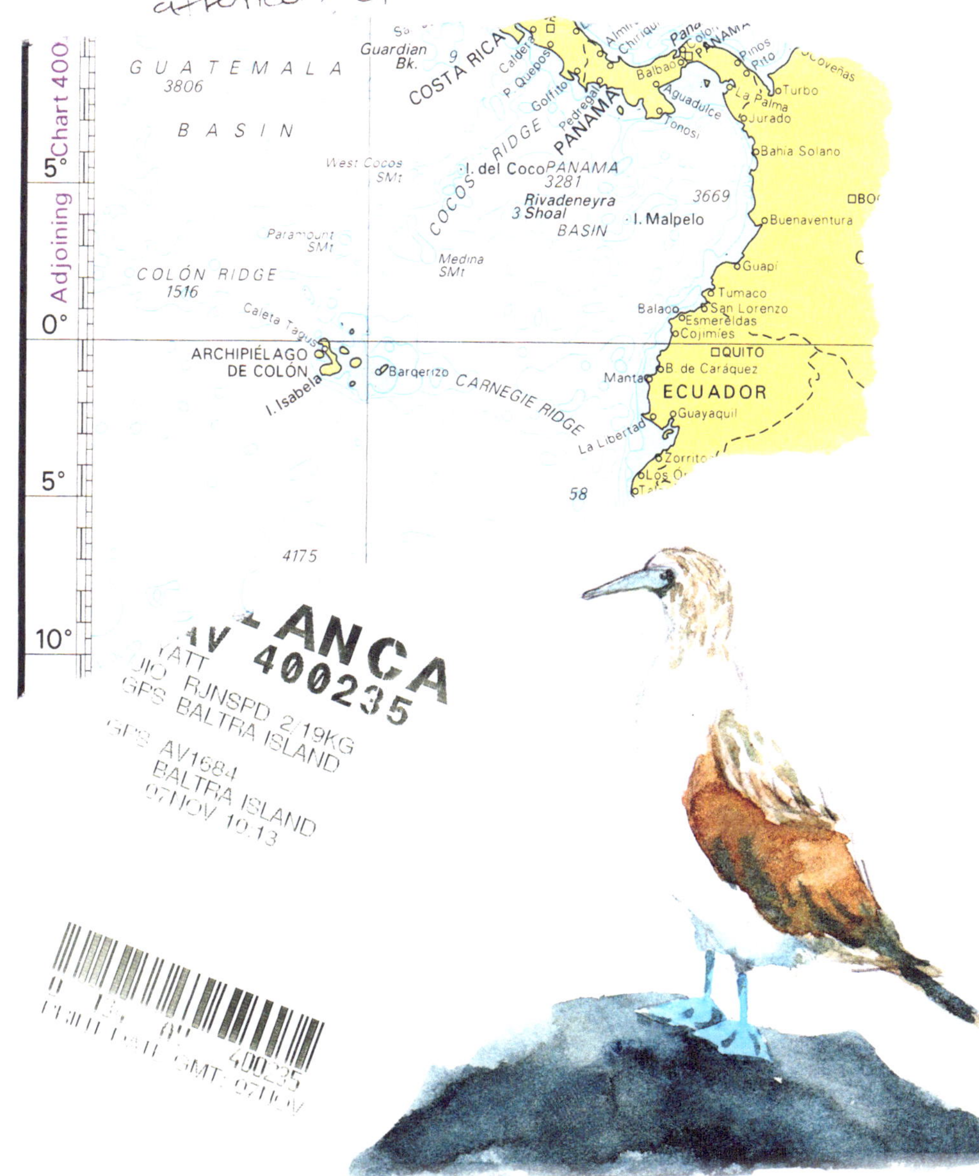

Puerto Ayora, Santa Cruz, Galapagos Islands

I've always wanted to visit these unusual islands which lie off the coast of Ecuador. They inspired Charles Darwin, host species of wildlife that are unique to the islands, and because of their recent geological age, give us a taste of what life on earth would have been millennia ago. When you stand on a volcanic island where foliage is only starting to appear and lizards are the only wildlife, it's like time travelling to our world when it was new.

I have to confess that I'm not a good traveller. I dislike flying, find airports stressful, and worry continually that I've forgotten to pack something essential. But when the anxiety of the journey is over, it's all worth it. Our small plane landed safely on a small island, my luggage turned up and I had the right paperwork. I negotiated a bus, ferry and a bumpy taxi ride in a pick up truck with a cheery driver who couldn't speak English and chatted away in French when I said I had no Spanish. After 30 hours travelling I could barely summon a word of French and made do with nodding and saying 'Ah oui, bien sur!' at regular intervals.

My hostel was basic but clean. There was no room key and the wiring on the shower looked decidedly dodgy, but it was only $25 a night and that was just fine. At last I could sleep as long as I wanted and then wake up hungry, work out whether it's morning or evening, what local time is and where I've hidden all my dollars. Then the magic begins. I take those first steps outside, not knowing what I'm going to see but hungry to see it, and knowing that a bar with a glass of wine and something to eat is also going to feature fairly soon. Do you know the intense pleasure of that first walk of discovery in a new country? All senses are alert, alive with colours, sights and smells. I'm aware of everything, the feel of my crumpled summer clothes and sandals, a soft warm breeze on my skin, the smell of the wind blowing off the sea. I take a delight in that first sight of a new place, knowing that in a few days the walk from hostel to harbour will be familiar, that I'll expect to find sea lions slumbering on the quayside benches and learn to step over large black marine iguanas basking on the sunny pavements.

It always takes me a while in a new place to get into the sketching habit but I took my painting gear out on the first day and stopped to draw the frigate birds squabbling like seagulls over the fish market. My first sketches are always a bit uncertain until I get used to a new place, but it's good to try and get colour on straight away. I found a bench near the fish market that wasn't occupied by a sea lion and made a start.

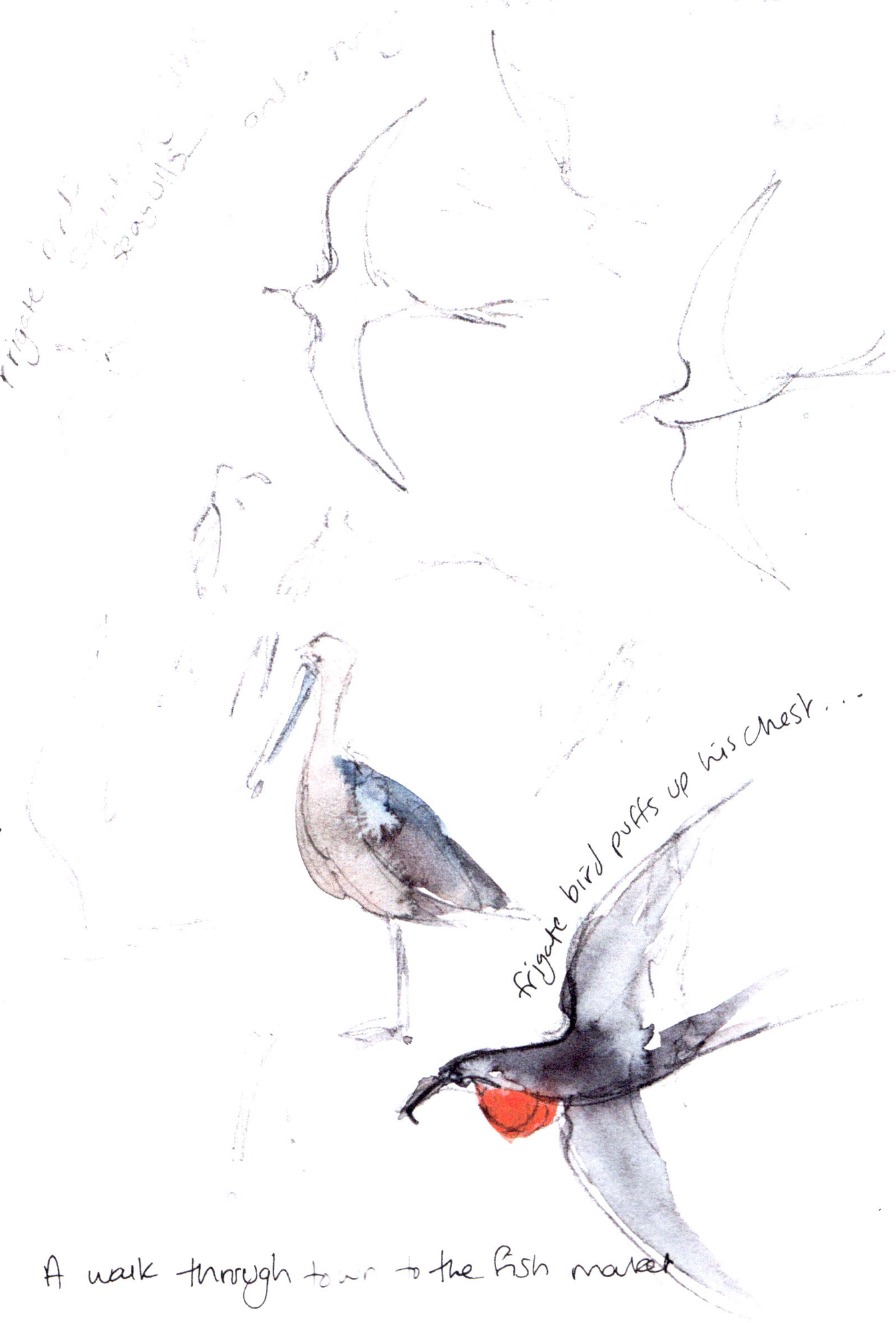
Frigate bird puffs up his chest . . .
A walk through town to the fish market

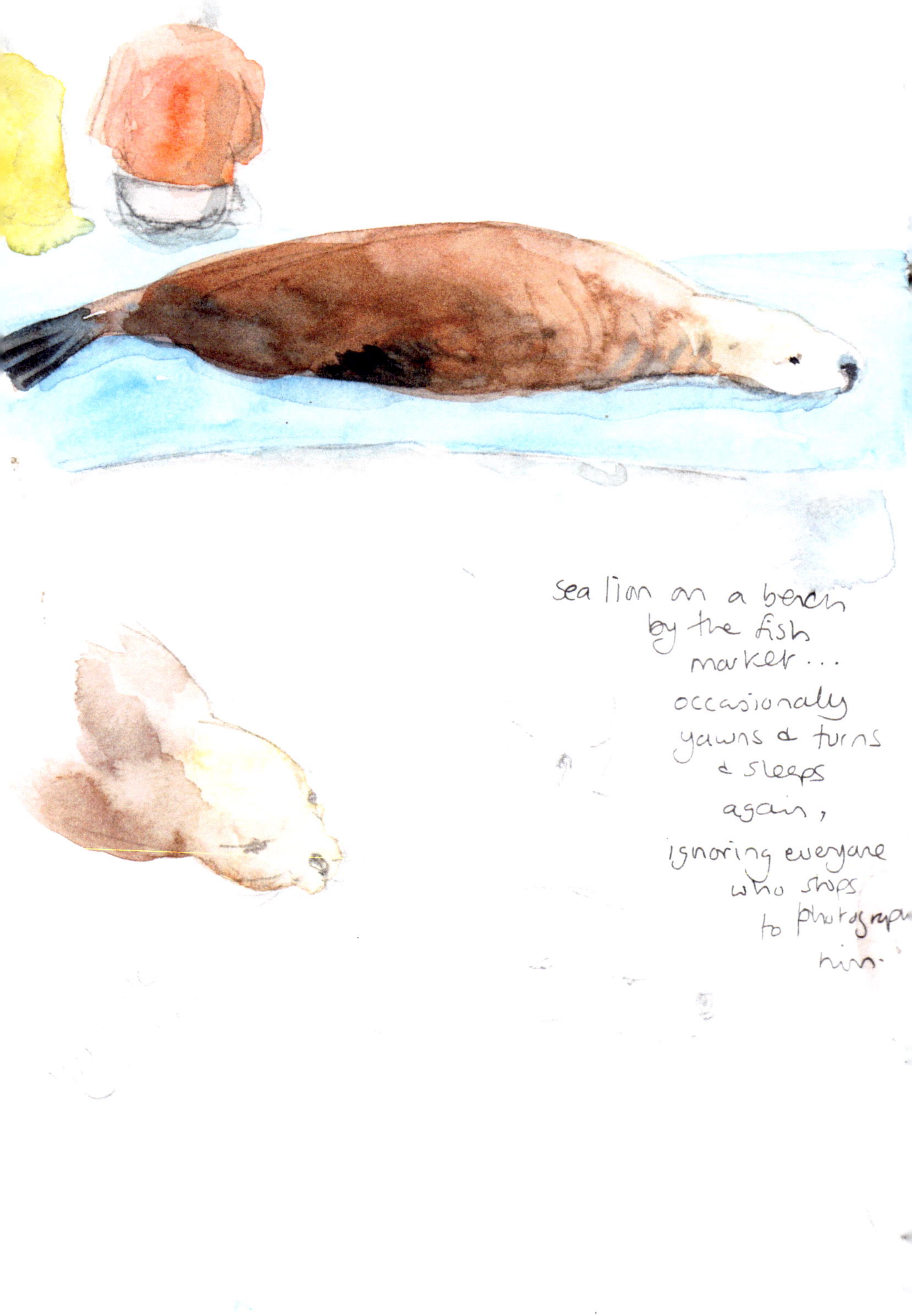
sea lion on a bench
by the fish
market...
occasionally
yawns & turns
& sleeps
again,
ignoring everyone
who stops
to photograph
him.

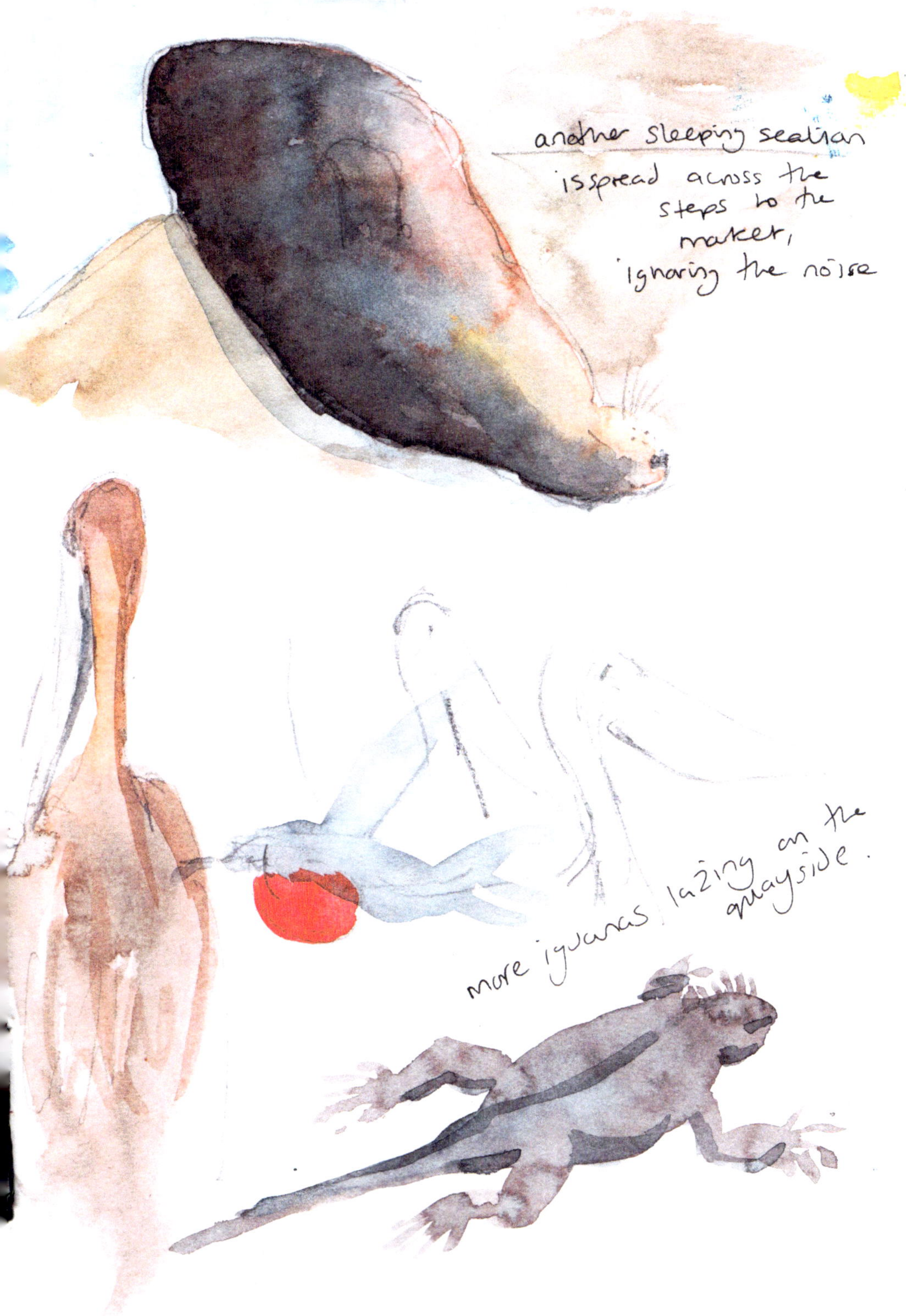

another sleeping sealion
is spread across the
steps to the
market,
ignoring the noise
more iguanas lazing on the
quayside.

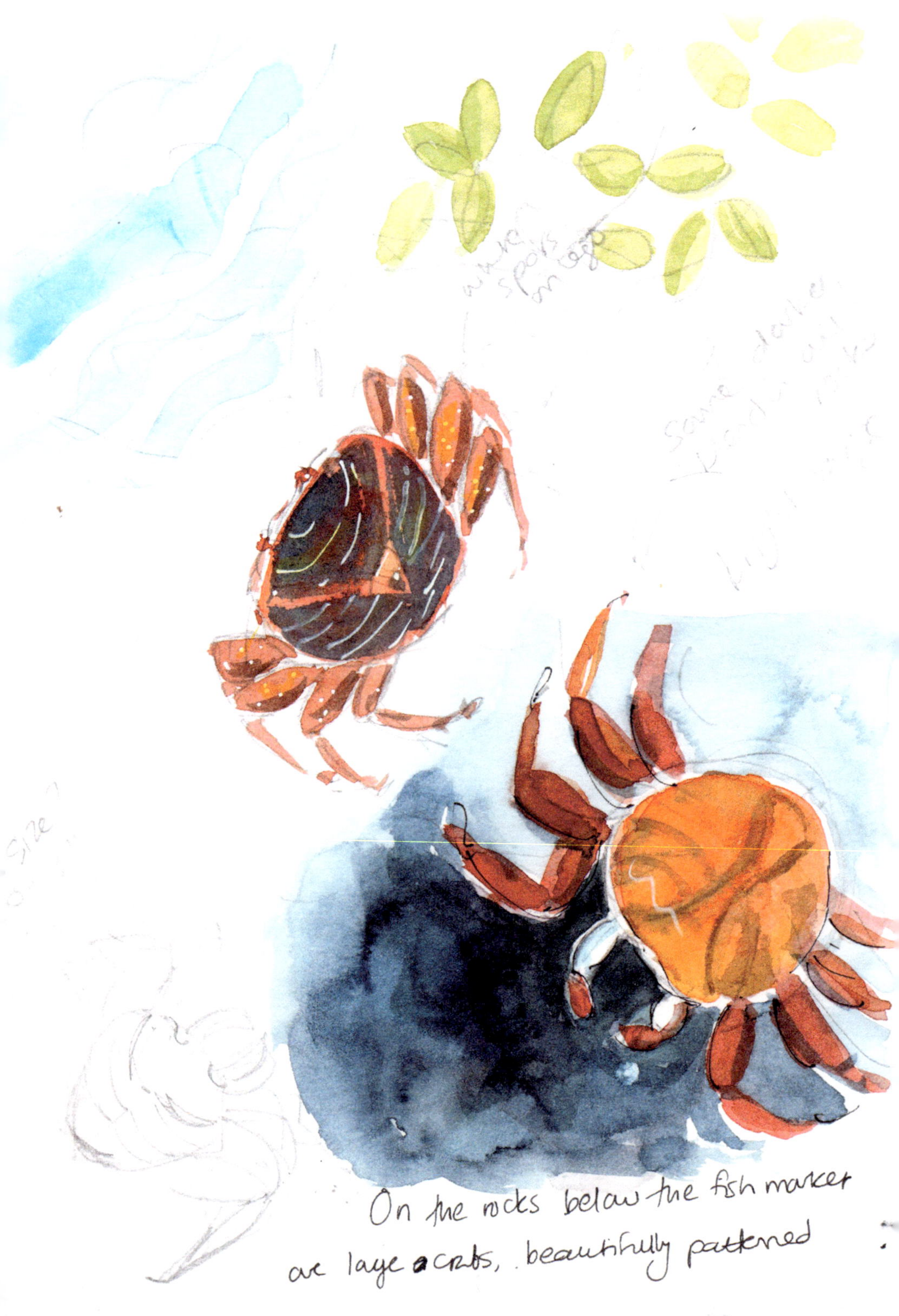

On the rocks below the fish market
are large crabs, beautifully patterned

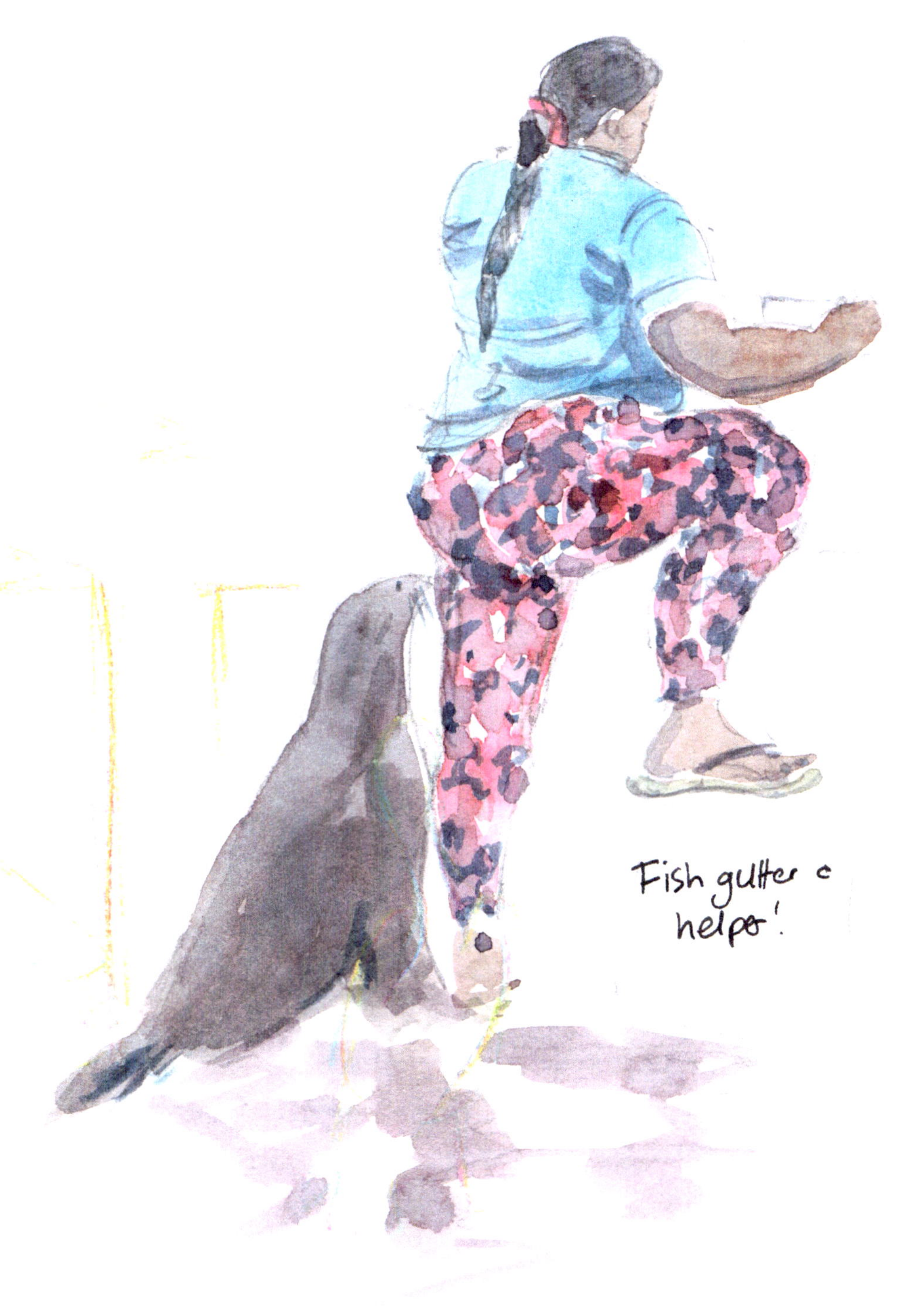
Fish gutter e
helper!

The Galapagos islands are all designated National Park and there are limits to how far you can explore alone. Outside the town you have to stick to the paths or take a tour with a National Park guide, but as for the most part the terrain is rocky and overgrown there is little temptation to stray from the paved route. Plenty of tour companies offer cruises of the islands and I'm so glad I had booked a three day trip on a small and well appointed ship around some of the more remote places. I was left with the feeling, especially on the uninhabited islands, that we humans are the visitors, the invasive species.

Our group was small, our guides knowledgeable, and in spite of being the only one who was sketching rather than photographing, I filled a few pages. I walked with sketchbook and pencil, drawing whenever we stopped to look at something and listen to our guide. Adding watercolours whilst standing is not easy, but I had a go. Sometimes I chose to make notes and add colour once I was back on the boat.

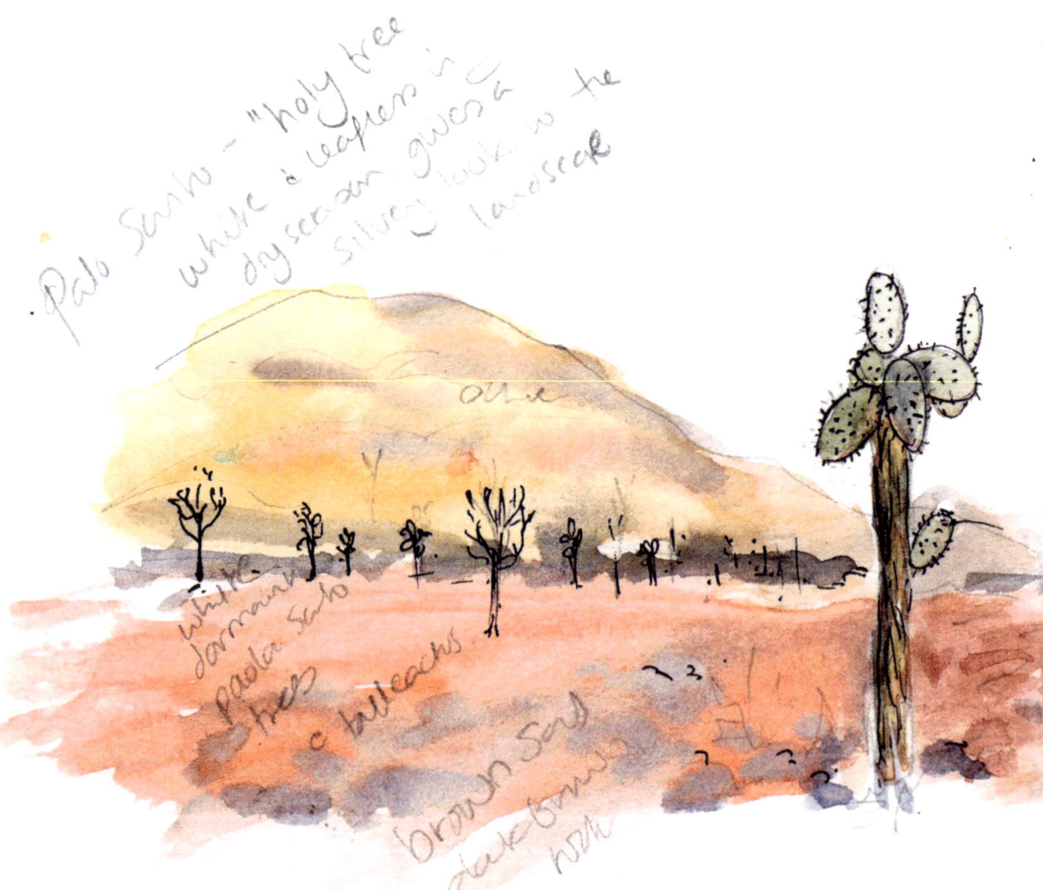

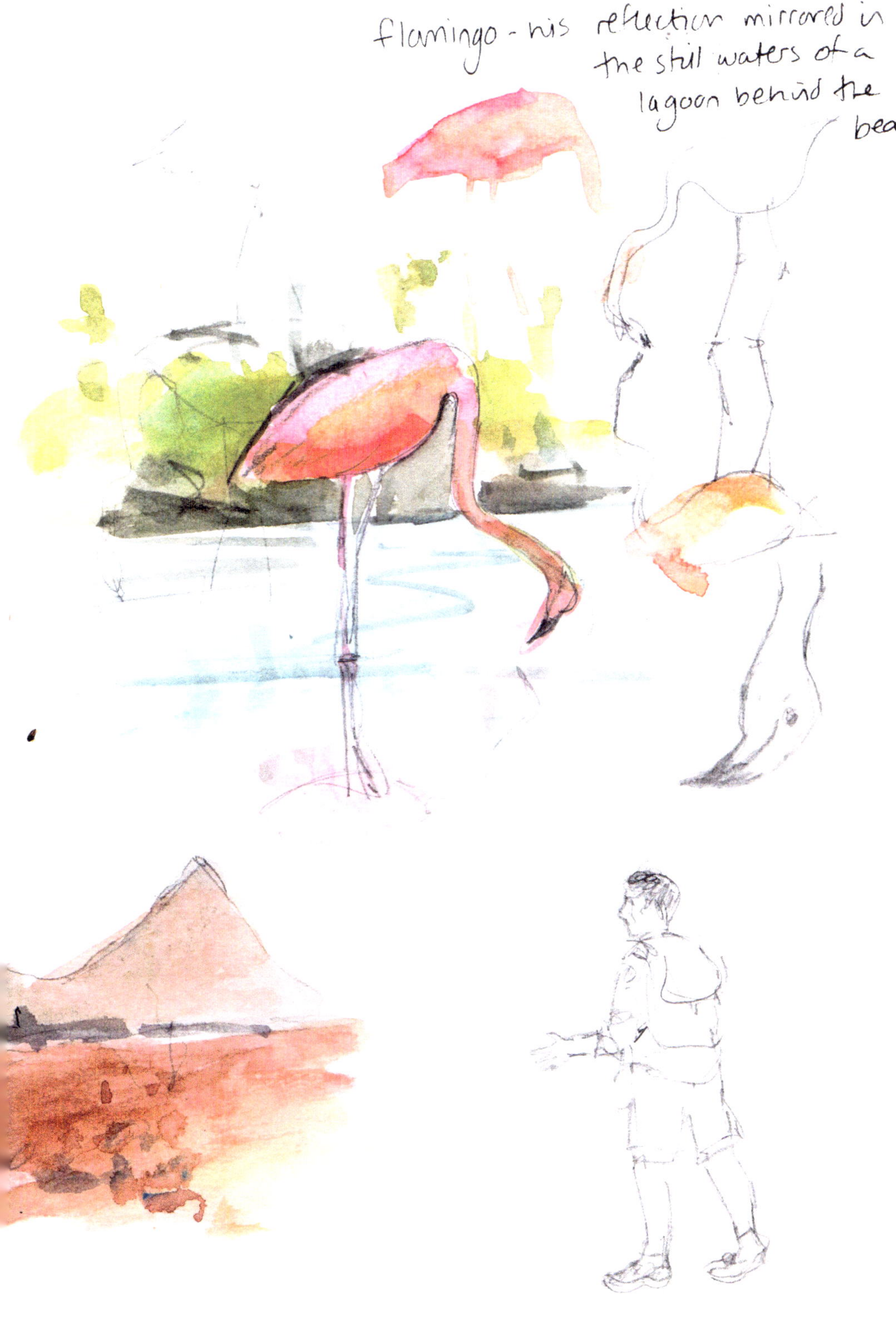

flamingo - his reflection mirrored in
the still waters of a
lagoon behind the
beach

Land iguanas are much harder to find than the smaller black marine iguanas, which are everywhere. Their colouring blends in with the surrounding countryside, and because we are not permitted to stray from the path, we depend on the guide to spot one if he can. Everyone else took their cameras out for this lovely specimen, which was about a metre long, so I didn't have much time. I drew the shape and made a few colour notes, then finished the drawing when we were back on board the ship. Not having much time to draw on the spot does wonders for your colour memory. If I'd taken a photo, it would have looked more accurate, certainly, but I think less exciting. Colour is as much an emotional response as a physical pigment.

I found the Darwin quote in a book on the ship. I thought it was a bit mean and rather unscientific of him to say the iguanas were ugly animals with a 'singularly stupid appearance'! But we mustn't forget that Charles Darwin was a young man when he visited the islands and he certainly at that stage in his life wasn't a scientist. He just had the benefit of an inquisitive mind.

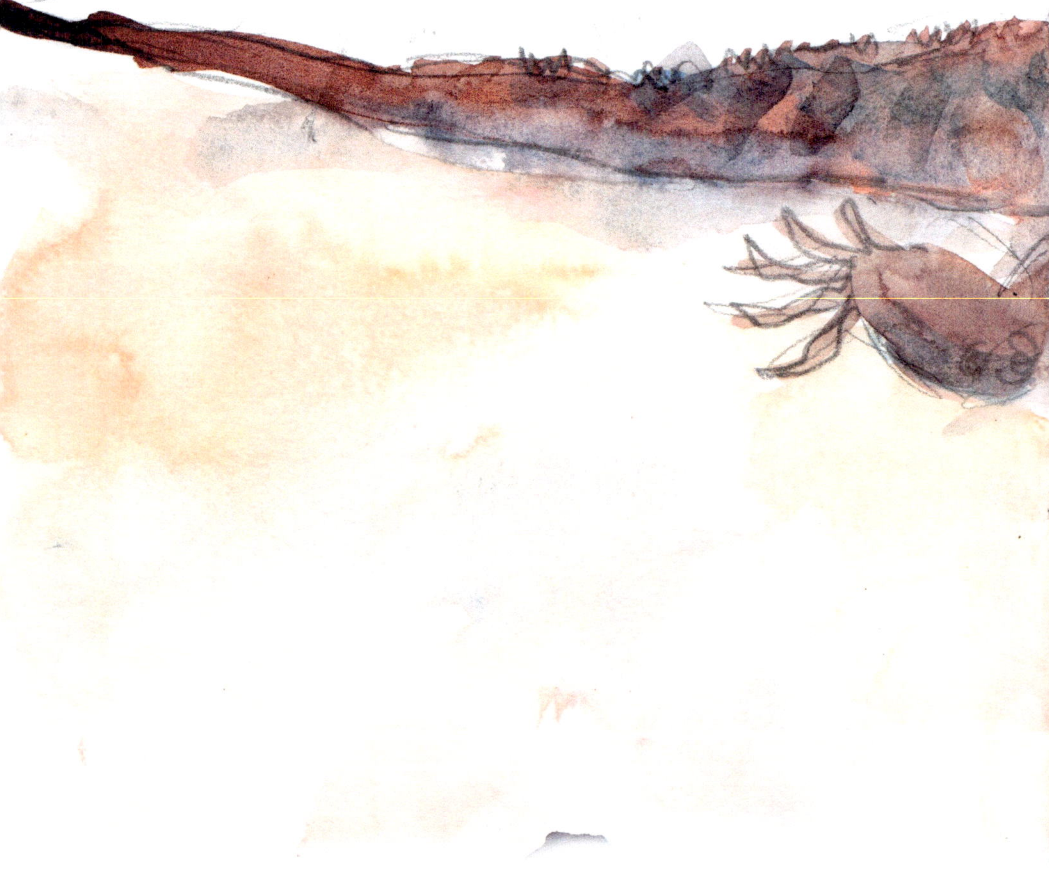

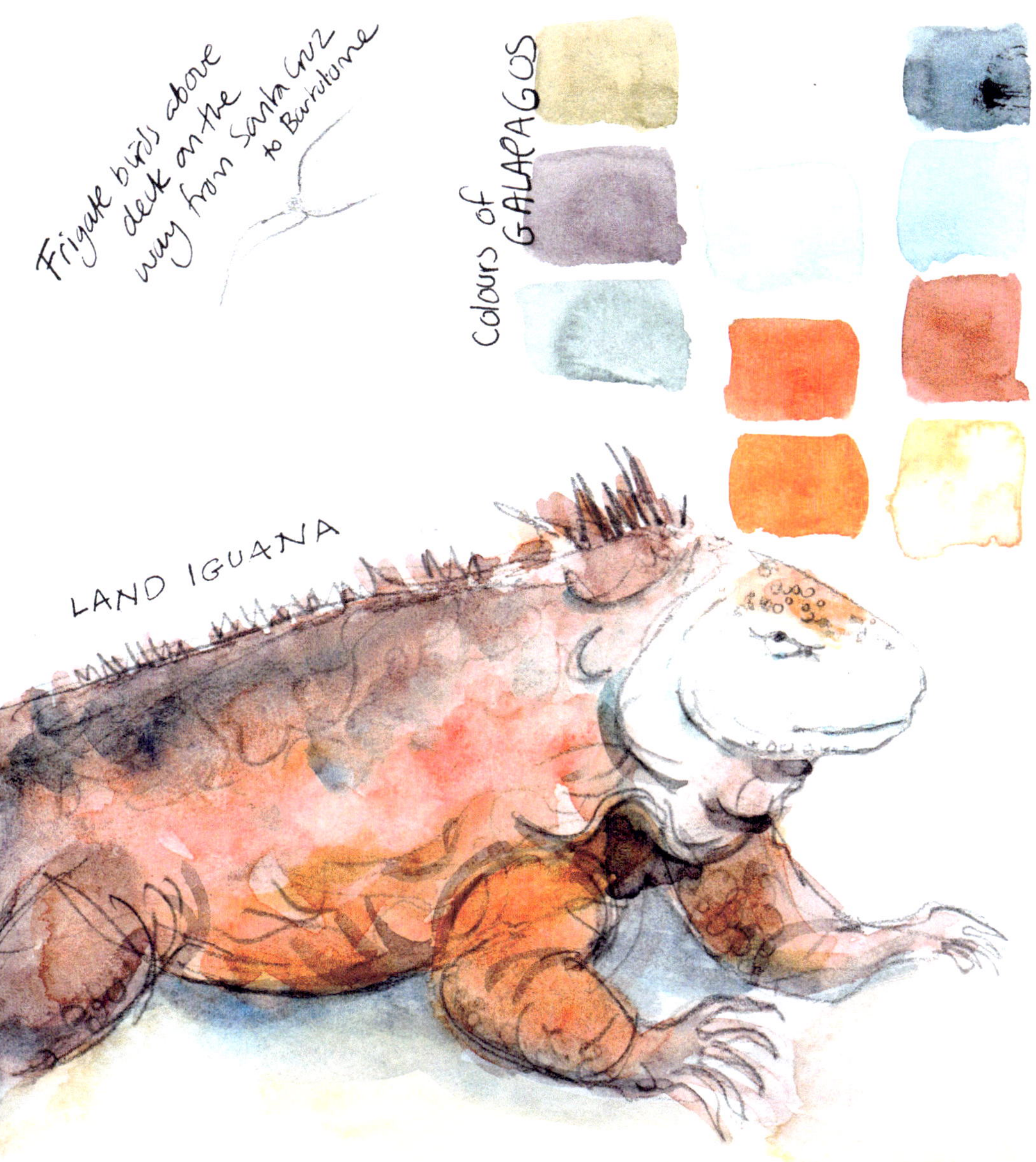

Frigate birds above deck on the way from Santa Cruz to Barrutone
Colours of GALAPAGOS
LAND IGUANA
"LIKE THEIR BROTHERS OF THE SEA-KIND. THEY ARE UGLY ANIMALS, OF A YELLOWISH ORANGE BENEATH, AND OF A BROWNISH RED COLOUR ABOVE: FROM THEIR LOW FACIAL ANGLE THEY HAVE A SINGULARLY STUPID APPEARANCE"
(Darwin, 1845)

RABIDA ISLAND

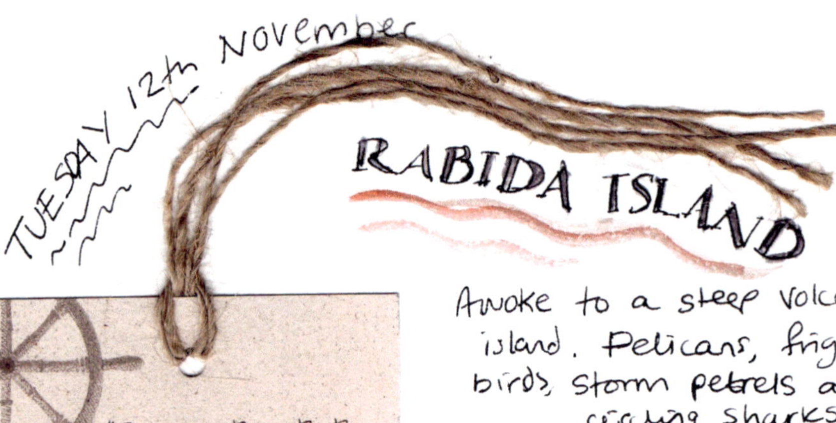

Awoke to a steep volcanic island. Pelicans, frigate birds, storm petrels and circling sharks ...

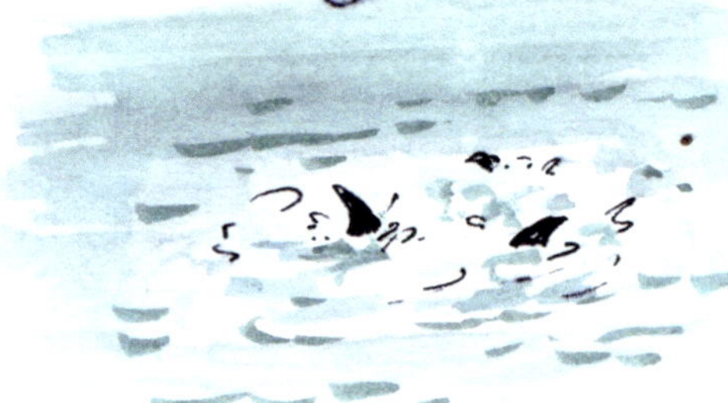

... worrying to see that we will be snorkelling this morning!

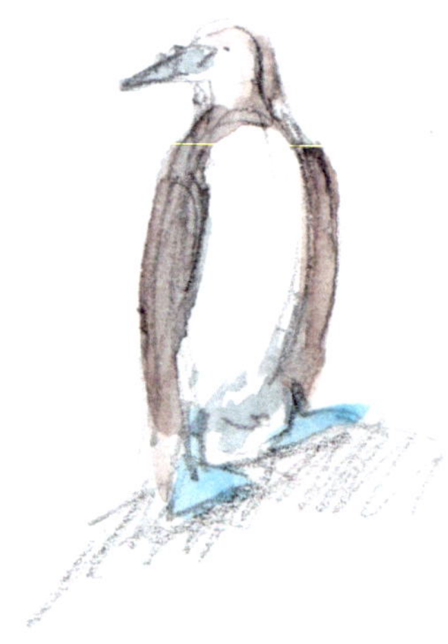

"I am not apt to follow blindly the lead of other men."

"Yo no estoy apto para seguir ciegamente las directrices de otros hombres."

"Eu não estou apto para seguir cegamente as diretrizes de outros homens."

"Es liegt mir nicht, den Vorgaben anderer blind zu folgen."

Laboratory of Evolution 1835

"Je ne suis pas apte à suivre aveuglément les directives d'autres hommes."

"Io non sono inclini a seguire ciecamente le linee guida di altri uomini."

Charles Darwin

ESPUMILLE BEACH, SANTIAGO ISLAND

Furred sealions, blue footed boobies, pelicans, ...
we take a dinghy tour & then spend time on a
long white sandy beach, backed by ~~bl~~ bleached-white
mangrove trees. water is crystal clear. As I snorkel
a large sea lion comes up close and swims around
me, just to show off

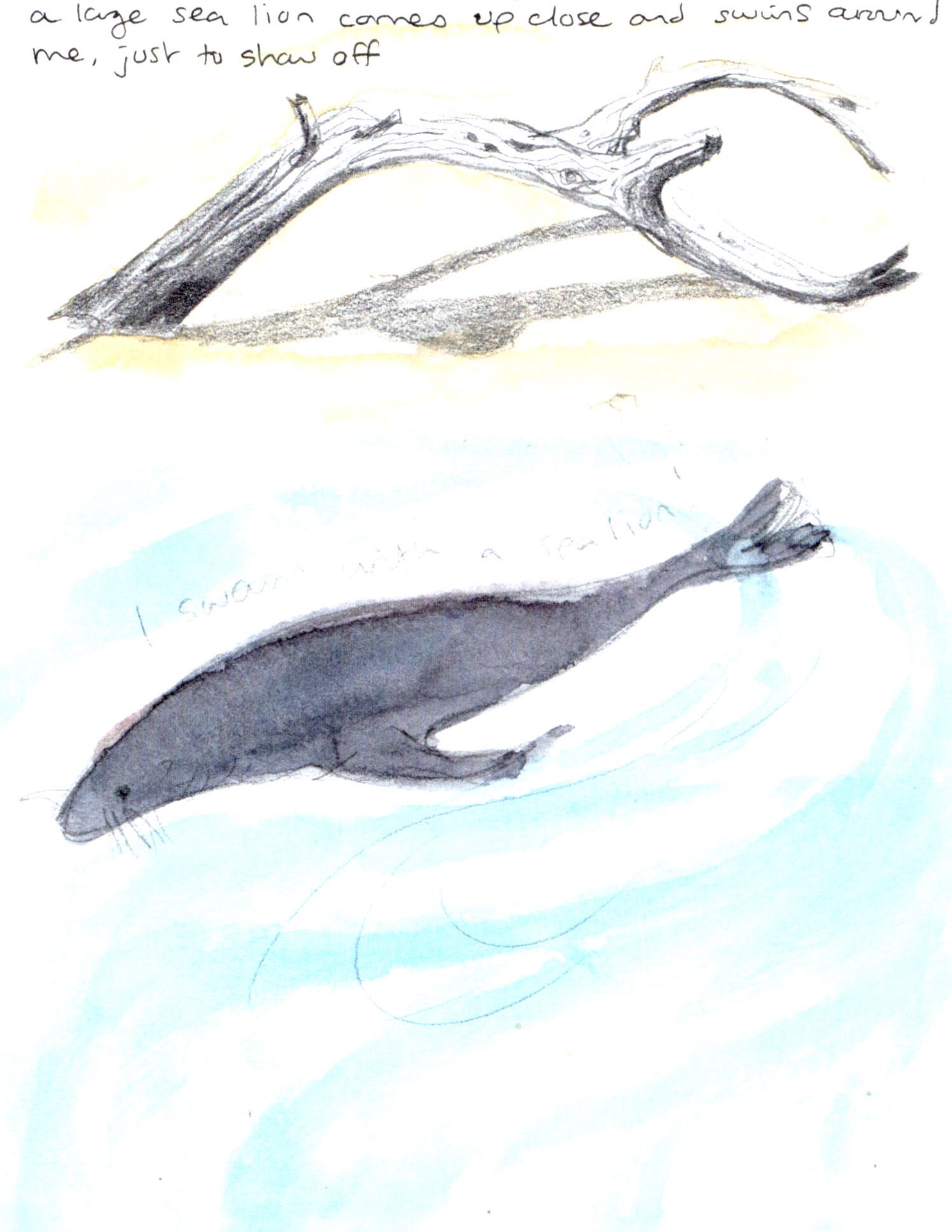

Wednesday 13th November   7.00am, a snoozing
                          visitor on the stern
                          of Coral I

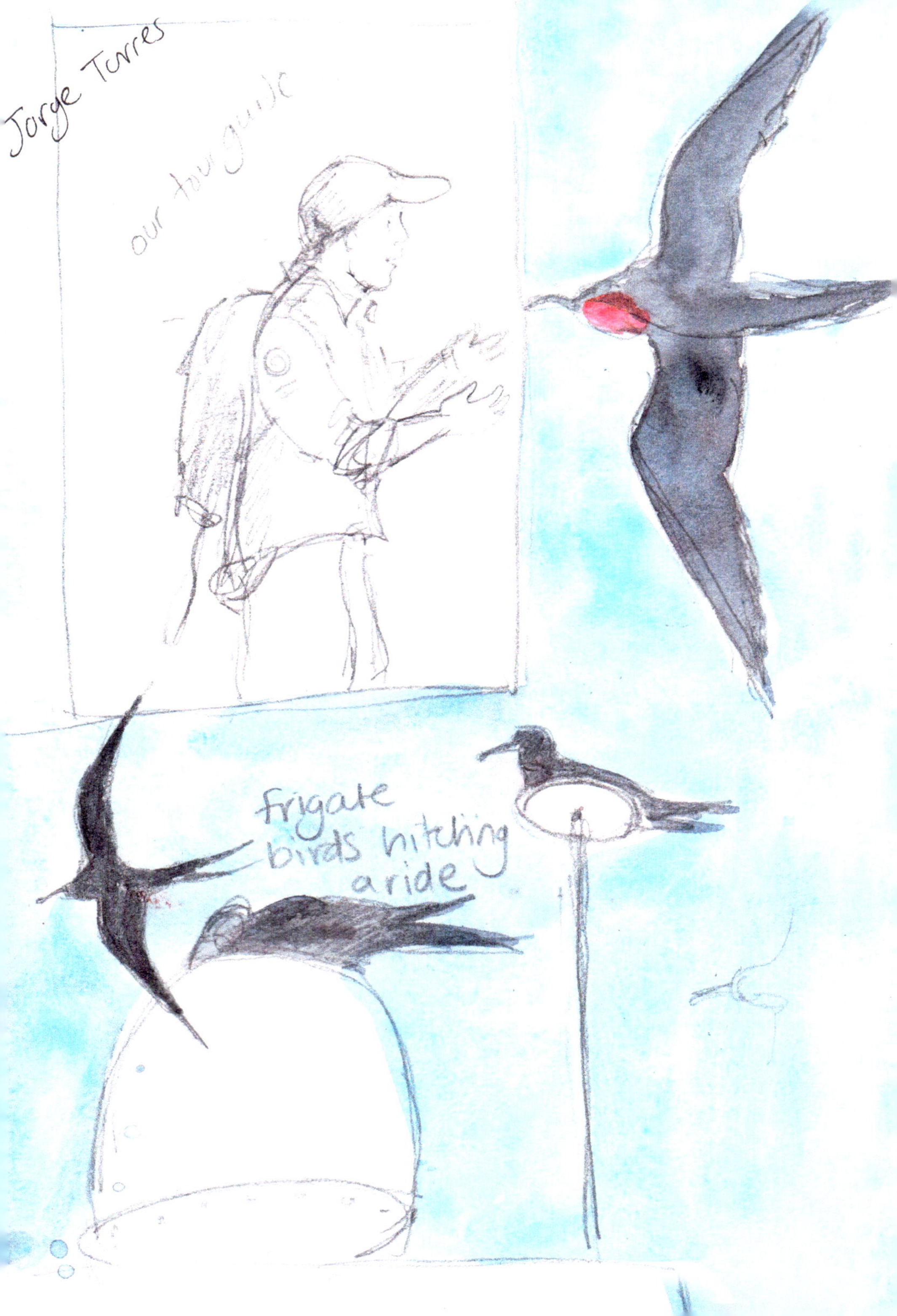

Jorge Torres

our tour guide

frigate
birds hitching
a ride

8.00am dinghy ride to Black Turtle Cove, Santa Cruz

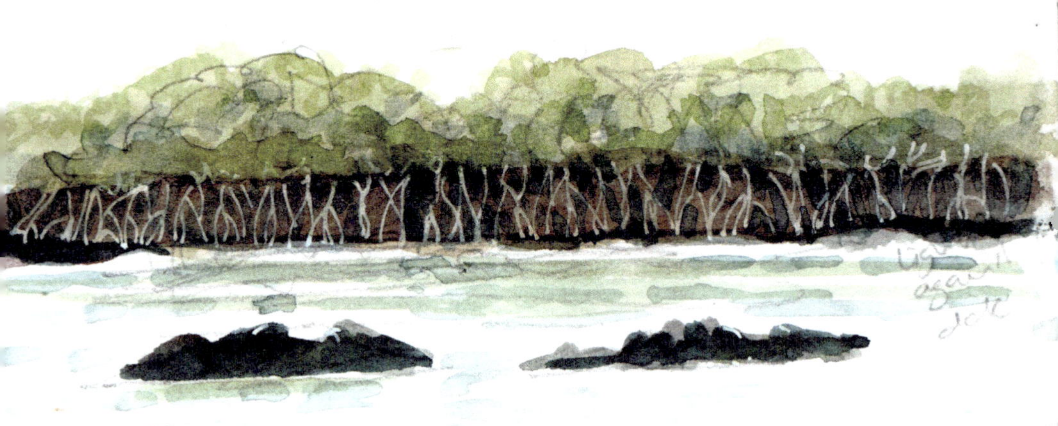

network of mangrove creeks, shallow water
alive with turtles, rays, white tipped sharks

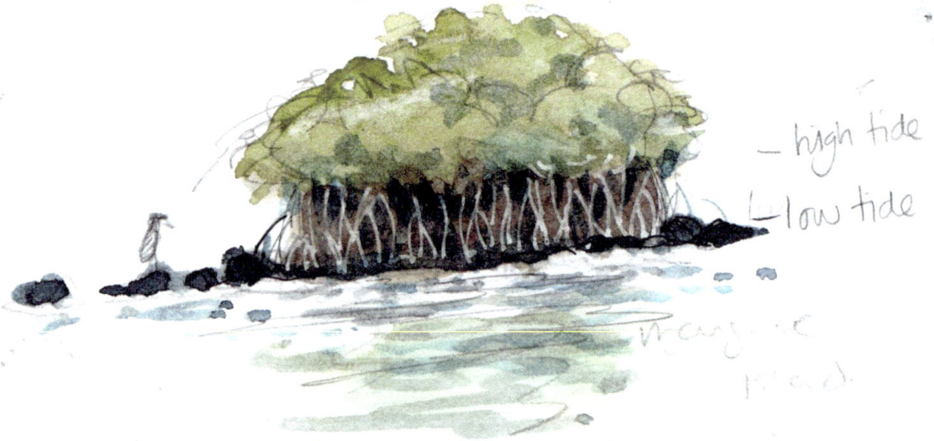

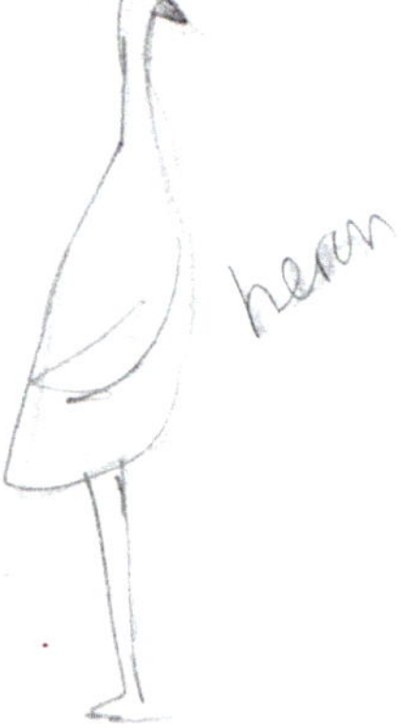

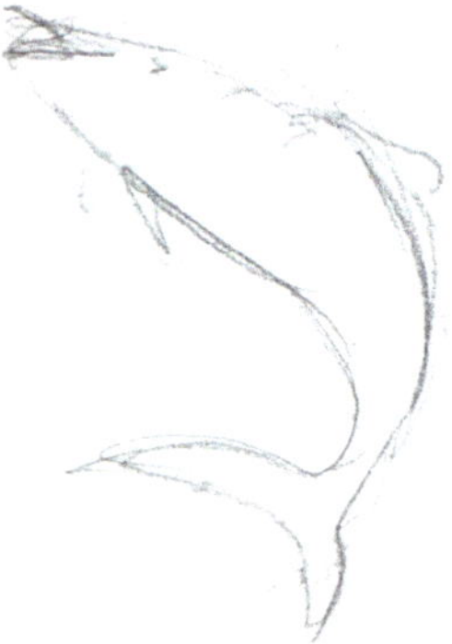

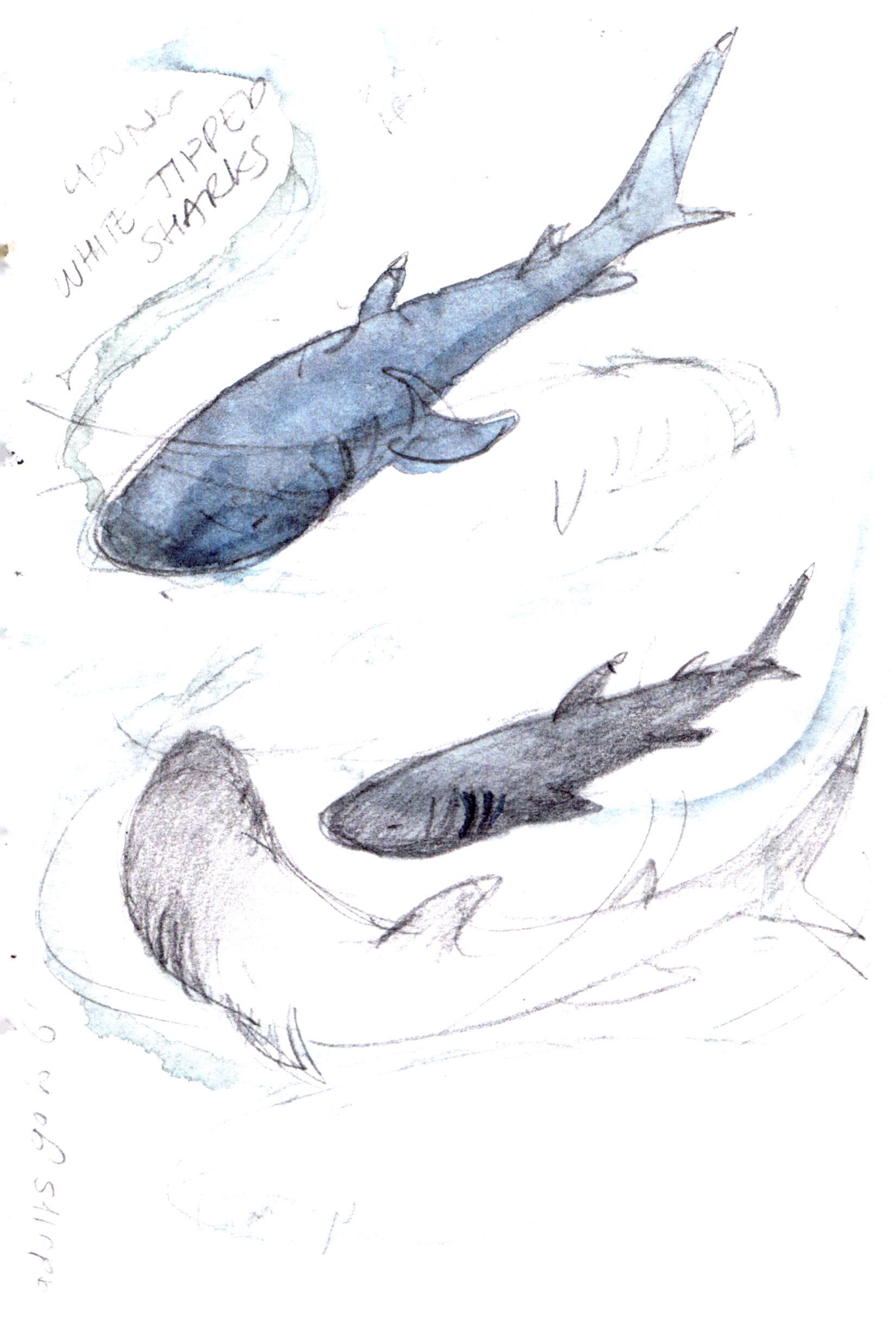

YOUNG
WHITE-TIPPED
SHARKS
adults gone ?

Beneath the surface at Black Turtle Cove

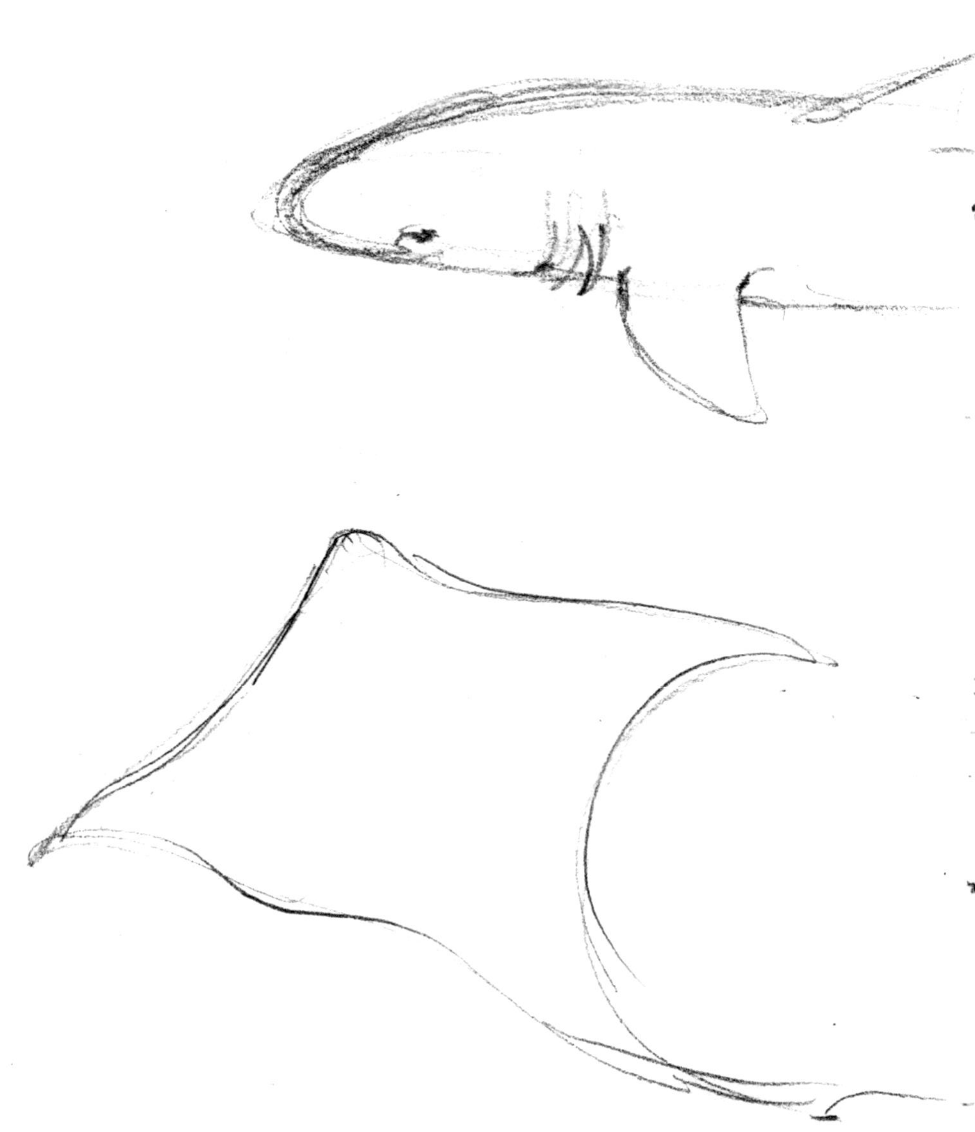

It was impossible to get my paintbox out whilst squashed into a small rubber dinghy with half a dozen others, so I just took a pencil and sketchbook on this tour of mangrove creeks then added colour later from memory on some sketches. Our guide knew just where to nudge the boat into the branches, cut the engine and wait. We talked in whispers to avoid scaring off the white-tipped sharks, rays and turtles that swam around and under us in the shallow water.

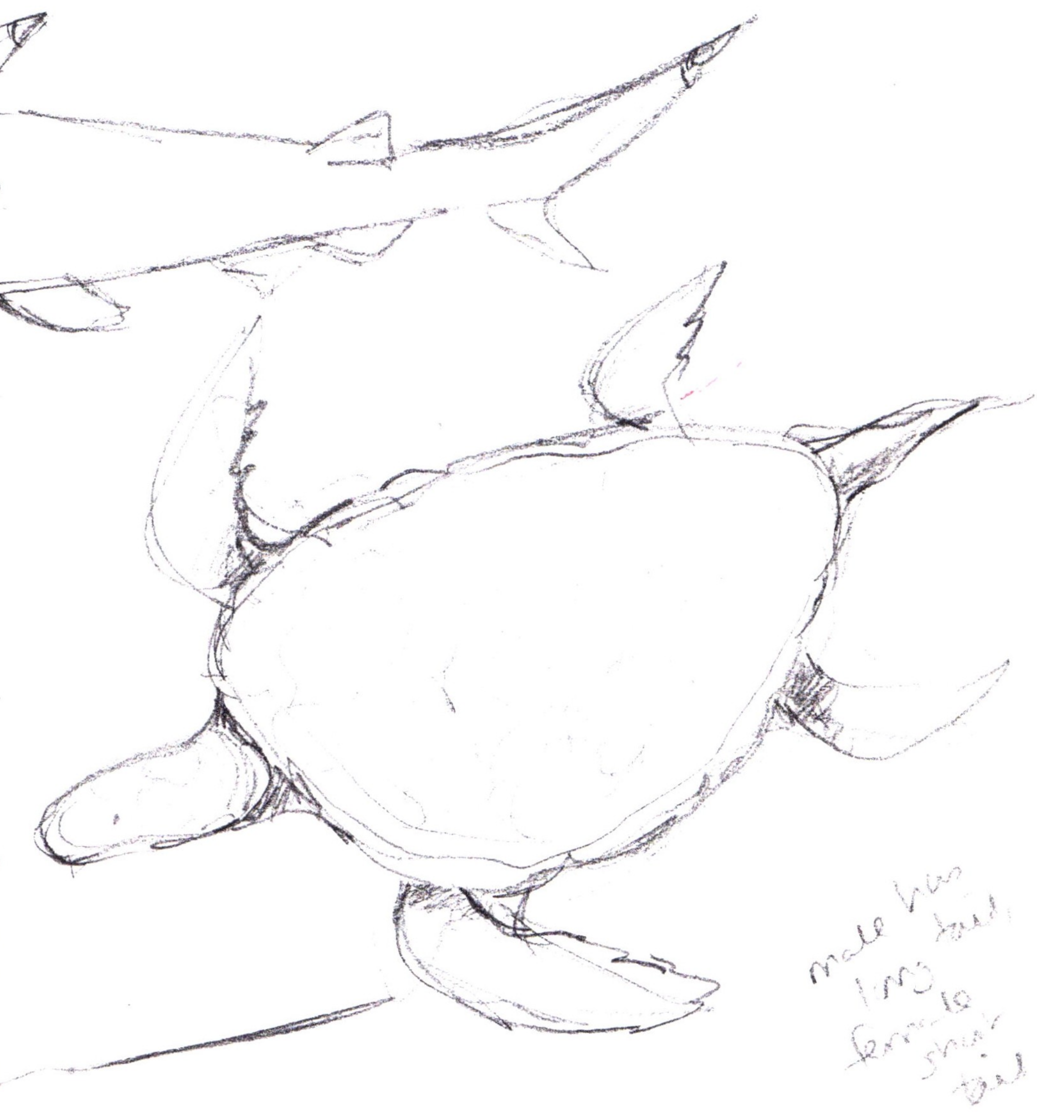

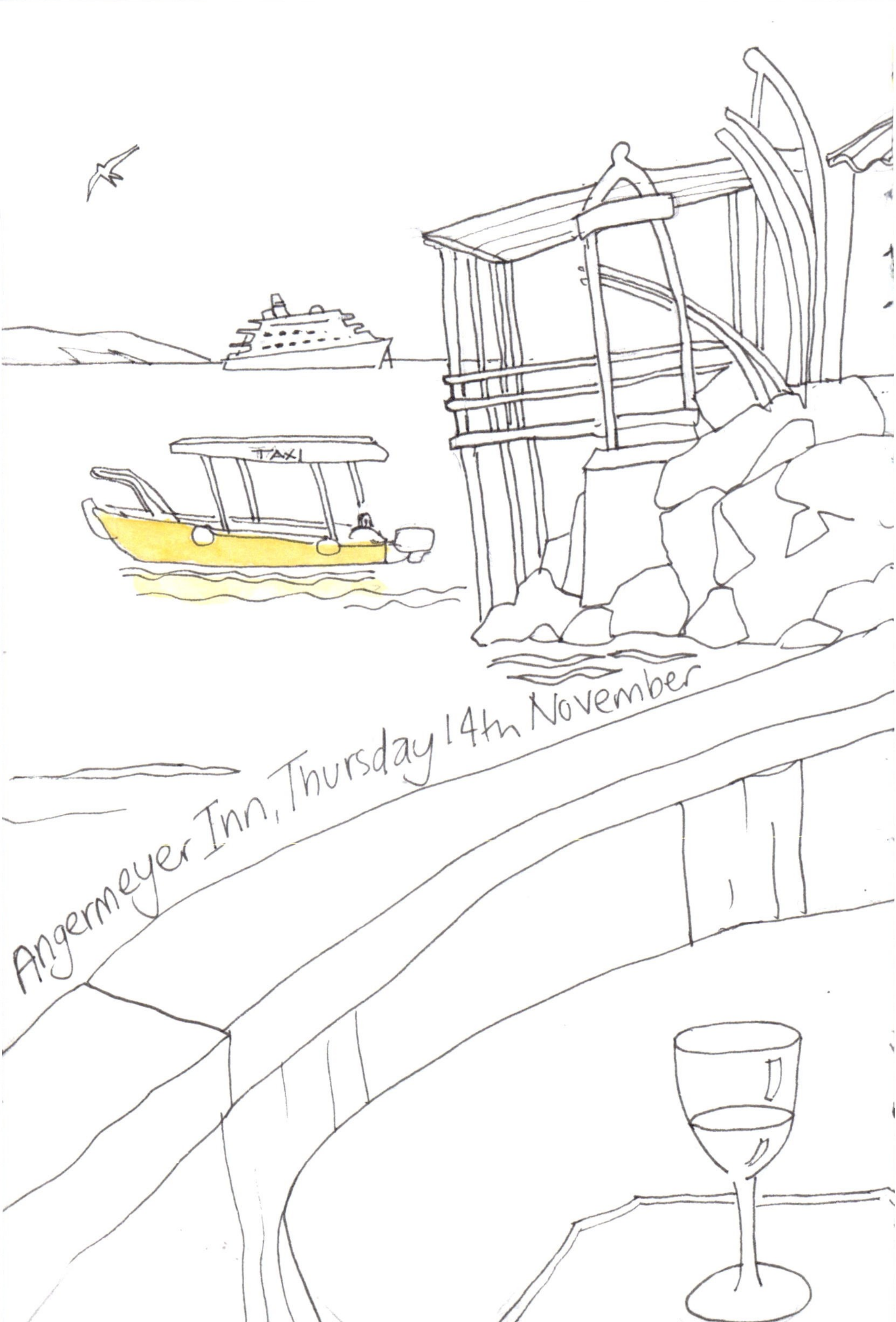
TAXI
Angermeyer Inn, Thursday 14th November

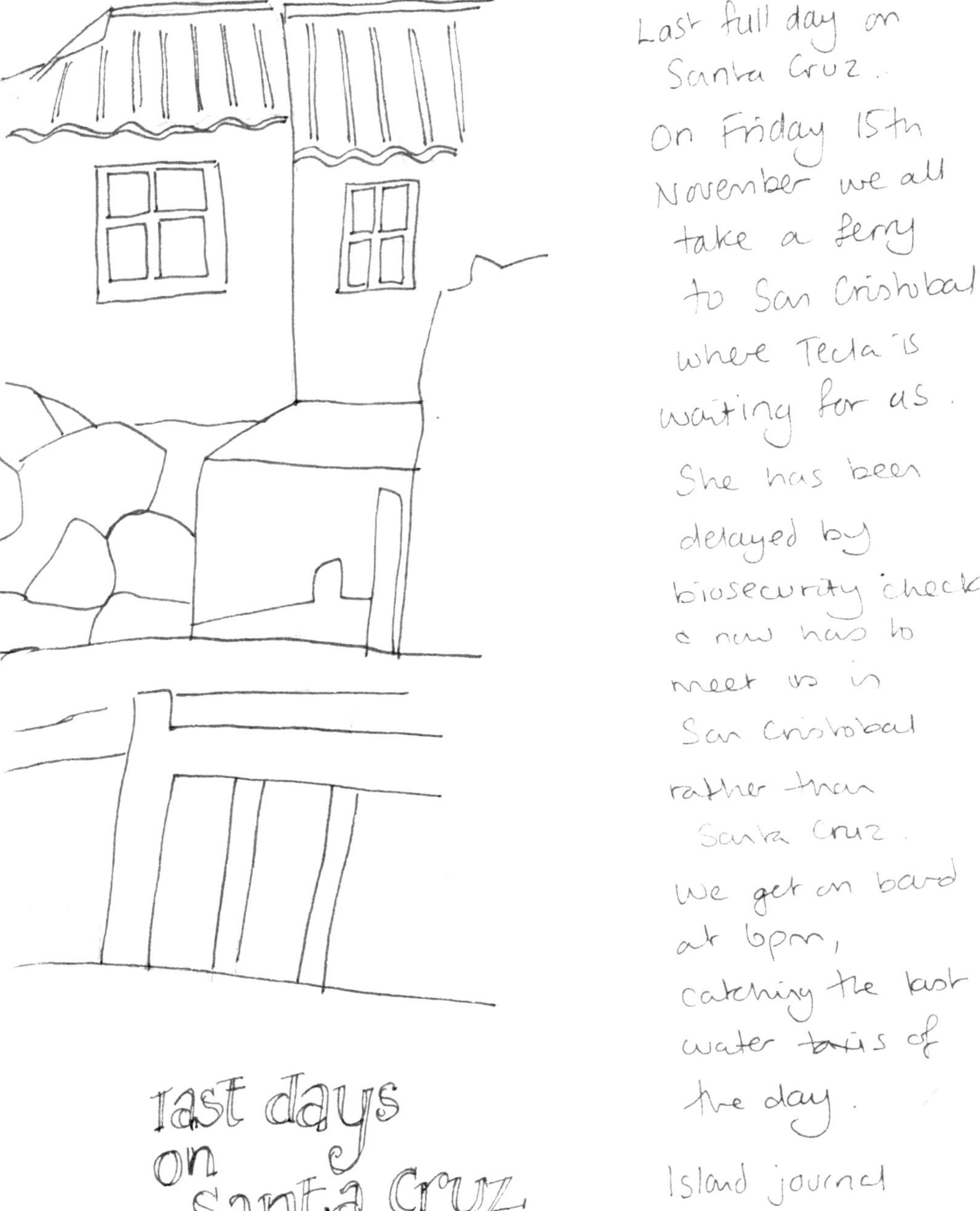

Last full day on Santa Cruz.

On Friday 15th November we all take a ferry to San Cristobal where Tecla is waiting for us. She has been delayed by biosecurity checks & now has to meet us in San Cristobal rather than Santa Cruz.

We get on board at 6pm, catching the last water taxis of the day.

Island journal resumes later....

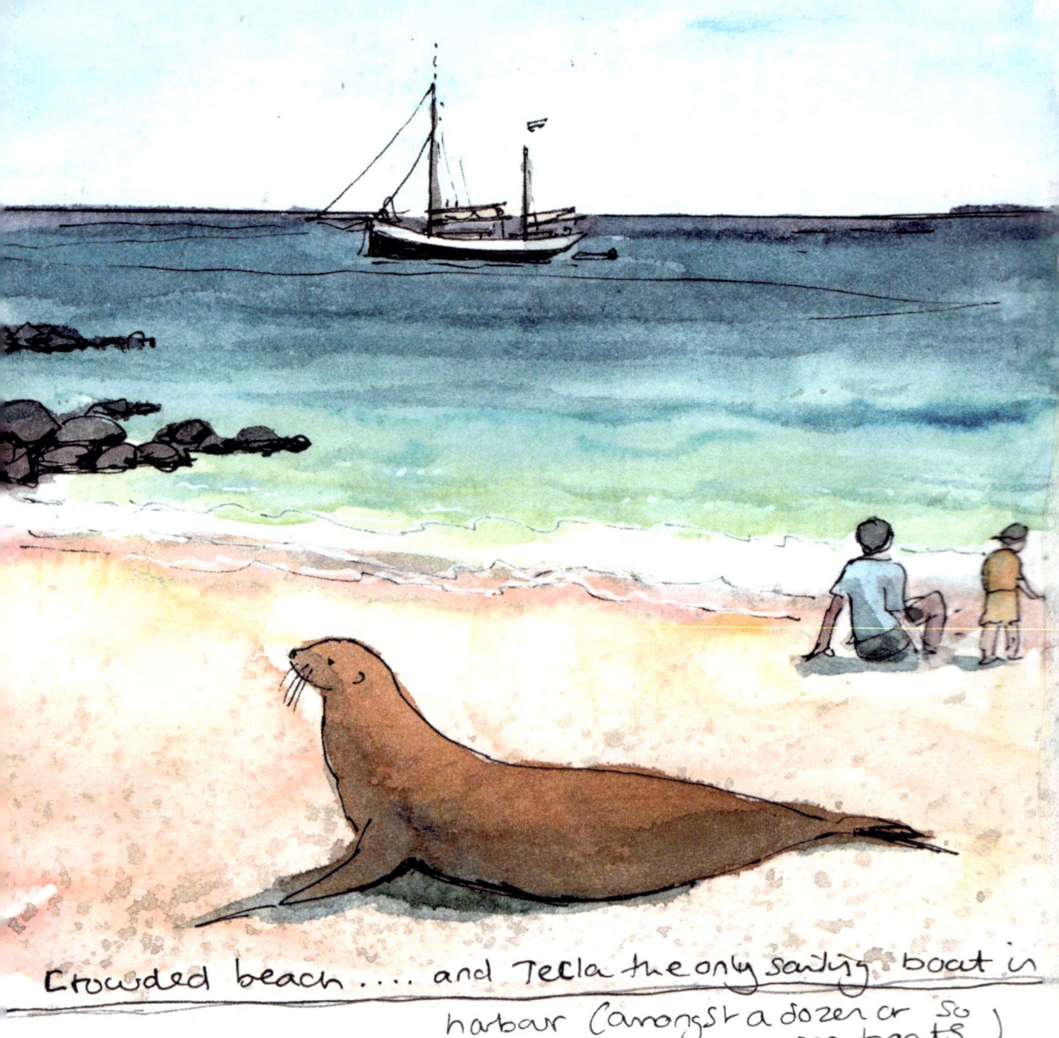

Back at my hostel in Puerto Ayora, my attention had been turning with anxiety and anticipation to the voyage to come. Gradually, I started to find my fellow shipmates as we had been making contact via social media and meeting up. From the Netherlands Janette kept us up to date with *Tecla*'s position as the bio-security measures that she was having to undergo on mainland Ecuador were causing delays. Eleven of us gathered with all our luggage on the quayside where we could see our little ship at anchor. We were a mixed lot – Irish, English, Scottish, New Zealand, American and Dutch, all excited and a bit nervous as we piled into a water taxi and headed out across the harbour. We climbed aboard to a helping hand, a welcome from the crew and an inviting smell of cooking from the hatchway.

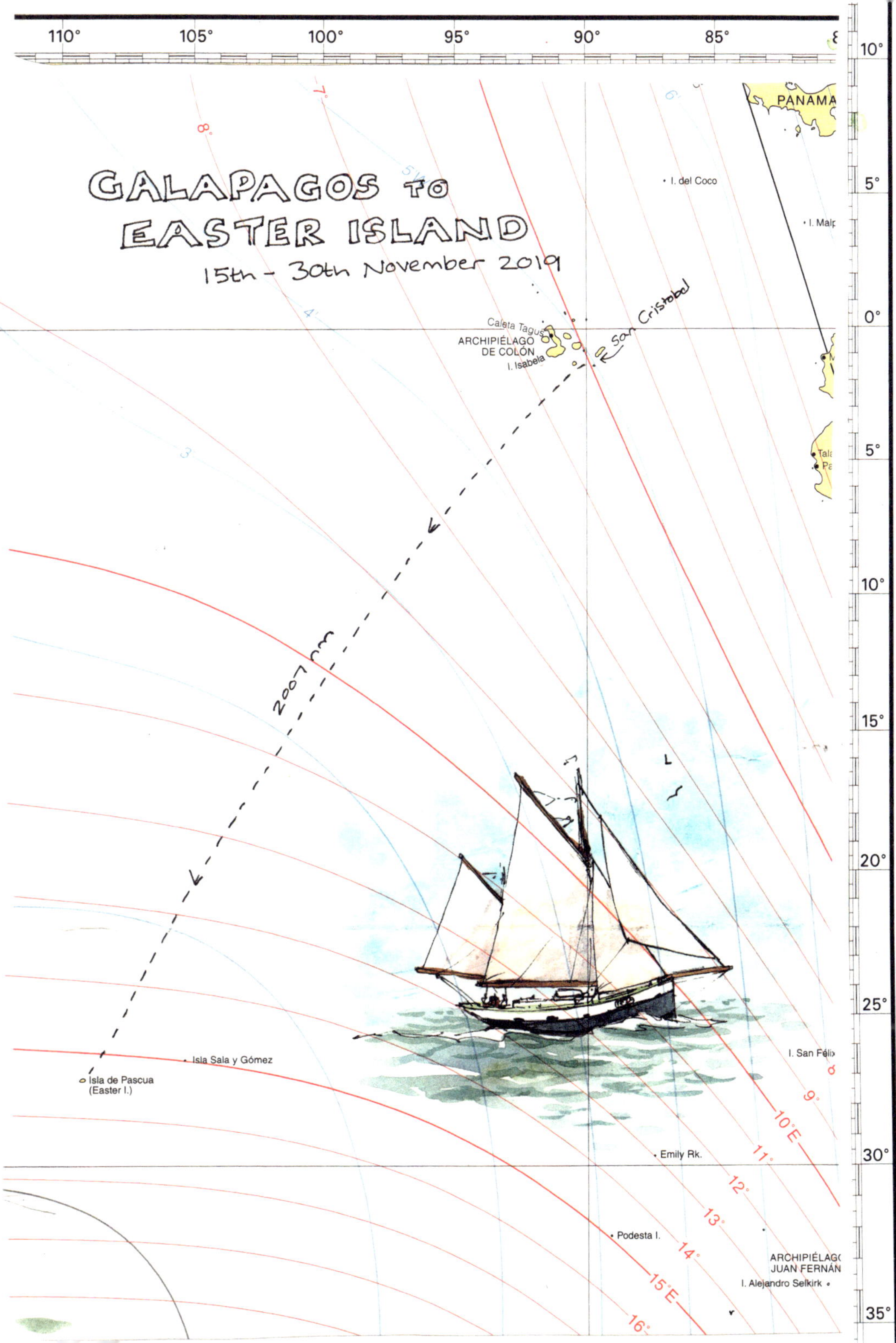

110°
105°
100°
95°
90°
85°
10°
5°

PANAMA
· I. del Coco
· I. Malp
0°
5°

GALAPAGOS TO
EASTER ISLAND
15th – 30th November 2019

Caleta Tagus
ARCHIPIÉLAGO
DE COLÓN
I. Isabela
R. San Cristobal
M

10°
Tala
Pa

2007 nm

15°

L

20°

25°
I. San Félix

Isla Sala y Gómez
Isla de Pascua
(Easter I.)

30°
· Emily Rk.

· Podesta I.
ARCHIPIÉLAGO
JUAN FERNÁN
I. Alejandro Selkirk ·

35°

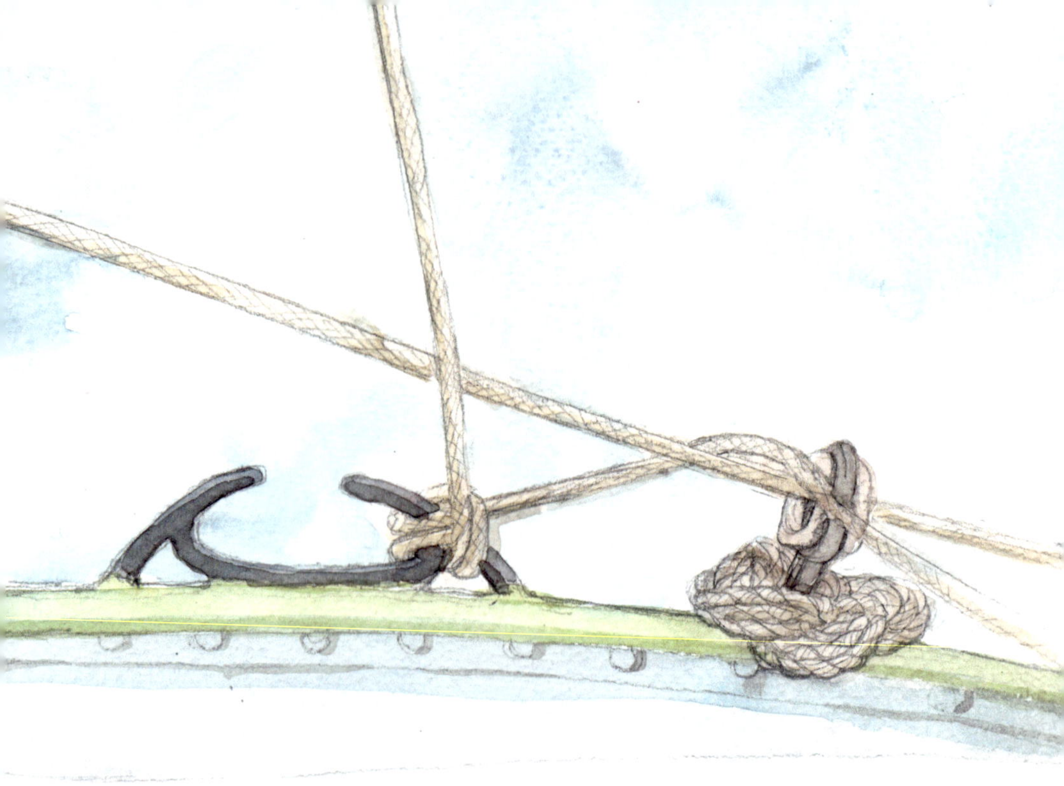

FRIDAY 15TH NOVEMBER

Came aboard 'Tecla' around 6pm after catching ferry from Santa Cruz to San Cristobal. Welcomed by Captain & crew with supper & wine

SATURDAY 16TH, SUNDAY 17TH NOVEMBER

At anchor. Not able to leave until Monday when we can clear with the authorities. I stay on board Saturday, take a walk ashore Sunday.

MONDAY 18TH NOVEMBER   DAY 1

By 2pm we have been ashore, had our passports stamped and are free to leave. Hoist all sail & weigh anchor. We're off! Close hauled on port tack

TUESDAY 19TH & WEDNESDAY 20TH NOVEMBER   DAY 2   DAY 3

Getting used to being at sea, gentle swell & southeasterly breeze, all sails up to begin with then motoring for a day or so as speed drops in light winds.

The voyage begins

It always takes a while to get used to an unfamiliar boat. Working out where all the ropes go (and there are so many of them on *Tecla*!), how the steering feels, how the captain likes things done, how to share out a small amount of cupboard space with your room-mate and how everything works. Our captain was Gijs (pronounced 'Heiss') and he also did all the cooking. The other professional crew were young, skilled in all aspects of ship life, and good company – Will (Tasmanian), Krista (Californian) and Nico (Dutch).

Whilst we were still at anchor I asked Will to name all the ropes for me so that I could make this sketch of the rigging layout and wonder how I was ever going to learn enough to find the right rope without having to be told. It took a while! The ones with asterisks were those I knew we'd need most often.

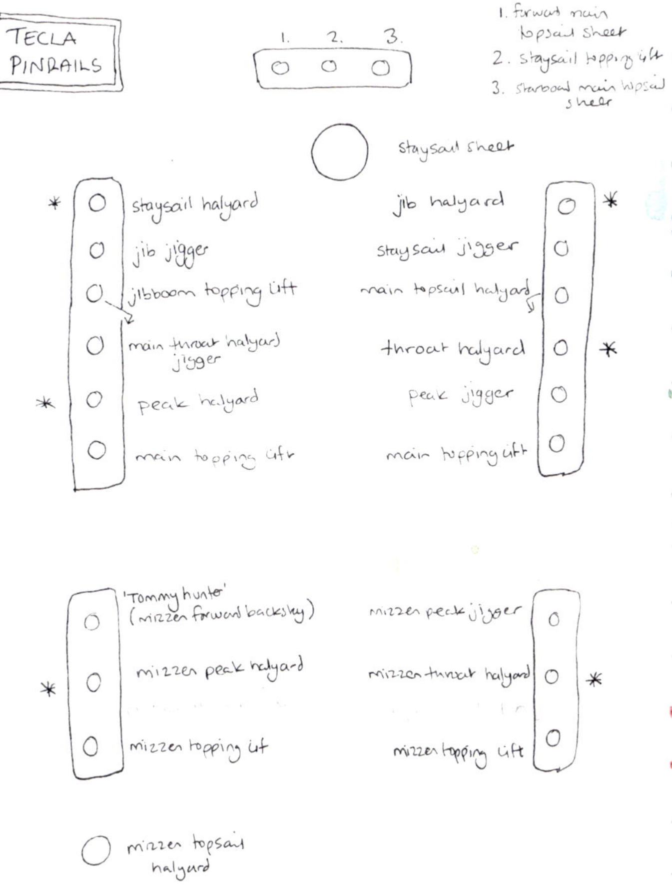

I am prone to seasickness but my hopes that the tropical seas would be kind on the stomach were well founded; after a few days of feeling a bit muzzy headed I was mostly fine. I can spot the symptoms well in advance and try to do something about it – like stay on deck and look at the horizon or lie down and sleep. Luckily on this ship there were no demands on my time when I was off watch (apart from helping with the washing up occasionally) so I managed to dodge the worst of the queasiness. By the time we had our first rough weather, about a week into the voyage, I was getting my sea legs.

I find it hard to draw when feeling queasy, though, so I waited for a few days before I brought my sketch book out. Winds were gentle on Day 4 and Gijs announced a 'swim stop'. The ship was hove to and a ladder lowered over the side for the timid swimmers like me – most of the crew dived over the side with yells of delight. I lowered myself cautiously, choosing the moment with the roll of the ship to let go and surrender to the sea. That first swim in the deep ocean was a revelation; the water was liquid crystal, sapphire blue and shot through with sunlight. The knowledge that the bottom of the ocean was over 3km below our wriggling feet exciting. It felt audacious, as if we shouldn't be there.

Also on that day I noted in my sketchbook the watch system, the routine that keeps the ship sailing round the clock. Allocated our watches at the beginning of the voyage, we stuck to them and no-one would have dreamed of being late or not turning up, seasick or not. The watch system for voyage crew was four hours on, eight hours off. I was on white watch, 4-8, which gave us dawn and sunset and not too many hours of darkness, though I could never get used to that wake up call at 3.40am!

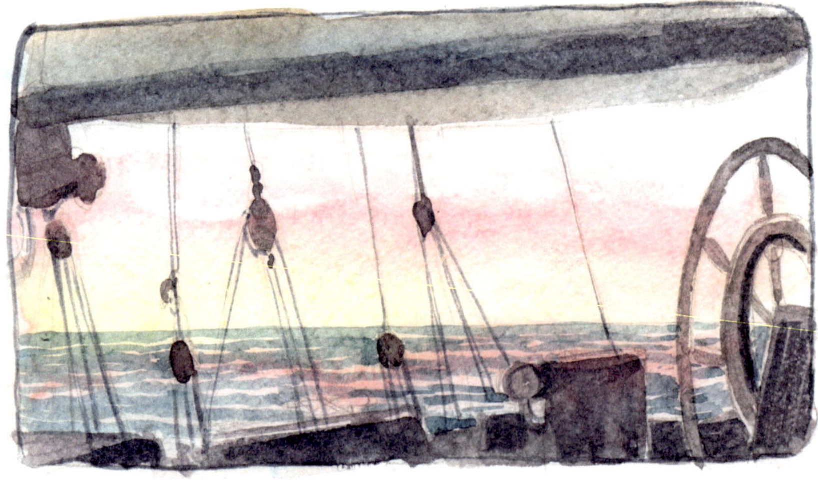

DAY 4

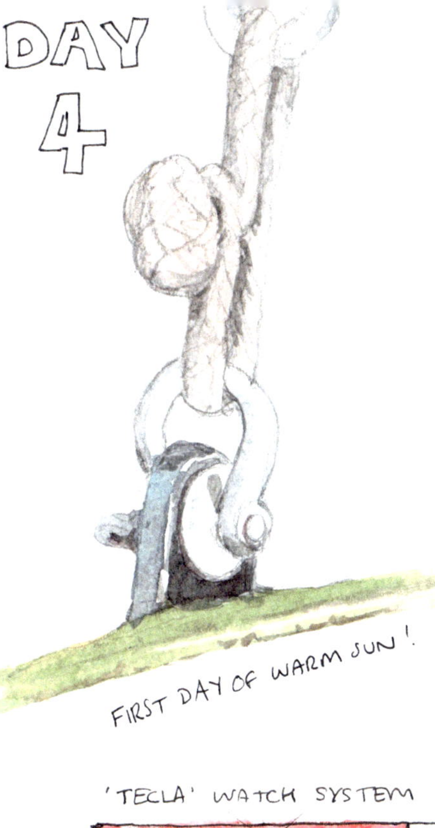

FIRST DAY OF WARM SUN !

Engine off and sailing again, close hauled with all sail up.

Before hoisting sail we hove-to after lunch for a swim. Perfect water temperature and gentle swell. Nearest land - 3km below !

Swimming at
6°12'8 S 094°53'6 W

Talk by Gijs this afternoon about Tecla's voyage through the Northwest Passage.

'TECLA' WATCH SYSTEM

RED WATCH	WHITE WATCH	BLUE WATCH
12 - 4	4 - 8	8 - 12
ANNETTE MARTY CHRIS ALISON	CLAUDIA GEORGE THEO MICHELLE	CARTER CHRIS B. ROBERT
GIJS & NICO 12-6		WILL & KRISTA 6 - 12

'Pacific Ocean' in Dutch is 'Stille Oceaan'. Living up to its name today !

Flying fish on deck at dawn

Cloudy, then sunny,
breeze fickle then
steady

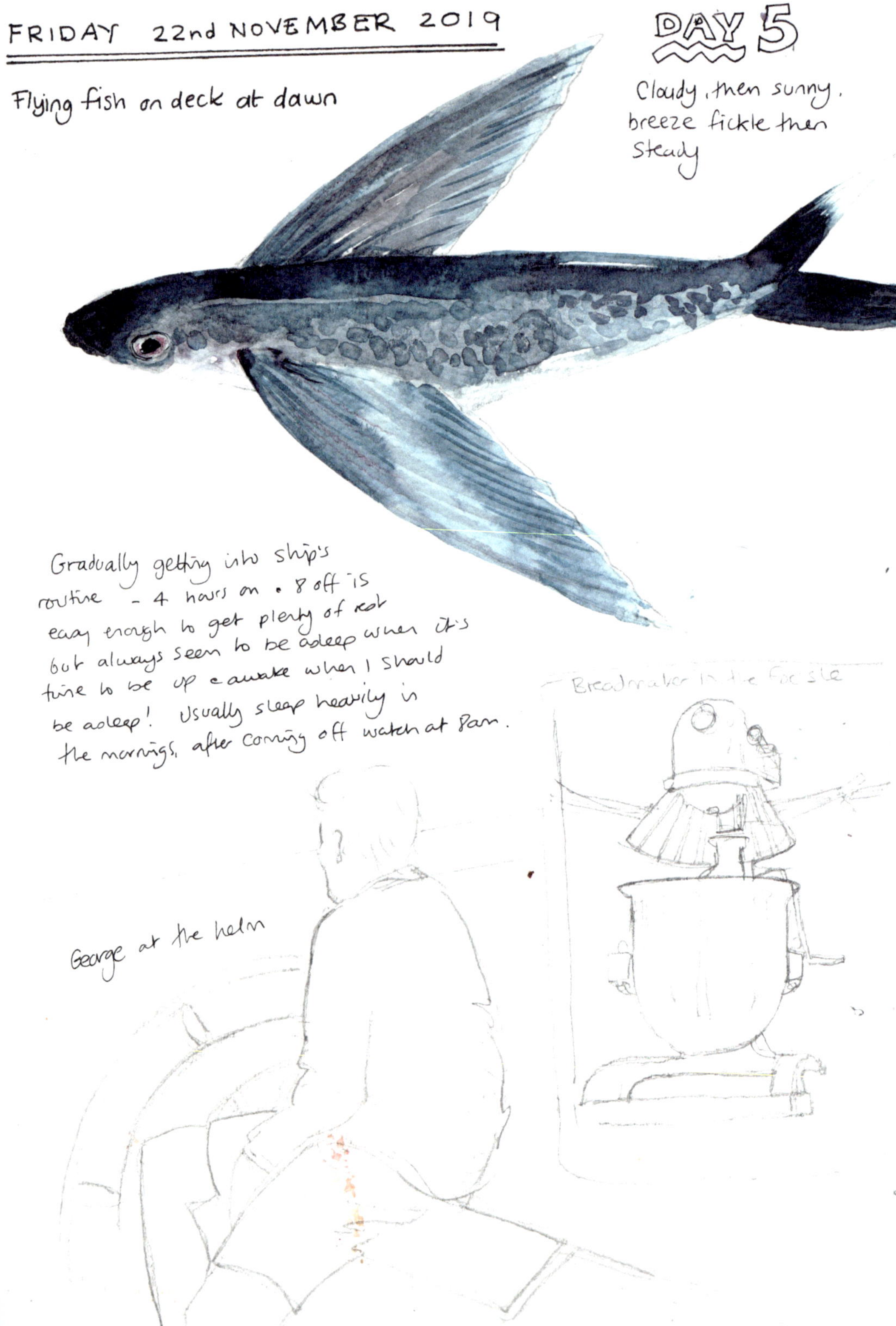

Gradually getting into ship's
routine – 4 hours on . 8 off is
easy enough to get plenty of rest
but always seem to be asleep when it's
time to be up & awake when I should
be asleep! Usually sleep heavily in
the mornings, after coming off watch at 8am.

Breadmaker in the fo'c'sle

George at the helm

No bird life ... gentle swell & white caps

Fresh baked bread every day

SATURDAY 23RD NOVEMBER

Distant sighting of whales just after
dawn ... a large and small spout close
together (mother & calf?)

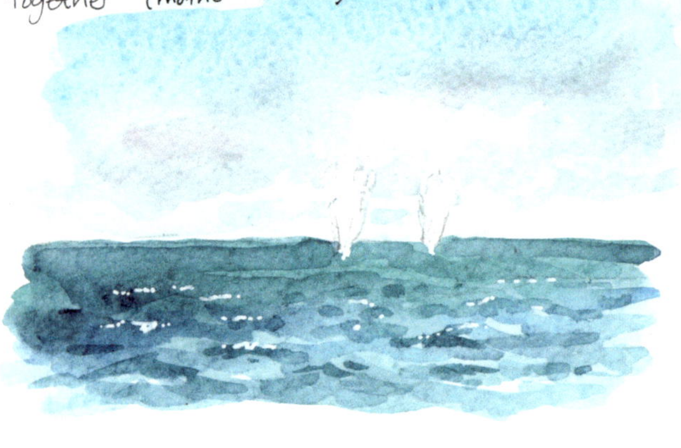

Fresh breeze,
on the beam.
Rolling along at
8 knots, topsails
taken down during
the night.

We discover the
hard way it's
difficult to have a
shower when heeled
over on port tack
as the water spills
over the lip of the
door & floods the
cabin!

Gradually feeling less
sleepy during the day,
found a heap of sails
to sit on & play some
music for a while.

'METICULOUS PLANNING
MAKES FOR A POSITIVE OUTCOME'
(Amundsen)

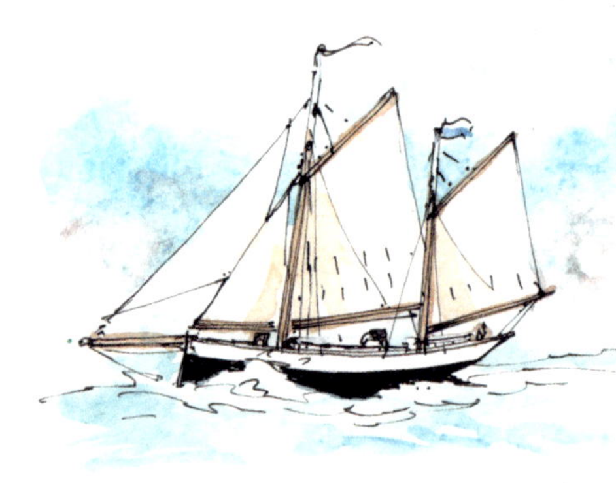

Where does one day begin and another one end?
We have two days in one - woken at 3.45
to get ready to go on watch at 4am.
Stumble on deck in the darkness, half hour at
the helm each. Dawn at about 6am, usually just
a lightening of the sky. Off watch at 8am,
a quick breakfast & then bed for a few hours.
Then lunch, and a talk by Gijs today about passage
planning & using ocean routeing charts. Plenty of time
to read, try a sketch (tricky today!) then back on watch at 4pm.

The captain and professional crew did six hours on, six hours off so there were always two of them on duty with four of us novices. Most of the time in tropical waters our time on deck was relaxed, unless a change in the weather called for sail handling. The four us took it in turns to steer, half an hour each, which gave plenty of time to gaze at the sea, chat, go below for supper, or do anything that needed doing on deck.

I had never sailed in tropical waters before and although it wasn't all easy sailing it was a delight after spending years messing about on small boats off the coast of Britain. Sailing in home waters is seldom warm and is rarely relaxing. There are lobster pots, tides, headlands, sandbanks, rocks, fishing boats, shipping lanes and windfarms to dodge, usually whilst trying to get the timing right for arriving at a drying harbour or getting over a shingle bar into a river at the correct state of tide. When I first took the helm on *Tecla* and asked the skipper how long we would be steering 210 degrees, he said 'Oh, about two weeks'!

Mealtimes became highlights of the day. This was a time when we all got together round the table apart from the crew members who took turns to steer whilst everyone ate. Food was excellent, plentiful and cooked by the captain, who coped well with having three vegetarians on board.

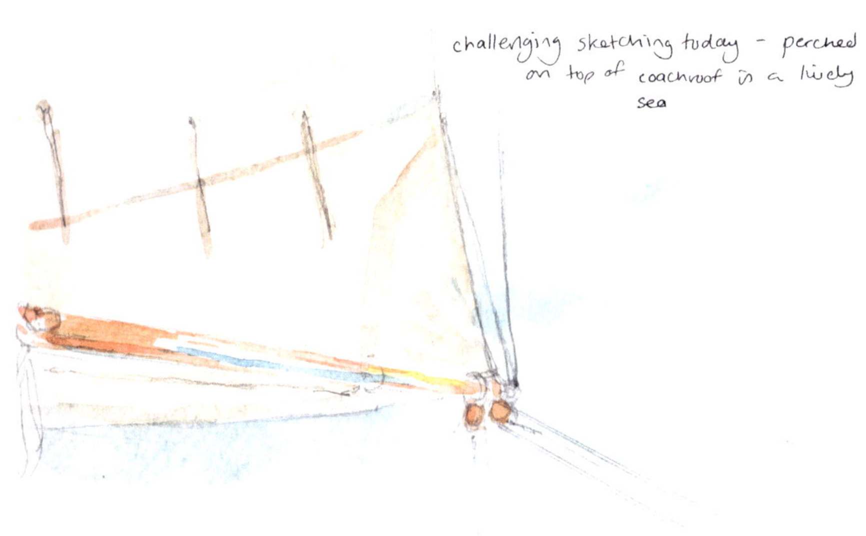

SUNDAY 24th NOVEMBER

DAY 7

Cool, windy, SE force
5 - 6.
Lively sea.

No 2 jib,
Staysail,
reefed
main &
mizzen

At daylight, Will goes aloft to fix a
problem with main backstay

Nico

Not very tropical gear!

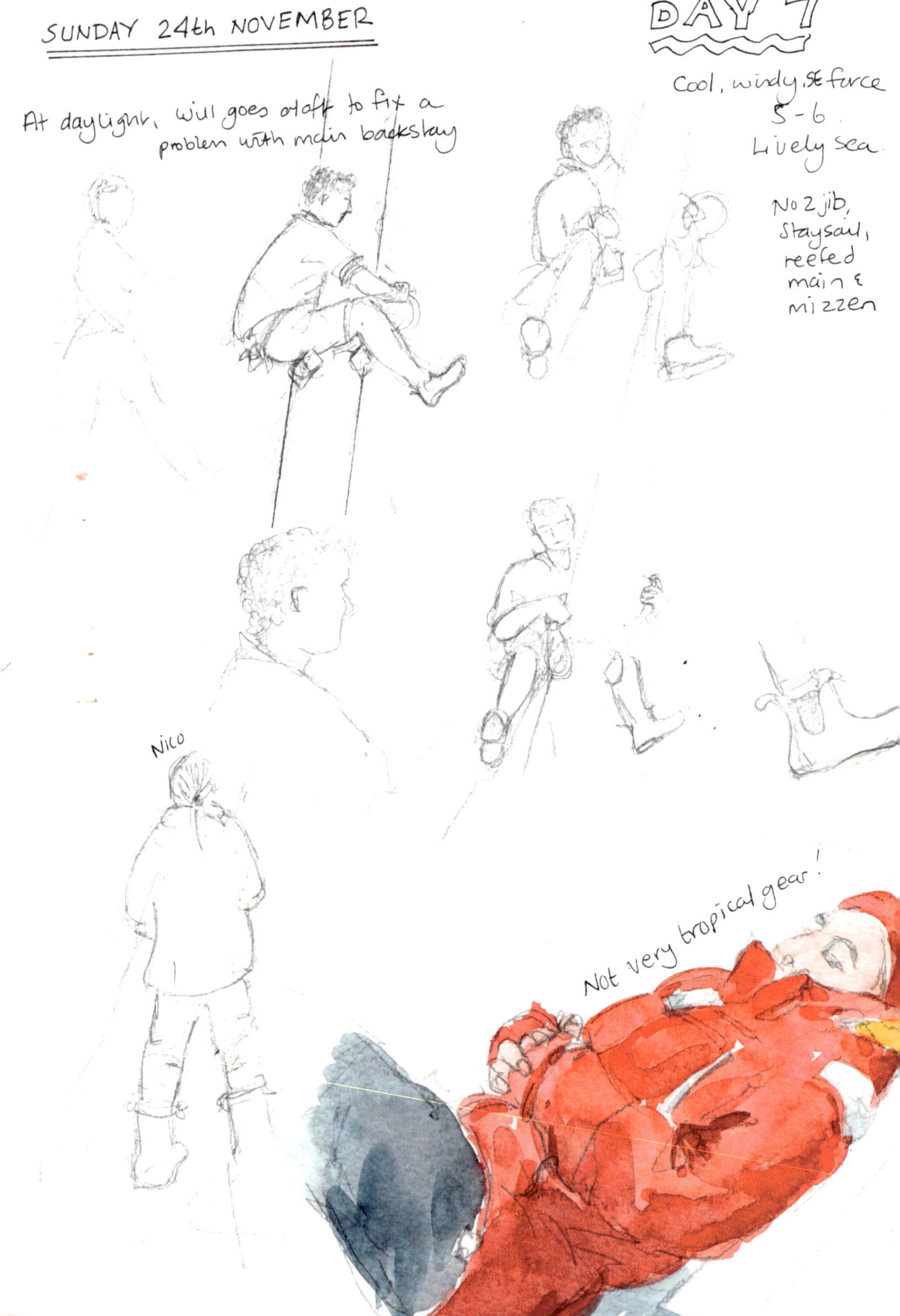

whales blowing
but no close sightings

warm sun, cool wind.

confused sea ... lumps of it keep landing on deck.
Time to unpack the sea boots?

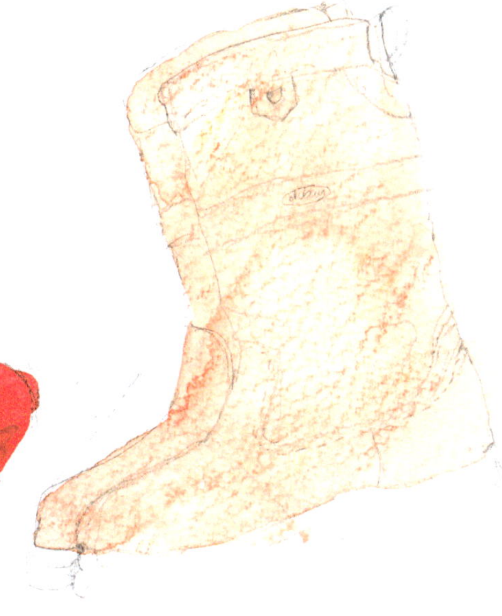

Annette gave a talk after lunch
about sailing the waka 'Haunui' (great wind
in Maori)
using only traditional polynesian
navigation methods, from
Santiago to Tahiti. ~~There is~~ There is
~~written~~ an e-book about it :-
Duncan Morrison - 'Hope or High water'

DAILY ROUTINE : (white watch

3.40am   woken by red watch
3.55 am   on deck, getting used
           to dark
4 am   on watch (includes
           2 half-hour sessions
           on helm)
8 am   hand over to blue watch
           Breakfast then sleep

midday-ish wake up, go on
            deck (or stay in bed!.)
12.30   lunch (skip this & stay
           in bed sometimes)
2 pm   occasional talk in saloon
2 - 4pm   on deck (if conditions
           allow)
4 - 8pm   on watch (supper at
           6.30, taken on watch)
8 pm   hand over to blue watch
8.10   sleep!

There was plenty of time to sit on deck reading, chatting, writing or just watching the sea. I was never bored. I gave myself the task of drawing either the sea, the sky or the set of the sails each day, or sometimes all three. We'd hoped for more wildlife, but only had a distant sighting of whales blowing, and a couple of tropic birds. Nothing else – no ships, no wildlife, no vapour trails in the sky.

Figure drawing doesn't come easily to me and I always need more practice. On Day 7 I sketched Will, who had shinned up the shrouds to mend something at the top of the mast. There are no ratlines (rope ladders in the rigging) on *Tecla*; Will and Gijs were both able to climb up hand over hand, their feet curled round the rigging, as easily as if they were taking a stroll.

The secret of drawing figures in motion is to rely on the power of repetition – grab a line, then wait until the pose is resumed, grab another. Later in the day, an easier subject was my Australian watch mate Shelley, huddled in her oilskins. We were still in the tropics but that wind was chilly!

We were in rough seas now, moving fast with spray on the decks. I find rough weather thrilling as well as unpleasant. Thrilling because I was on a safe, powerful ship in the world's biggest ocean. Thrilling because of all the shifting colours and shapes and beauty in every wave, so hard to paint on the move.

On Day 8 I sketched the netting that stopped us getting washed over the side if we lost our grip whilst sail handling, or were knocked by an extra big wave. Luckily we all stayed safely on board. *Tecla*'s decks are wide and her bulwarks high, but the nets were a reassuring presence.

The part of me that is not thrilled by rough weather is, shamefully, wishing that it would all calm down so that I could walk around normally and not worry about how to hold a steady course when it's my turn to helm. The compass swings wildly and the captain always seems to glance at it when we wobble off course. With huge pressure in the sails there is little margin for error.

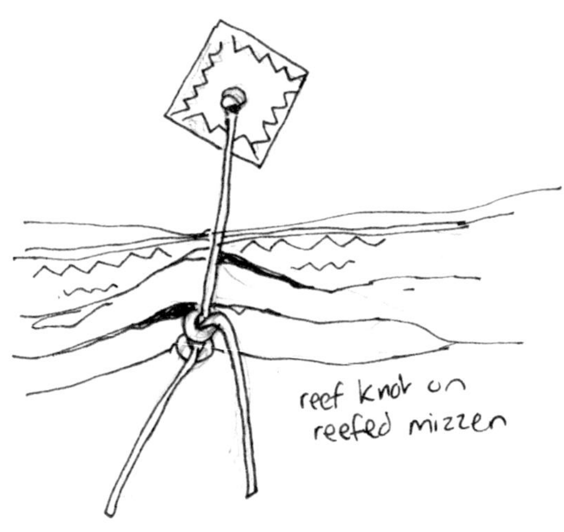

I also worry about how I can contribute to reefing those big sails when the wind increases. It's a difficult job involving plenty of hands and good teamwork as we lean over the boom, struggling to find the reefing lines to tie round unwieldy folds of terylene to make the sails smaller on a wet sloping deck. Meanwhile the waves try their best to shake us off. There is a saying 'one hand for yourself and one for the ship', but most sail handling tasks need both hands. You do your best to brace yourself against something solid if you can.

What wimpish thoughts! We all work together and the job gets done and if I'd wanted an easy ride I wouldn't have come on the voyage. When the work is done we feel wet, exhausted and hugely satisfied.

There was plenty of sail handling to do, as the wind was playing games with us — plenty of it one minute, none at all the next. There were frequent squalls, full of rain and wind.

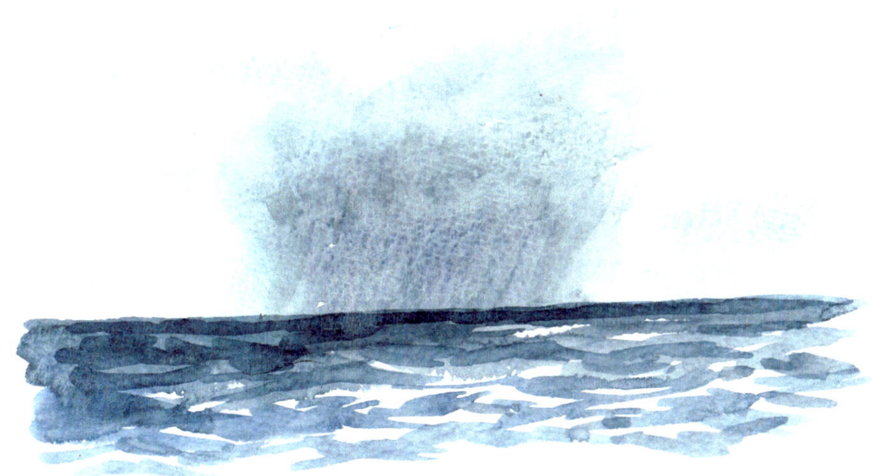

This squall missed us, luckily · · · ·

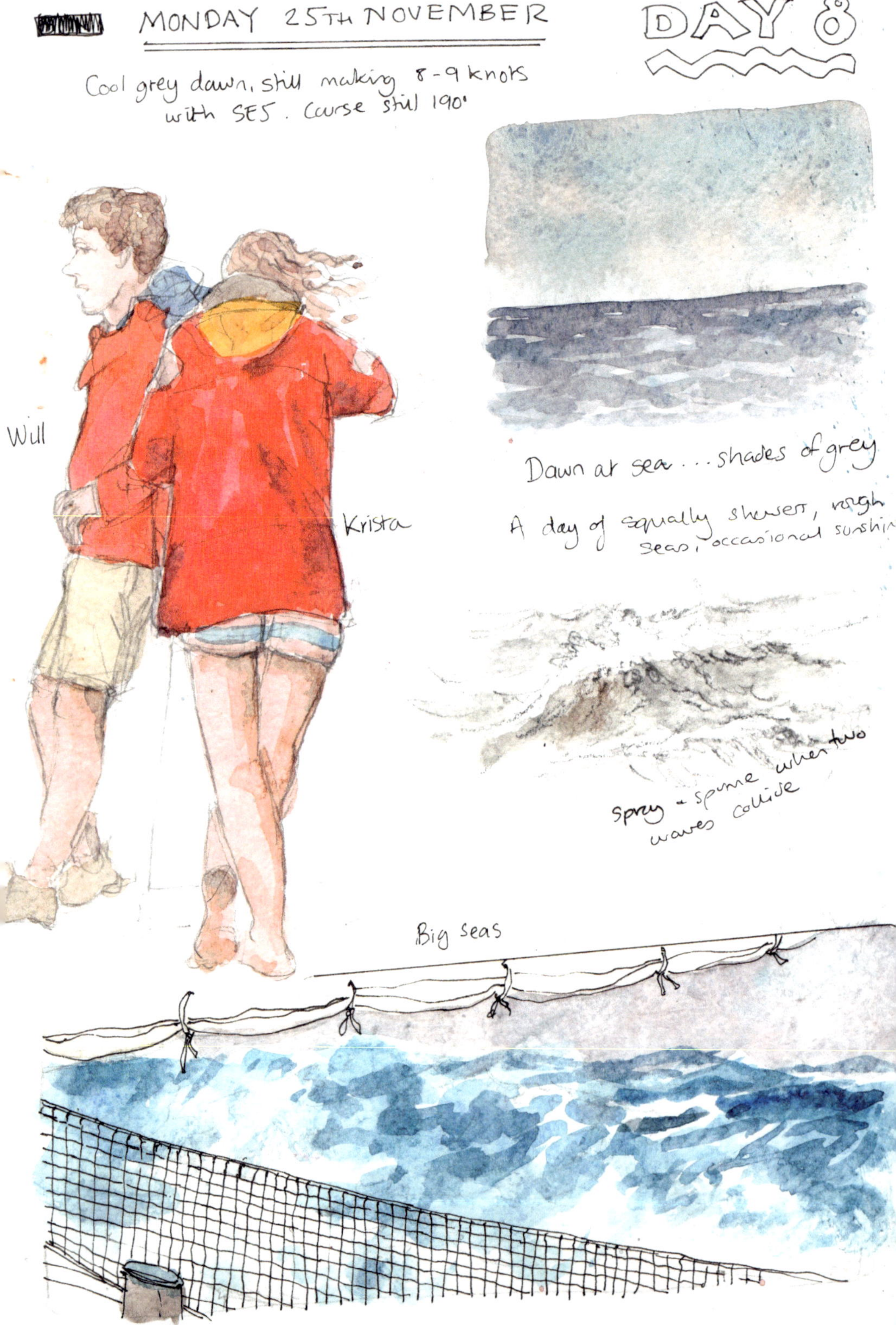

MONDAY 25TH NOVEMBER
DAY 8

Cool grey dawn, still making 8-9 knots
with SE5. Course still 190°

Will

Krista

Dawn at sea ... shades of grey

A day of squally showers, rough
seas, occasional sunshine

spray & spume when two
waves collide

Big seas

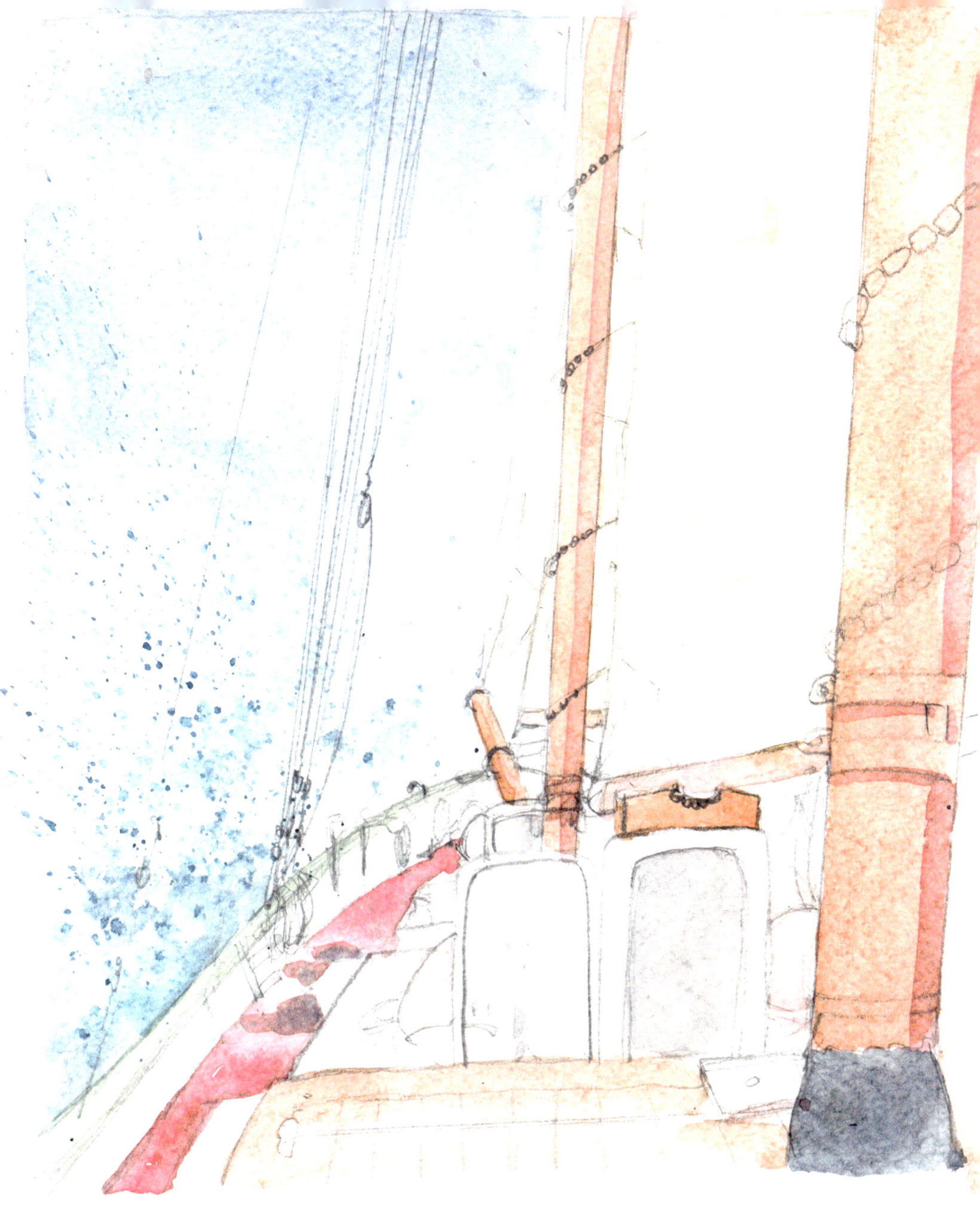

A rough night, wind force 6 on the beam but with heavy squalls & torrential rain in the squalls. Sea is rough & very uneven, making ~~better~~ steering challenging. Glad to be off watch!

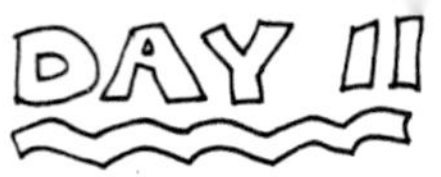

Still motoring through a lumpy swell this morning, another cool & cloudy dawn. Thoughts are turning to our arrival on Rapa Nui, now just over 300nm away.

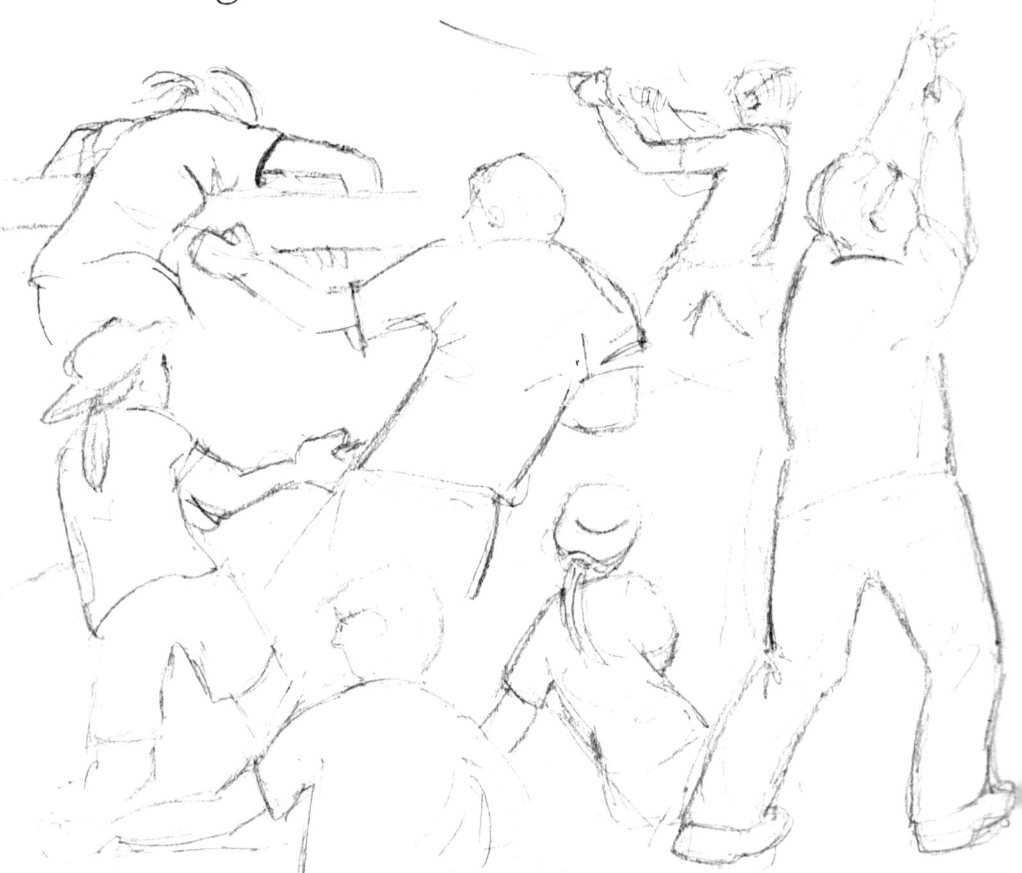

After lunch, a breeze arrives, sails go up again...

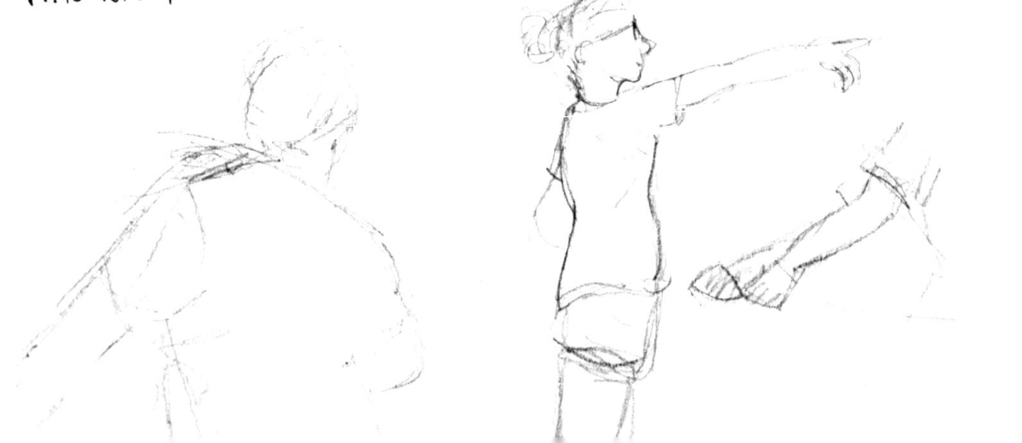

Chris and Alison practising sun sights

.. by mid afternoon, the sun has come back, it's warm on deck and the sea has returned to a welcome shade of blue. Crew morale has improved!

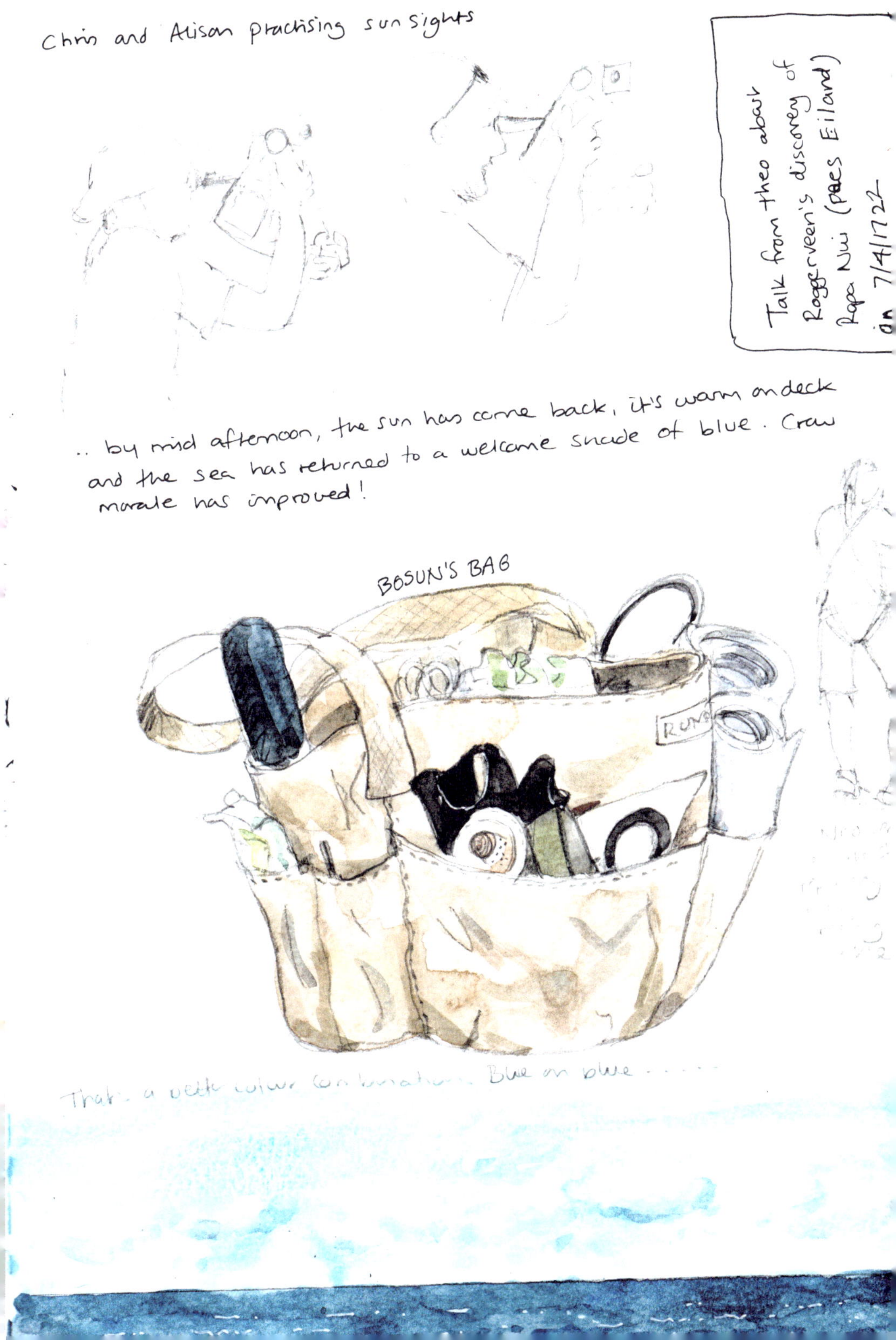

That's a better colour combination. Blue on blue . . . . .

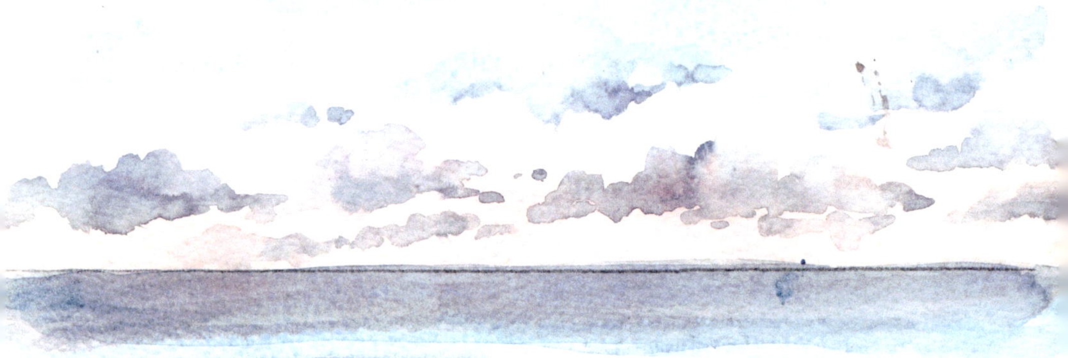

Attempts to catch the colours of sunset   – first non – cloudy sunset for
        several days !

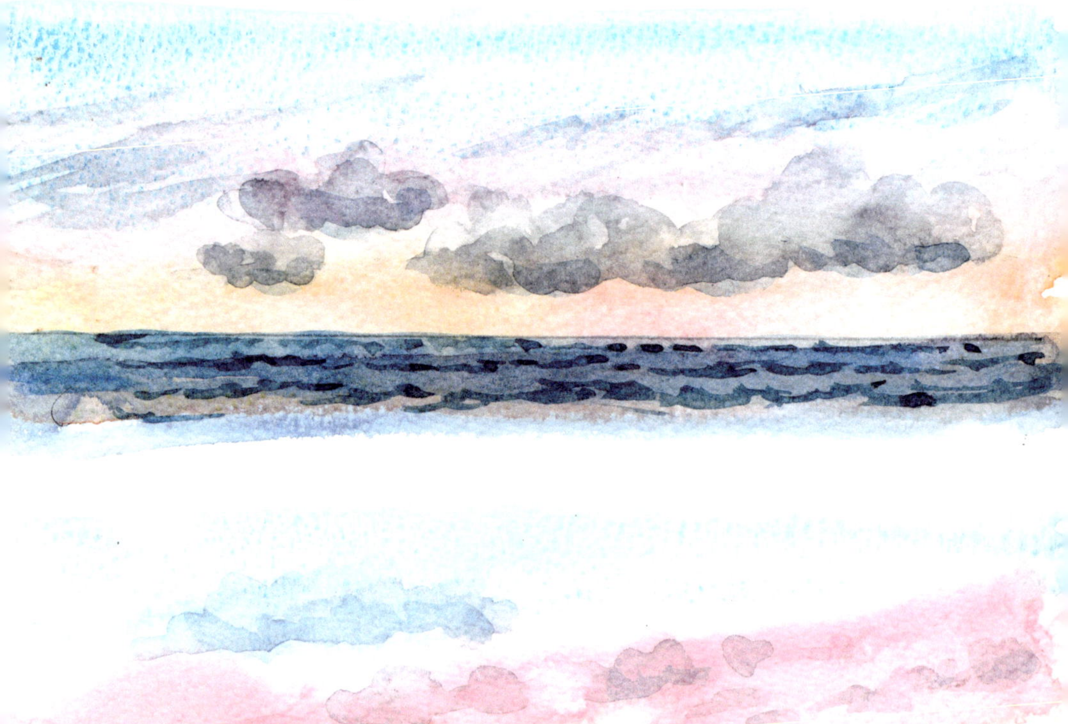

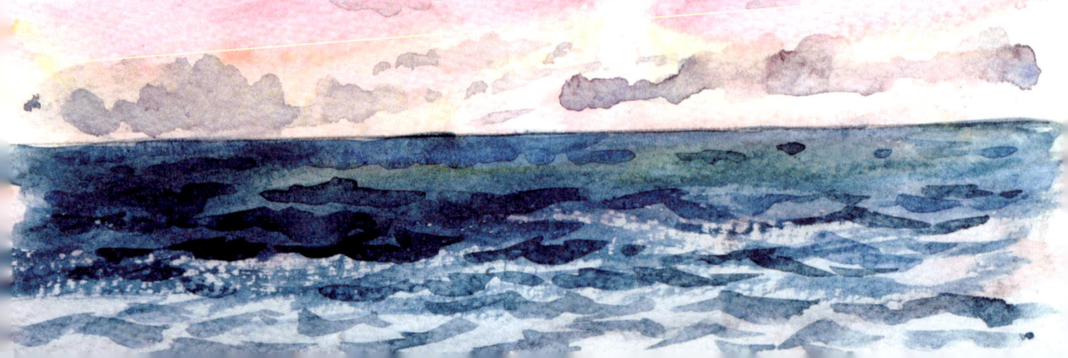

DAY 12

The wind died overnight, we heard the engine go on just before our 4am watch. Our first task - to take down main & mizzen in the dark. Wisely, the crew knew we won't be able to find the right halliards in the dark - they hand us a line with instructions to ease/pull/belay. The day dawns bright & sunny with a gentle swell.

motoring for a while, warm and sunny

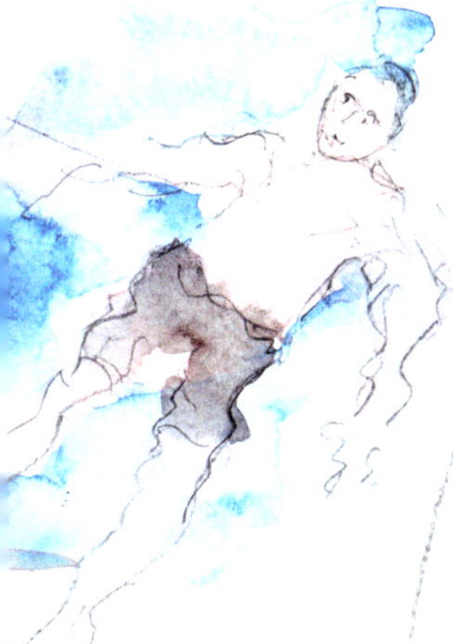

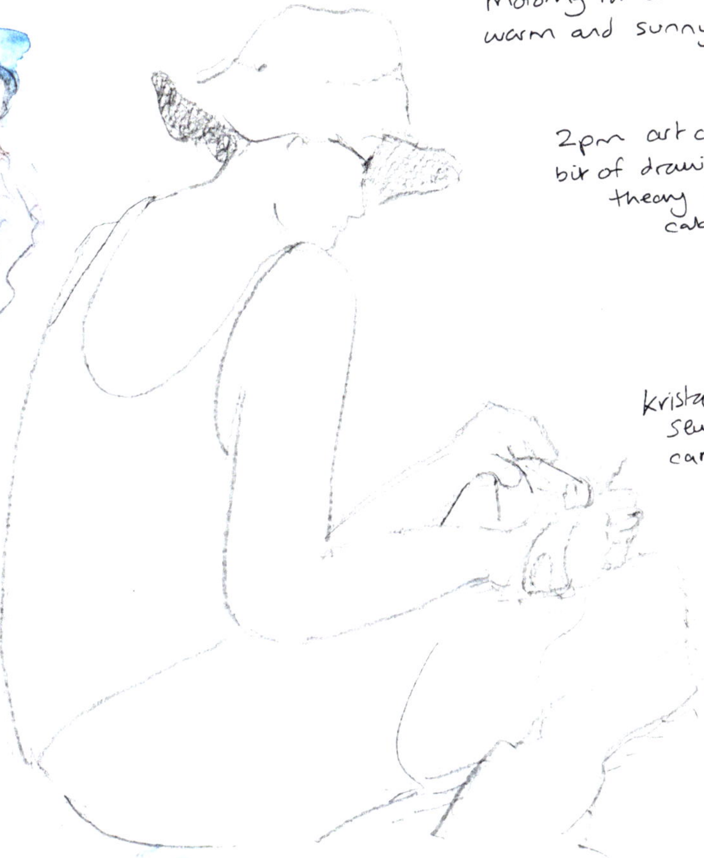

2pm art class! bit of drawing theory in the cabin

krista sewing canvas

1pm swim stop!

fabulous .. clear blue water, 4km deep

24° 22 S
107. 39 W

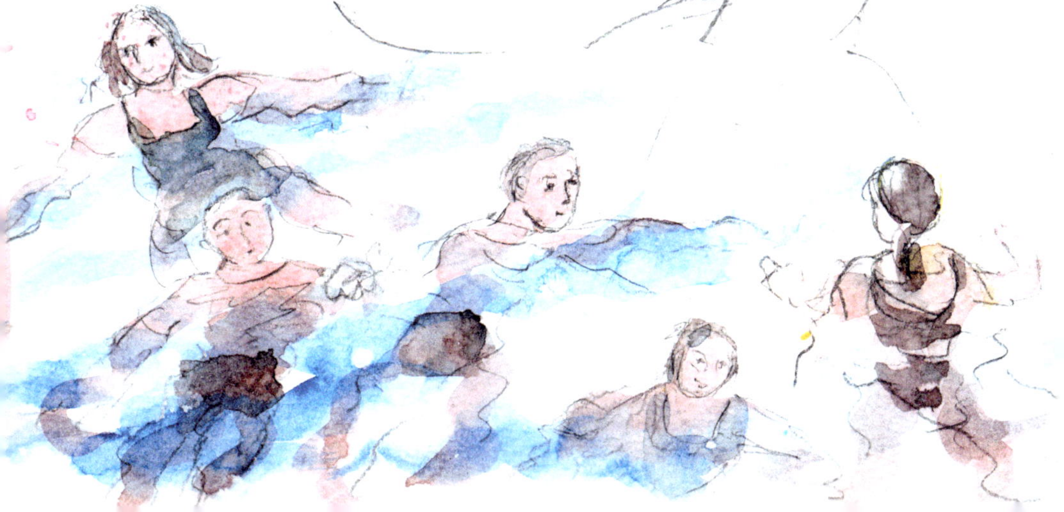

As a complete contrast to yesterday ....
our first task at 4am was to reef the
mainsail. Rain increased steadily all day, alternating strong winds
& calms. All hands on deck to lower main
& jib in a deluge after lunch.

At 8am, the end of our morning watch,
Rapa Nui was 90 nm away.

LAND-HO!

1530 ... a slight grey lump on horizon ----
possibly!
occasional glimpses through the drizzle

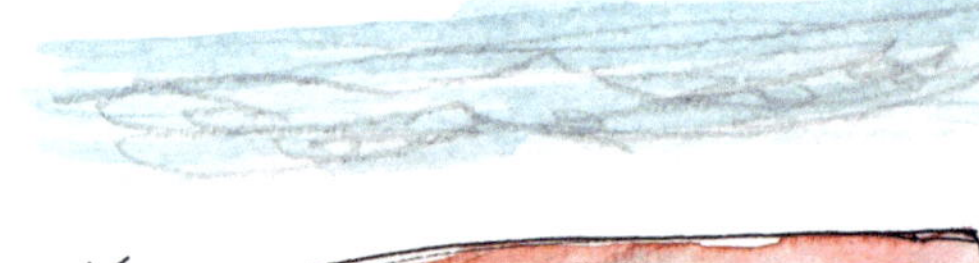

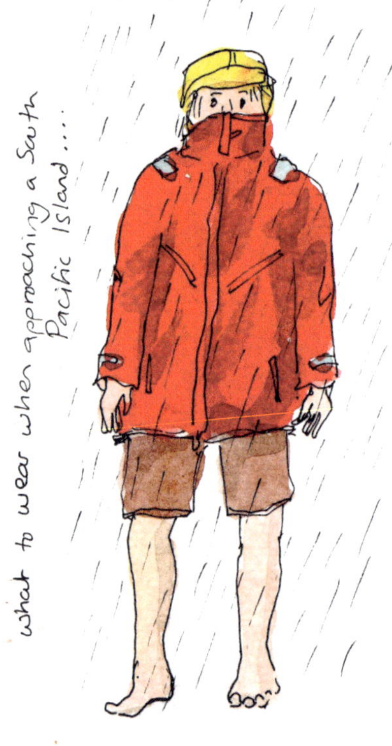

what to wear when approaching a South
Pacific Island .....

19.45

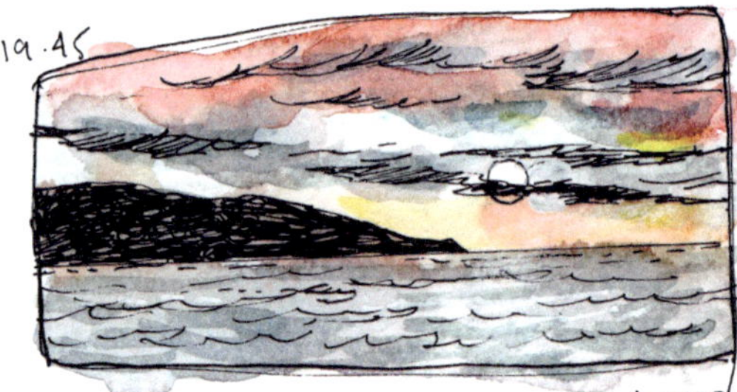

Heavy rain, lumpy grey
sea, cold wind all day. Most
of the day motorsailing into headwind
with mizzen & staysail set. Cold!

5.30

Finally anchored 2100.
Wind & sea now calm &
rain stopped. All on deck
for celebratory drinks
(including skipper's potent
bottle of Dutch liqueur)

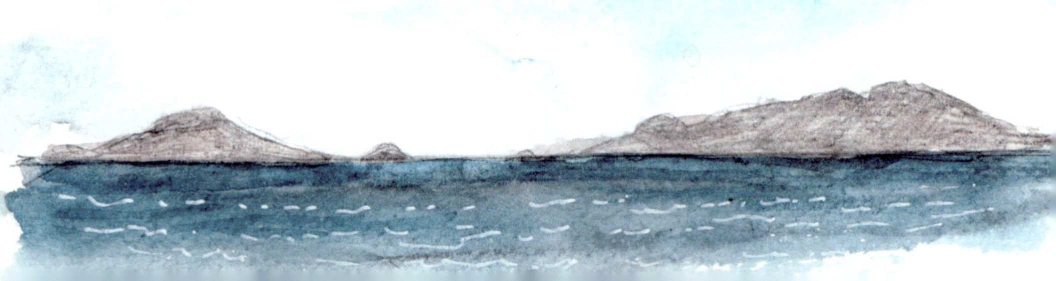

Landfall – Rapa Nui (Easter Island)

On the chart, Easter Island is a tiny dot in a very large ocean, 22km across and 11km wide. It was first inhabited by Polynesians who sailed there from other islands and started a settlement sometime between 800 and 1200 AD. They named the island Rapa Nui. We know that the Polynesians were (and still are) phenomenally good navigators, but the question remains how did they know the island was there? It lies over a thousand miles from the nearest island, over two thousand from the mainland of Chile, an unlikely lump of rock in the middle of nowhere.

The first European to stumble across Rapa Nui was a Dutchman called Roggeveen, whose arrival on Easter Sunday in 1722 inspired its European name. The sight of land on the horizon must have given the sailors a shock in the middle of thousands of miles of apparently empty ocean. He could also have been very unlucky and run into it on a dark night. There would have been no warning as the island rises steeply out of the sea. On board *Tecla* we of course knew exactly when and where to expect to sight land and we all wanted to be the first to see it. It turned up as a very faint smudge of grey in the drizzle when our chart plotter showed us we were about 30 miles off. Standing on deck in oilskins on a cold, grey day, was not how we visualised our approach to a tropical island! We anchored after dark, deepening the sense of mystery.

Our first daylight view of Rapa Nui the next morning reminded me of Scotland – green flowing hillsides and a misty rain. We sailed round the headland to anchor off the town of Hanga Roa, and then waited for our visit from the immigration and bio-security authorities.

SUNDAY 1ST DECEMBER

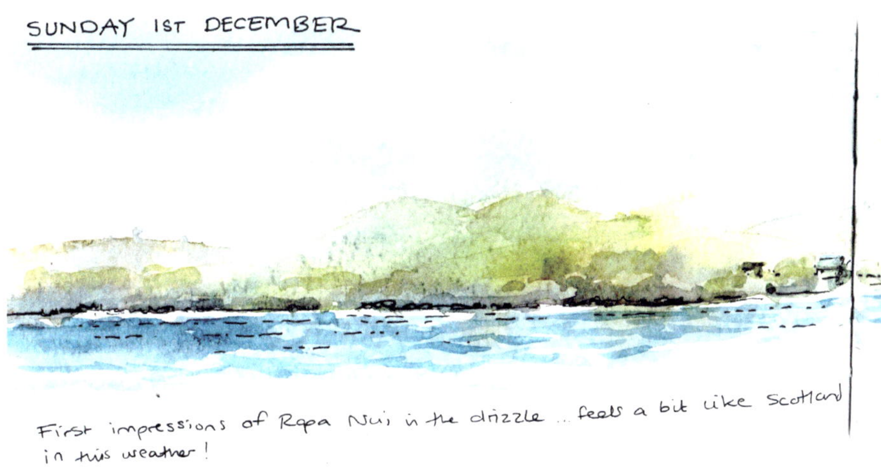

First impressions of Rapa Nui in the drizzle ... feels a bit like Scotland in this weather!

It was late afternoon before we could go ashore, and this was not straightforward. There is no harbour on the island, just an open anchorage which is unsafe in an onshore wind. Krista and Will had explored by dinghy so they knew where to take us ashore, heading through a gap in an alarming wall of surf and then turning sharp left into a small sheltered fishing quay. Hanga Roa is a sprawling network of narrow roads, single storey buildings amongst trees and hibiscus bushes, full of colour and a relaxed Polynesian atmosphere in the many cafes but a surprising amount of traffic (where were they all going? we wondered).

The people are a mix of Polynesian and Chilean – with a sense that the fiercely proud Polynesian side of the culture resented its Chilean ownership as much as it desperately needed its support, goods and services. Are there any remote islands that are able to be independent? I suspect not. Isolation is both a blessing and curse.

I teamed up with shipmate George and stayed ashore for a night in a small and inexpensive hotel. George hired a car and we took a trip around the island. Car hire on Rapa Nui is straightforward; every car is a white Suzuki jeep and the booking procedure goes like this: 'Can you drive?' 'Yes' 'Good. Here are the keys. There is no insurance.'

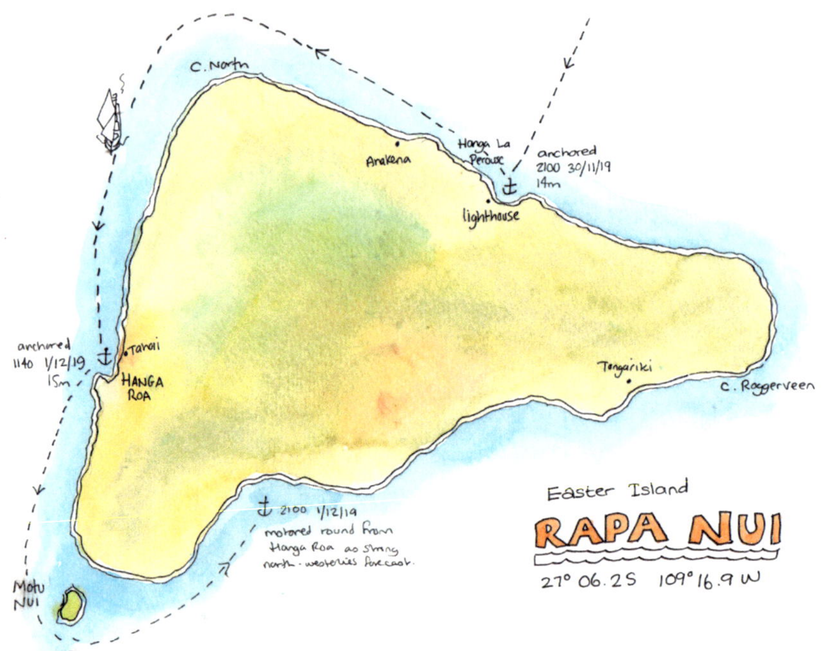

RAPA NUI

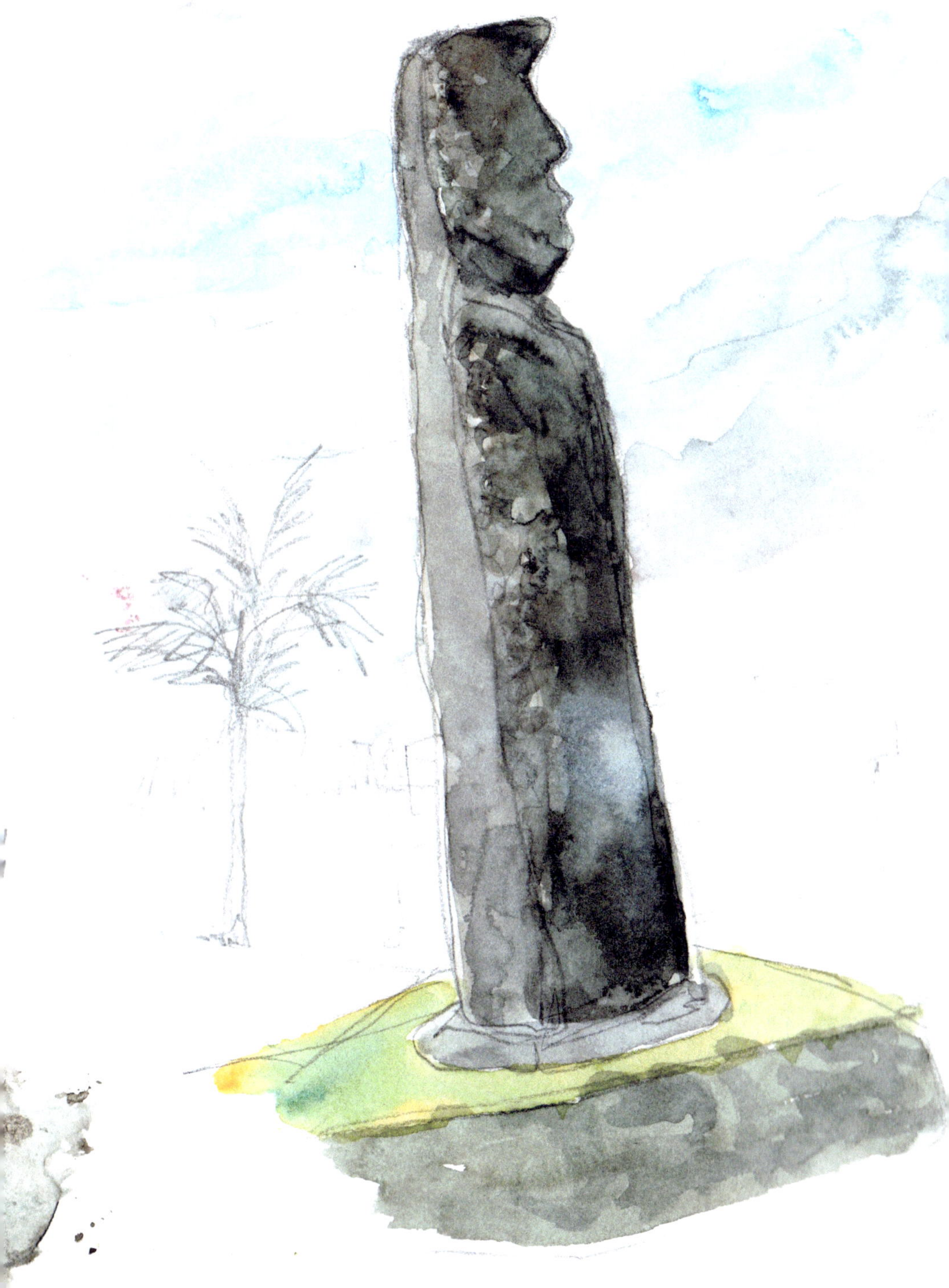

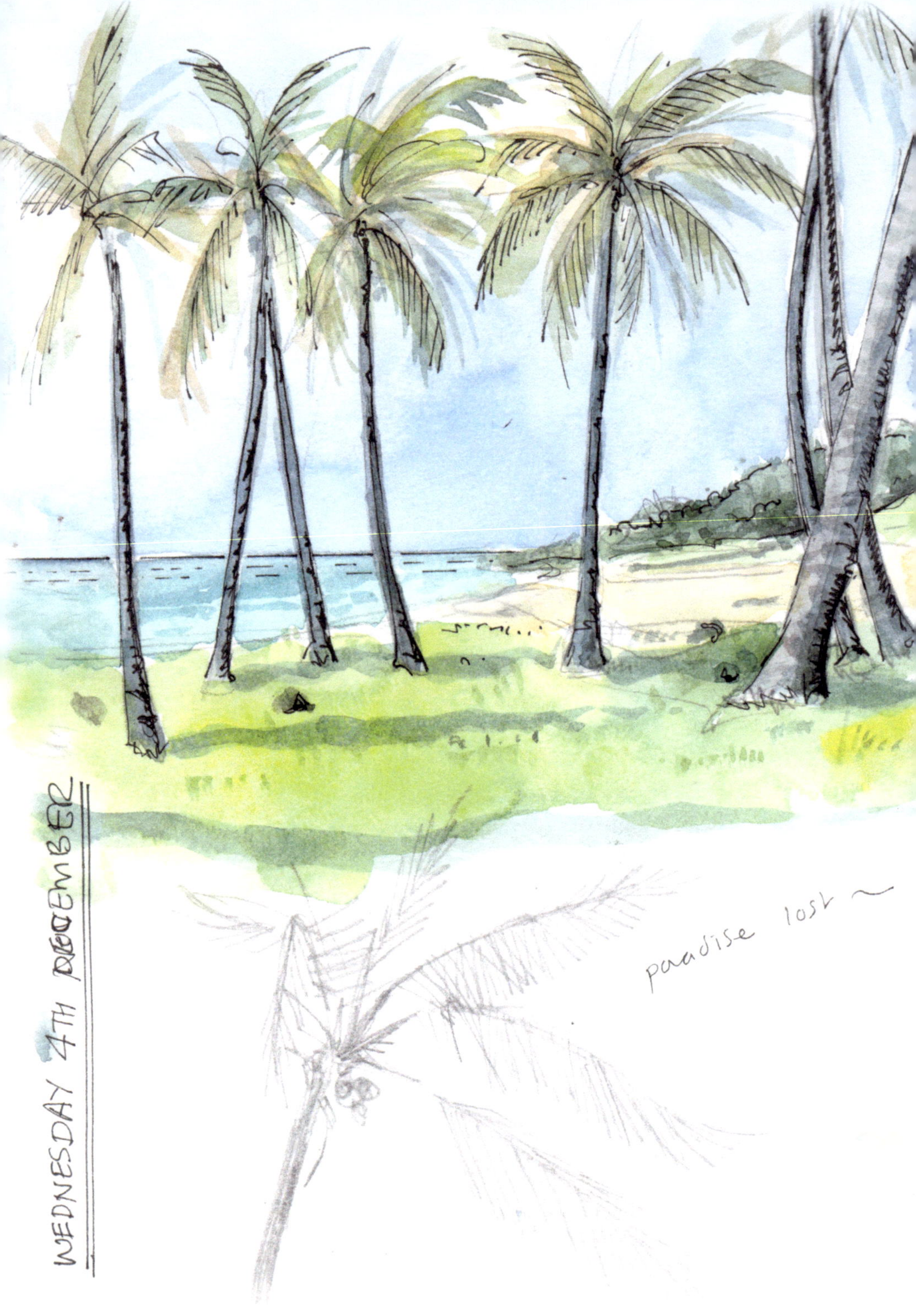

WEDNESDAY 4TH DECEMBER
paradise lost ~

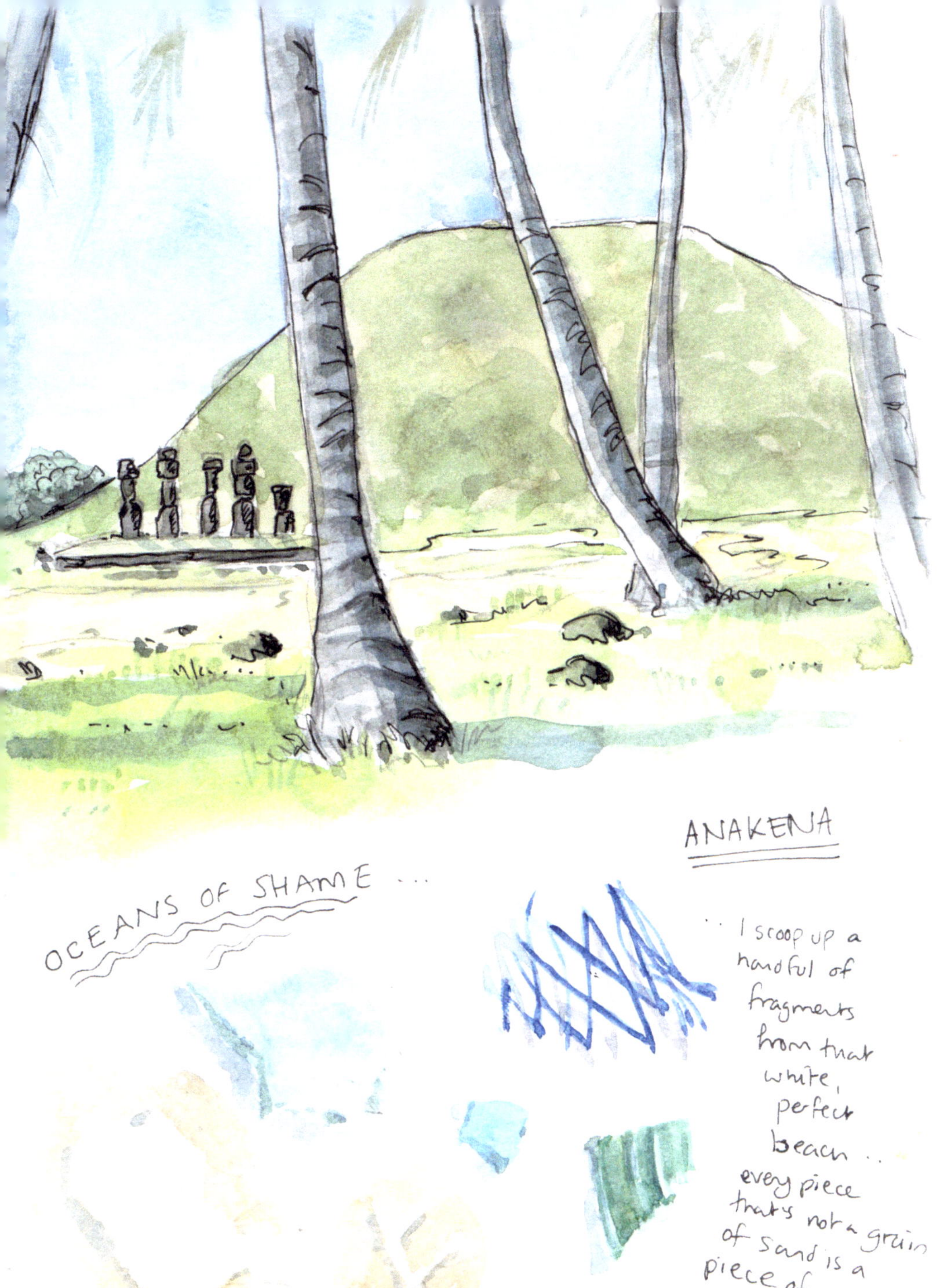

ANAKENA

OCEANS OF SHAME ...

... I scoop up a
handful of
fragments
from that
white,
perfect
beach ...
every piece
that's not a grain
of sand is a
piece of
PLASTIC

ANAKENA
first landing place of Rapanui people

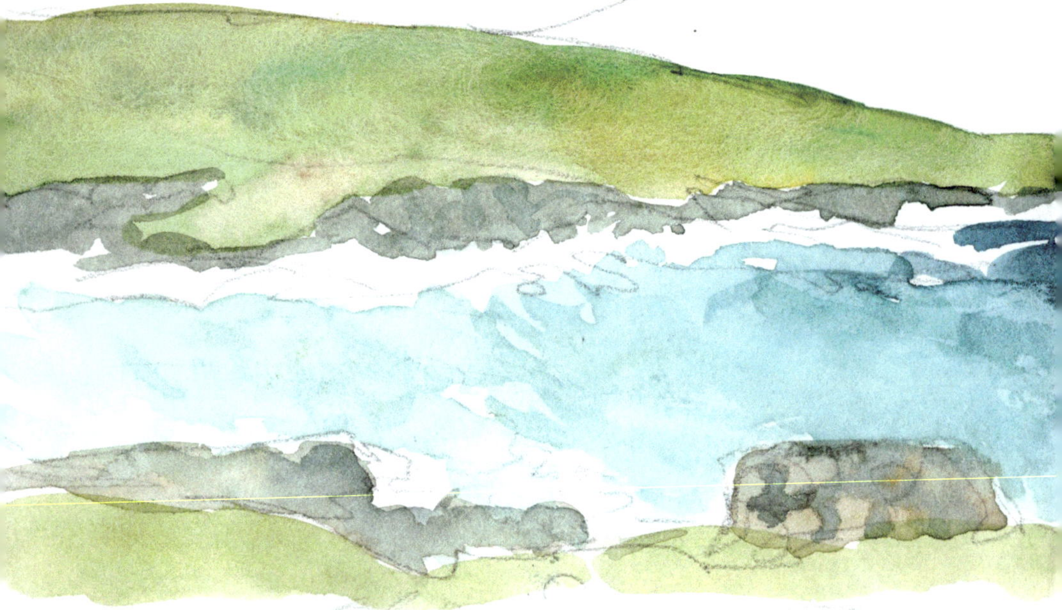

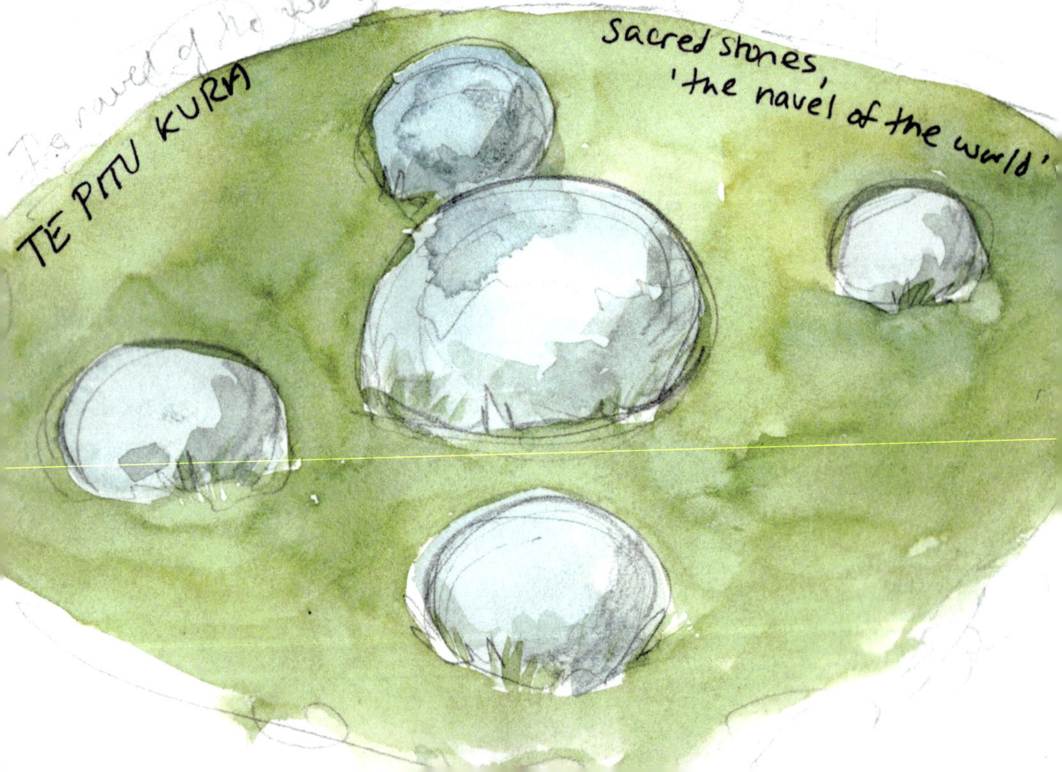

The navel of the world
TE PITU KURA
sacred stones,
'the navel of the world'

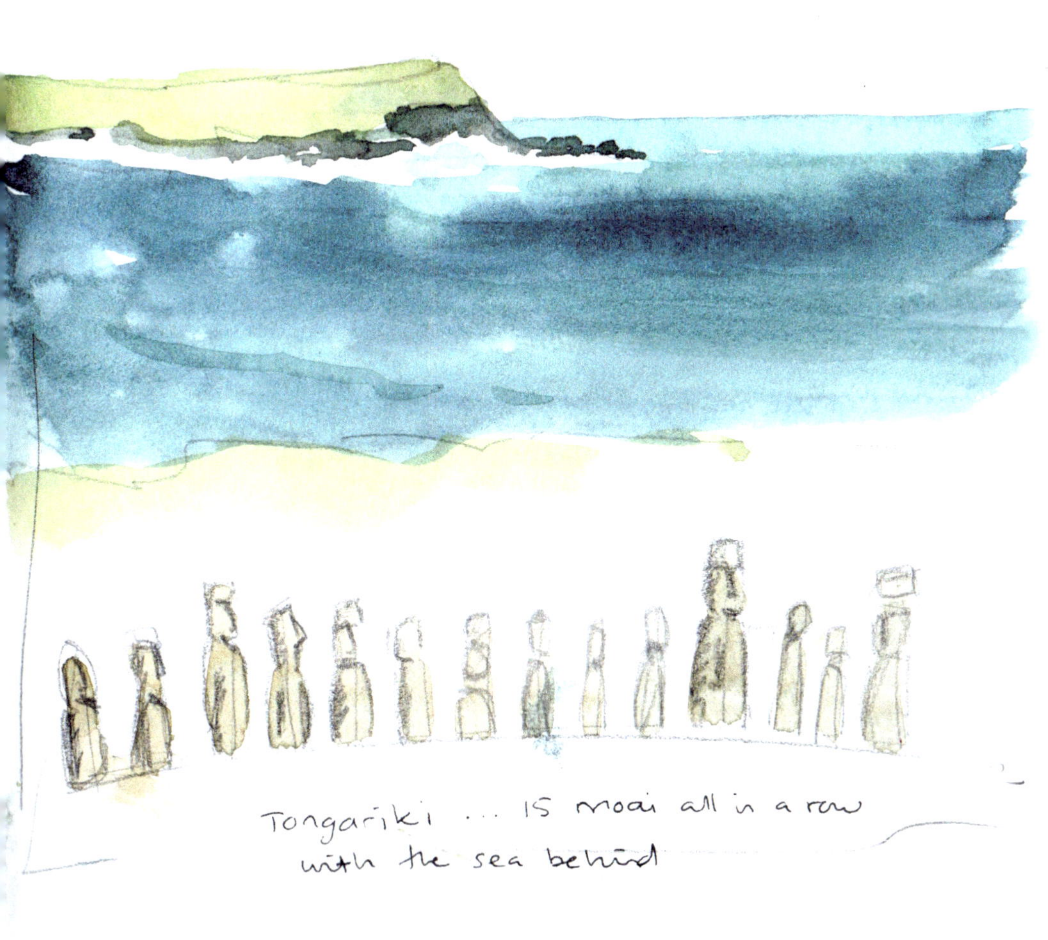

Tongariki ... 15 moai all in a row
with the sea behind

WEDNESDAY 4th ~~November~~ December! – road trip with George

THURSDAY 5th DECEMBER – ~~raining~~ raining hard, then easing to drizzle by lunchtime. Leisurely breakfast in town, then short drive to see the moai at Tahai – Tecla now anchored in the bay again.

Also visit the museum.

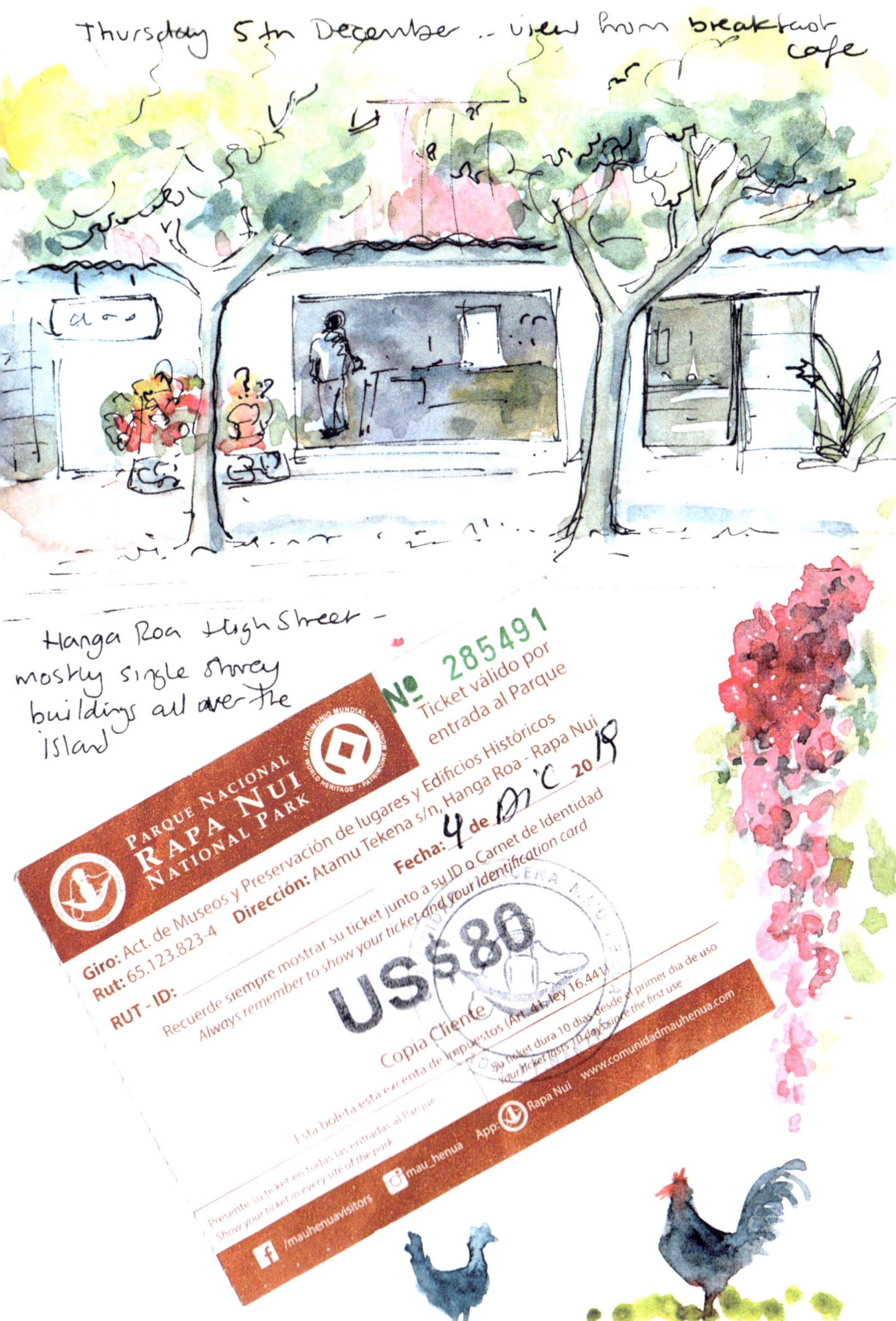

Thursday 5th December .. view from breakfast cafe
Hanga Roa High Street —
mostly single storey
buildings all over the
island
Nº 285491
Ticket válido por
entrada al Parque
PARQUE NACIONAL
RAPA NUI
NATIONAL PARK
WORLD HERITAGE · PATRIMOINE
PATRIMONIO MUNDIAL
Act. de Museos y Preservación de lugares y Edificios Históricos
Giro: Act. de Museos y Preservación de lugares y Edificios Históricos
Rut: 65.123.823-4
Dirección: Atamu Tekena s/n, Hanga Roa - Rapa Nui
RUT - ID:
Fecha: 4 de Dic 2019
Recuerde siempre mostrar su ticket junto a su ID o Carnet de Identidad
Always remember to show your ticket and your identification card
US$80
Copia Cliente
Esta boleta esta excenta de Impuestos (Art. 41, ley 16.44)
Su ticket dura 10 días desde el primer día de uso
Your ticket lasts 10 days since the first use
Presente su ticket en todas las entradas al Parque
Show your ticket in every site of the park
/mauhenuavisitors
@mau_henua
App: Rapa Nui
www.comunidadmauhenua.com

There is one straight road down the centre of the island and several more wriggling round the coastline. In the time we had we went to the far side of the island and round the coast, stopping briefly at a few of the sights along the way. There was not much time to sketch, which is why these pages are unfinished, but it gave me a good feel of the place. When you're short of time it's tempting sometimes to think 'It's not worth getting the paints out, I'll just take a photo instead', but I'm glad I had a go. These hasty sketches made me observe and take in the scene and when I look at them now, I'm taken right back to those big skies, rolling hills and a background of indigo sea.

Most of the island is National Park and before visiting the places of interest you have to buy a pass in town for $80. The islanders are keen to preserve their natural and human landscape, but remoteness and National Park status is no defence against the bigger problem of ocean pollution. The brightly colour fragments I found on the pristine-looking beach at Anakena all turned out to be not shells or stones but ocean-weathered pieces of plastic. The stone statues – the moai – dominate the island and they are impressive. It's hard to imagine the tenacity, time and effort the islanders invested into creating them. Many toppled or were knocked down during the island's history, but most have now been restored and put back in position. Some have had their blue and white coral eyes replaced.

I'd like to have stayed longer but time was running out. During the afternoon of 5th December I said a final goodbye to my Galapagos companions as I was the only one staying on for the next voyage. I'd already met a couple of my new shipmates around town (I made sure to wander around wearing my 'Tecla Crew' hoodie tied round my waist). Down on the small fishing quay at the appointed time I looked for people hovering nervously with luggage, gazing out at where Tecla was anchored for sign of the tender coming over to meet us. We were not difficult to spot - there's a chap with deck shoes and a large kit bag. 'Excuse me, are you joining Tecla? Me too!'

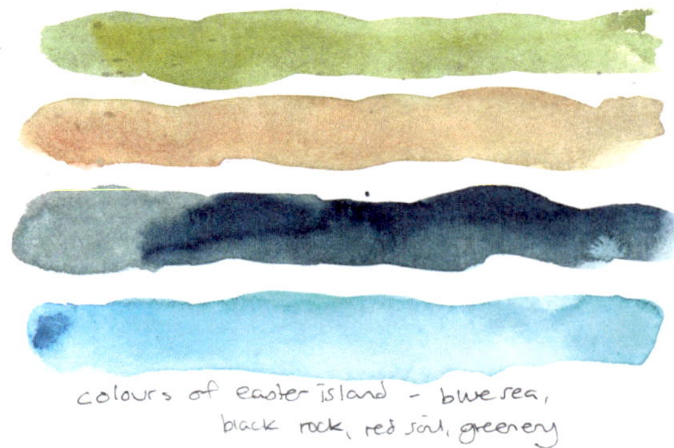

colours of easter island - blue sea,
black rock, red soil, greenery

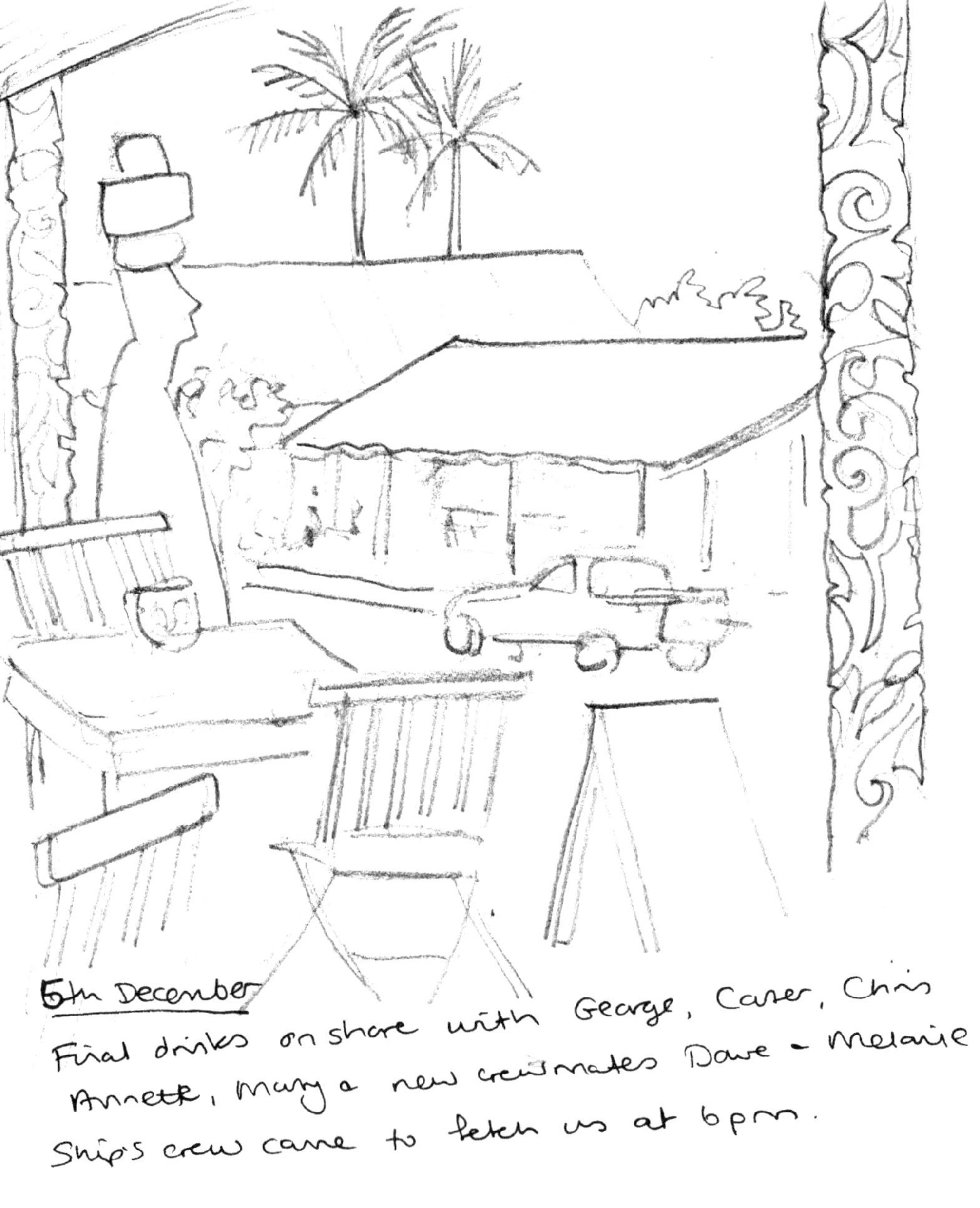

<u>5th December</u>

Final drinks on shore with George, Carer, Chris, Annette, Mary & new crewmates Dave + Melanie. Ships crew came to fetch us at 6pm.

FAREWELL RAPA NUI

We set sail from Hanga Roa on **FRIDAY 6TH DECEMBER 2019**

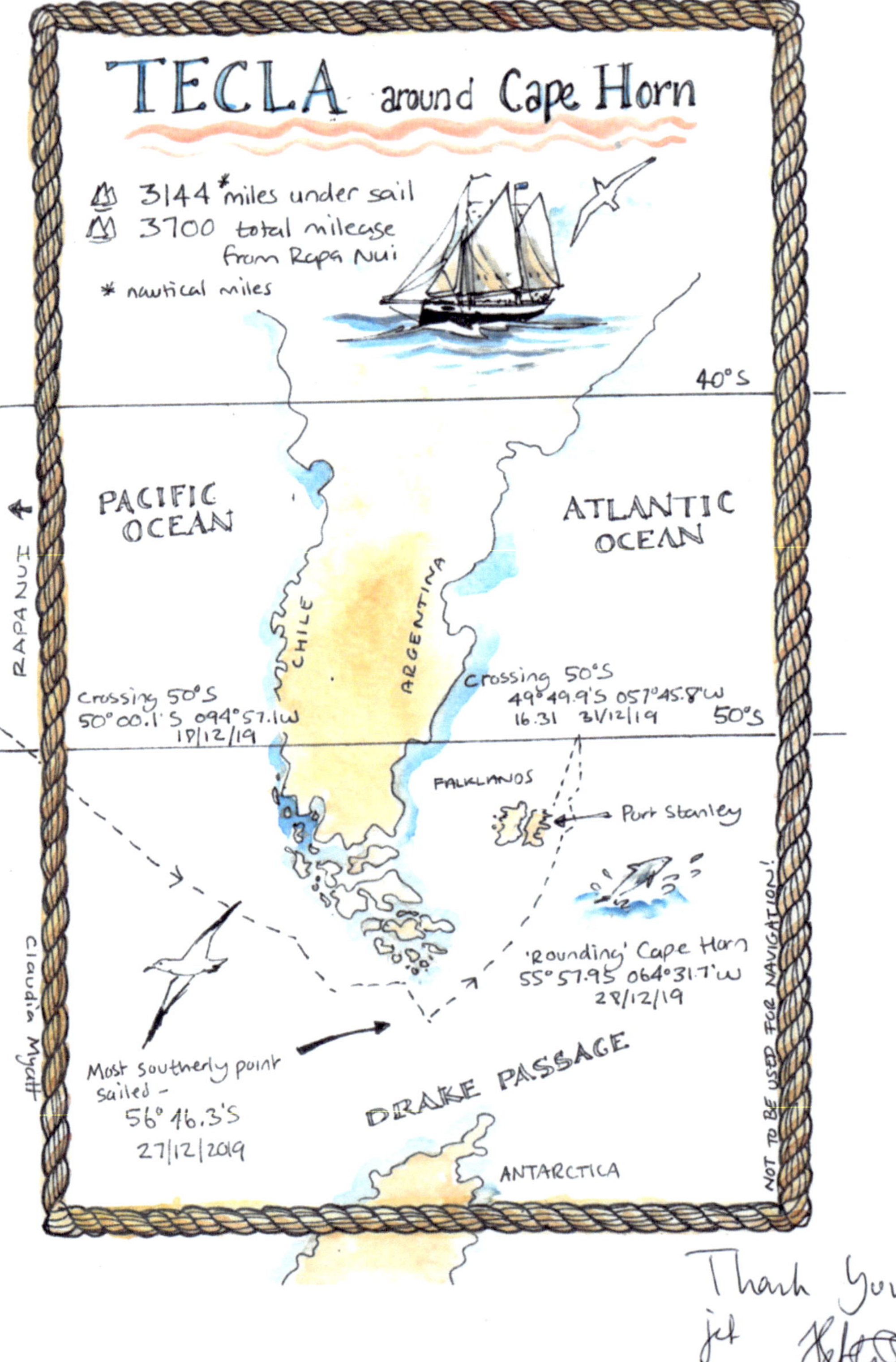

TECLA around Cape Horn
3144 * miles under sail
3700 total mileage from Rapa Nui
* nautical miles
40°S
PACIFIC OCEAN
ATLANTIC OCEAN
RAPA NUI
CHILE
ARGENTINA
Crossing 50°S
50°00.1'S 094°57.1W
18/12/19
Crossing 50°S
49°49.9'S 057°45.8'W
16.31 31/12/19
50°S
FALKLANDS
Port Stanley
'Rounding' Cape Horn
55°57.9S 064°31.7'W
28/12/19
Most southerly point sailed –
56°16.3'S
27/12/2019
DRAKE PASSAGE
ANTARCTICA
Claudia Myatt
NOT TO BE USED FOR NAVIGATION!
Thank You!
jet

Farewell Rapa Nui

We had a new captain – Gijs had flown home and his sister Jet (pronounced 'Yet') was leading the next voyage. Our crew ranged in age from twenty-something to sixty-something, a mix of English, Dutch, French, German, New Zealand, American, Chinese and Tasmanian. We were nine voyage crew altogether, three of us on each watch. I was on blue watch, 8-12, which still meant getting all the sunsets as we were heading south and the sun set later each night. I was lucky enough to be the only one with a cabin to myself.

It was easier getting into the ship's routine this time as I was familiar with it, but I was more nervous about what lay ahead. This voyage was longer and conditions were going to get colder and more difficult. Just cope with it one watch at a time, I told myself, noticing gratefully that there was a radiator in each cabin and the promise of heating being turned on when it became chilly. I think we appreciated sailing through moonlit tropical nights at the beginning of the voyage knowing that we would soon be heading into colder waters.

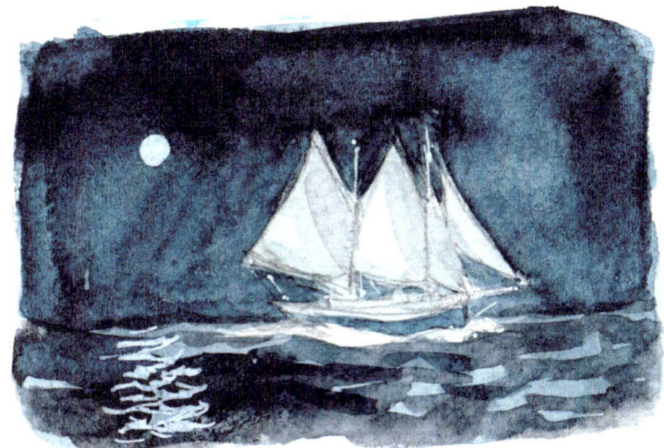

Heading for Cape Horn

If you mention 'Rounding the Horn' to a small boat sailor it's like mentioning Everest to a mountaineer – it's the big one. When I told friends and fellow sailors what I was planning to do the reactions were extreme: either 'Oh, amazing, I've always wanted to do that!' or 'You're crazy, rather you than me!'

There are plenty of small cruise ships working the south coast of Chile and taking passengers to Antarctica so you no longer have to endure thousands of miles under sail to see the fabled Cape. Hardy sailors with a well equipped boat can sail the islands from the sheltered waters of Ushuaia or Punta Arenas. Indeed in good weather you can anchor off Horn Island and go ashore to the small lighthouse that marks the southernmost point of the Americas. With this in mind, the International Association of Cape Horners (www.capehorners.org) tries to maintain the spirit of achievement by setting qualifying conditions to a ship and crew wanting to call themselves Cape Horners:

'Membership is open to individuals of all nationalities who have rounded Cape Horn under sail as part of a non-stop passage of at least 3,000 nautical miles which passes above the latitude of 50° South in both the Pacific (or Indian) and Atlantic Oceans and is completed without the use of engines for propulsion'.

It is about 3,500 nautical miles from Rapa Nui to Falkland. As long as we had a good margin of over 3,000 miles to go, we used the engine in the calms at the beginning of the voyage to give ourselves more time later. The weather was fickle right from the start and this trip would involve the captain in careful planning based on the daily satellite forecast, threading our way through the pattern of low and high pressure systems all around us. We would try to avoid very strong winds and calms whilst keeping our stern to the swell and heading in the right direction – not easy as the forecast was not always correct.

There was a more businesslike atmosphere on board than the easy-going holiday feel of the last leg. We were all taking the time, under Will's guidance, to get more familiar with the ropes so that we could go straight to the correct ones when needed in a hurry or at night. The professional crew spent time on maintenance, checking the rigging and digging out storm sails. We even plugged the anchor chain pipes with cement (what a messy job!) to stop water getting into the chain locker in big seas.

The weather became cool quickly, especially at night. We were kept busy with fickle winds, and inspired by some spectacular sunsets. As the weather became cooler, our appetites increased and Jet's cooking did not disappoint. I notice that food starts to feature more and more in my sketchbook. On the first leg I had often skipped breakfast or lunch. But now I was astonished to see a large bowl of porridge disappear at 8am followed at 12 by a large helping of cooked lunch, then the same at supper with second helpings, and still be keen for snacks at midnight. Fresh fruit ran out early on as supplies had been limited in Rapa Nui, but *Tecla's* larder and freezer were very well stocked and I don't recall having the same meal twice.

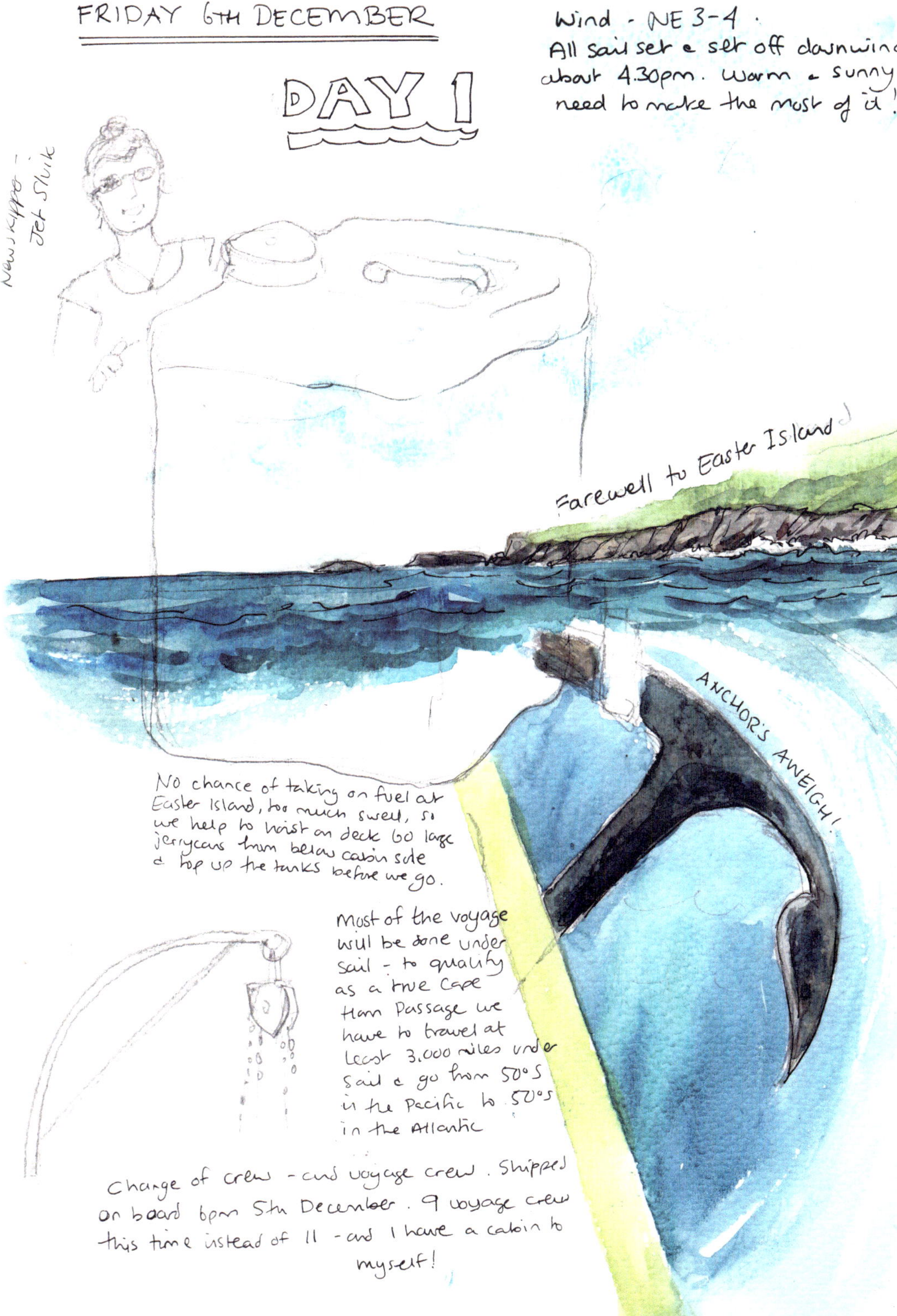

FRIDAY 6TH DECEMBER

DAY 1

Wind - NE 3-4.
All sail set & set off downwind
about 4.30pm. Warm & sunny -
need to make the most of it!

Farewell to Easter Island

ANCHOR'S AWEIGH!

News Kippa -
Jet Stink

No chance of taking on fuel at
Easter Island, too much swell, so
we help to hoist on deck 60 large
jerrycans from below cabin sole
& top up the tanks before we go.

Most of the voyage
will be done under
sail - to qualify
as a true Cape
Horn Passage we
have to travel at
least 3,000 miles under
sail & go from 50°S
in the Pacific to 50°S
in the Atlantic

Change of crew - and voyage crew. Shipped
on board 6pm 5th December. 9 voyage crew
this time instead of 11 - and I have a cabin to
myself!

SATURDAY 7TH DECEMBER

DAY 2

Still heading just west of south with a fresh breeze astern,
sea gentle this morning, getting a bit livelier during the day.
Preventers are on the rig but helming takes concentration!

Will is keeping us busy on watch - this morning we cemented the
anchor pipes to keep water out of the boat in big seas, also decks
scrubbed.

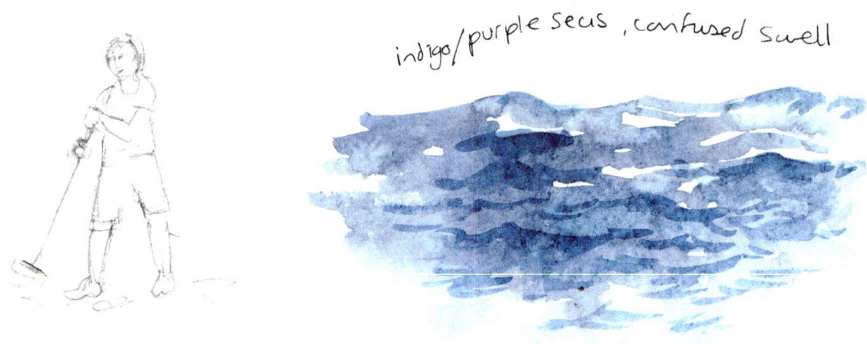

indigo/purple seas, confused swell

RED WATCH	WHITE WATCH	BLUE WATCH
Kate Paul David	Kersten Dennis Melanie	Claudia Siyu Russell
12-4 0200 - 1600	4 - 8 1600 - 2000	8 -12 2000 - 0000
12 - 6 Jet •	Erik 6 -12	Will • Krista

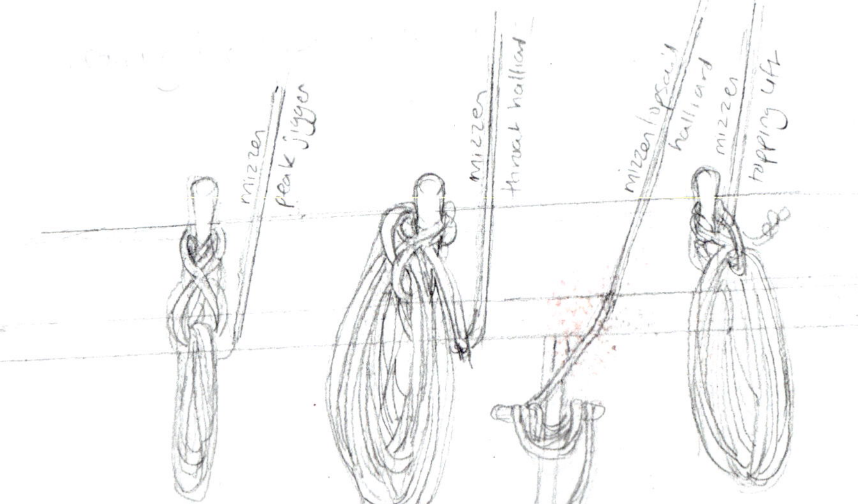

7 am, sun trying to
break through

After two days of good sailing, we came on morning watch to
motoring into a lumpy sea. Raining, then cloudy. Still warm, but
oilskins and boots are on!

Later ... all sorts of weather today, evening watch
much rougher & cooler. Reef in, reef shaken out, sailing
slowly over lumpy sea. Not much drawing opportunity
today

Frustrating evening trying to
sail with fickle headwinds.
Give up eventually, take all
sail down, & motor.

Lovely moonlit night.
Krista gets out her birthday
ukulele!

Still on Rapa Nui time
so it's 9.15 am &
sun is not yet set.

Yellow dusk, changing
to pink & purple

DAY 4

Cool, clear start with a headwind, motoring with staysails & mizzen

Chilly wind!

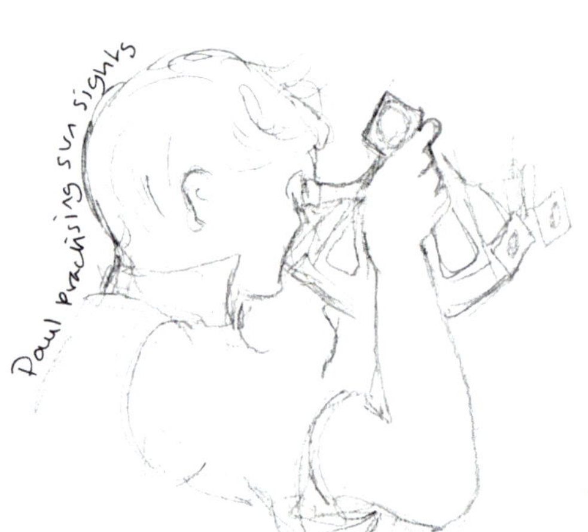

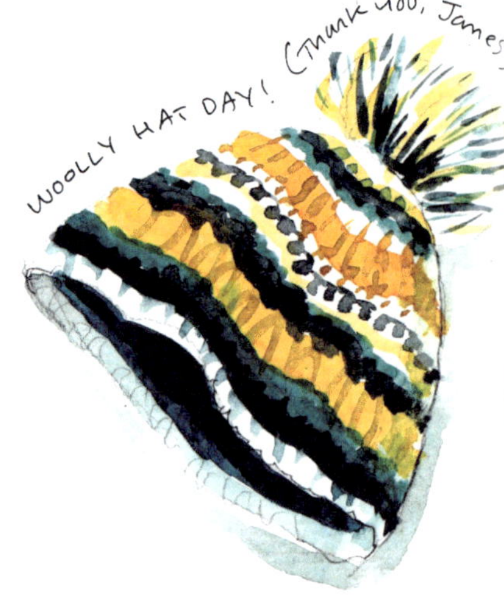

evening watch... perfect weather but no wind!

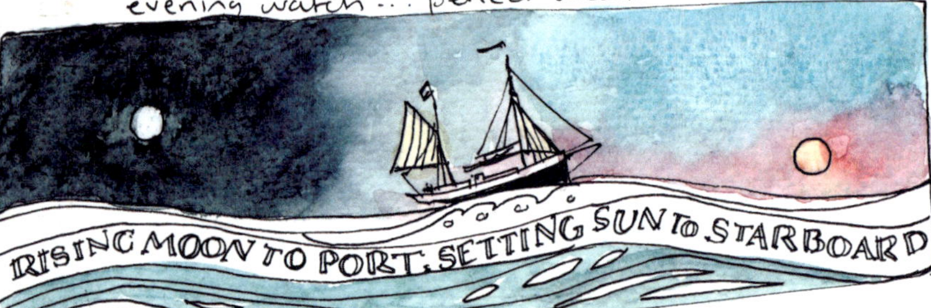

musical interlude on watch - krista on guitar, me on 'harp', but hard to hear ourselves with engine noise
9.30 PM

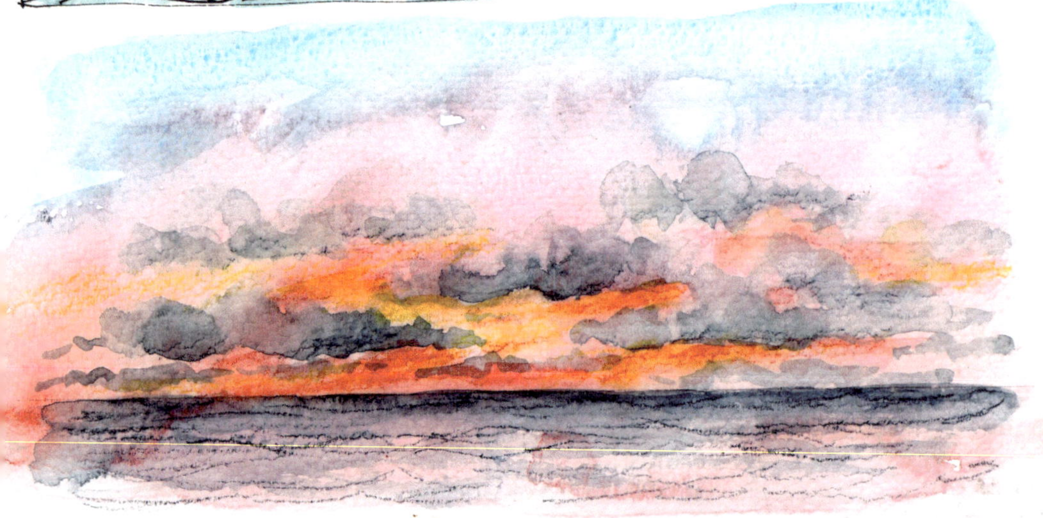

<u>TUESDAY 10TH DECEMBER</u>

DAY 5

wind again at last, fitful from SW,
but picking up gently. muffins for breakfast (thank you krista!)
and a cool day with bits of blue sky, long swell from the SW
will reads us extracts from the nautical almanac to
keep us amused (a tsunami travels 300-500 knots at sea)

<u>CLOUDSPOTTING · · · ·</u>   alto-cumulus (probably!)

cumulus

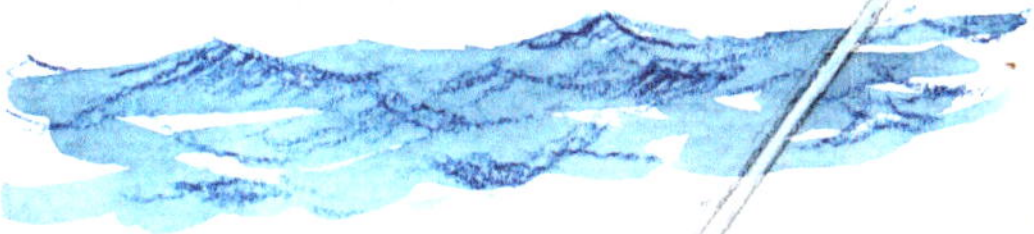

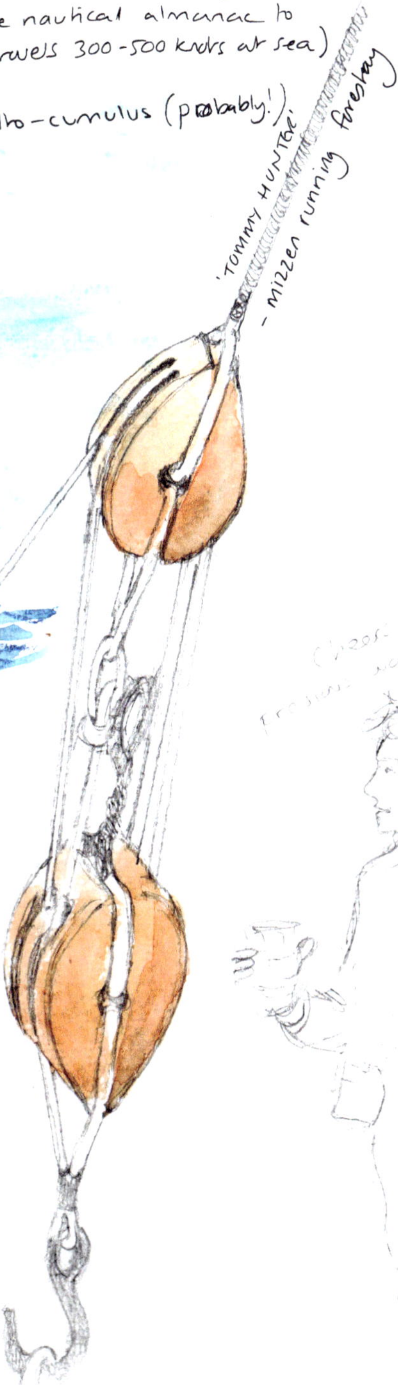

'Tommy Hunter'
– mizzen running forestay

evening watch –

sailing at 7 knots
in lively sea, one
reef in main,
wind on beam.
Previous watch have
set us a challenge to
beat their 29 knots
in 4 hours

(we did! 32.4 nm
   in 4 hours.
   lively sailing!)

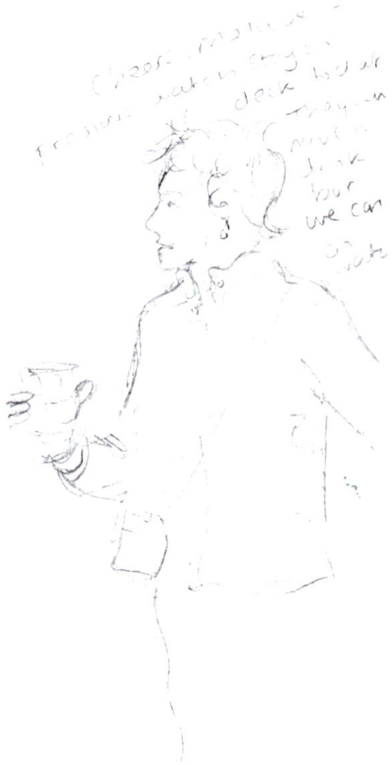

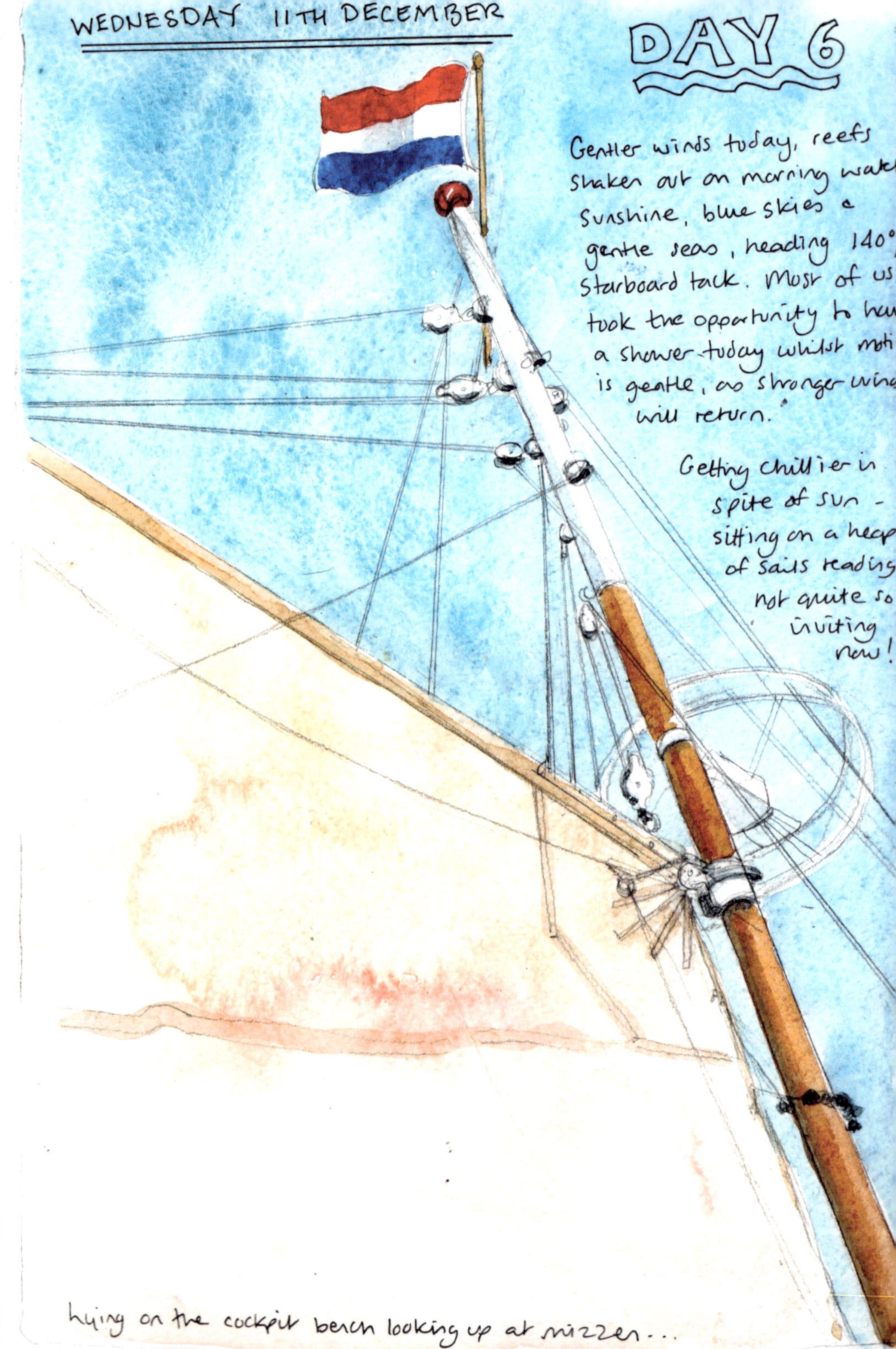

WEDNESDAY 11TH DECEMBER

DAY 6

Gentler winds today, reefs
shaken out on morning watch
Sunshine, blue skies &
gentle seas, heading 140°
Starboard tack. Most of us
took the opportunity to have
a shower today whilst motion
is gentle, as stronger winds
will return.

Getting chillier in
spite of sun -
sitting on a heap
of sails reading
not quite so
inviting
now!

lying on the cockpit bench looking up at mizzen...

THURSDAY 12TH DECEMBER

DAY 7

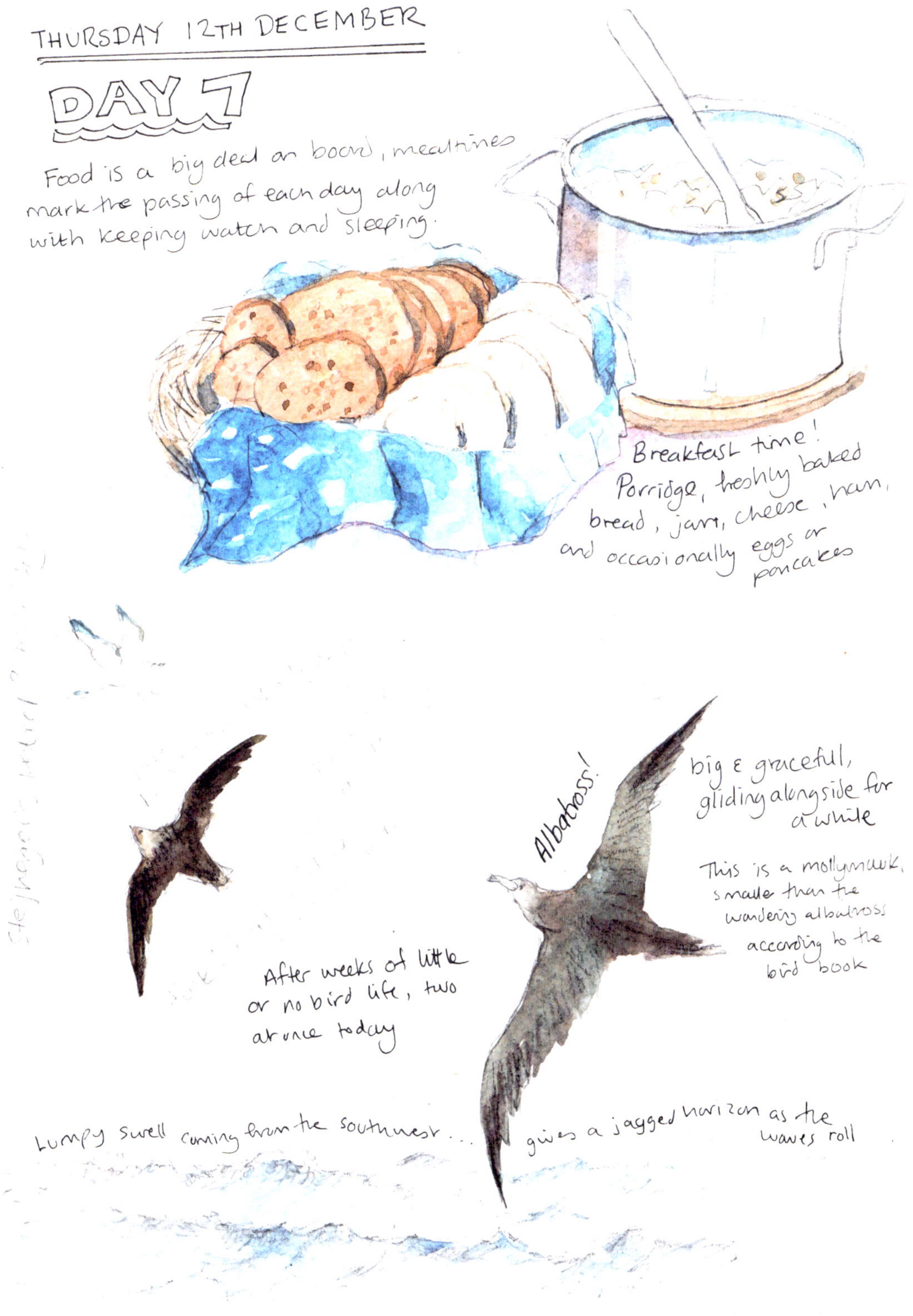

Food is a big deal on board, mealtimes mark the passing of each day along with keeping watch and sleeping.

Breakfast time! Porridge, freshly baked bread, jam, cheese, ham, and occasionally eggs or pancakes

After weeks of little or no bird life, two at once today

Albatross!

big & graceful, gliding alongside for a while

This is a mollymawk, smaller than the wandering albatross according to the bird book

Lumpy swell coming from the southwest... gives a jagged horizon as the waves roll

DAY 8

Passed 40°S overnight - now officially in the Roaring Forties. Not roaring too much at the moment, doing 6 - 7 knots with reefed main. Big swell running. Cold!

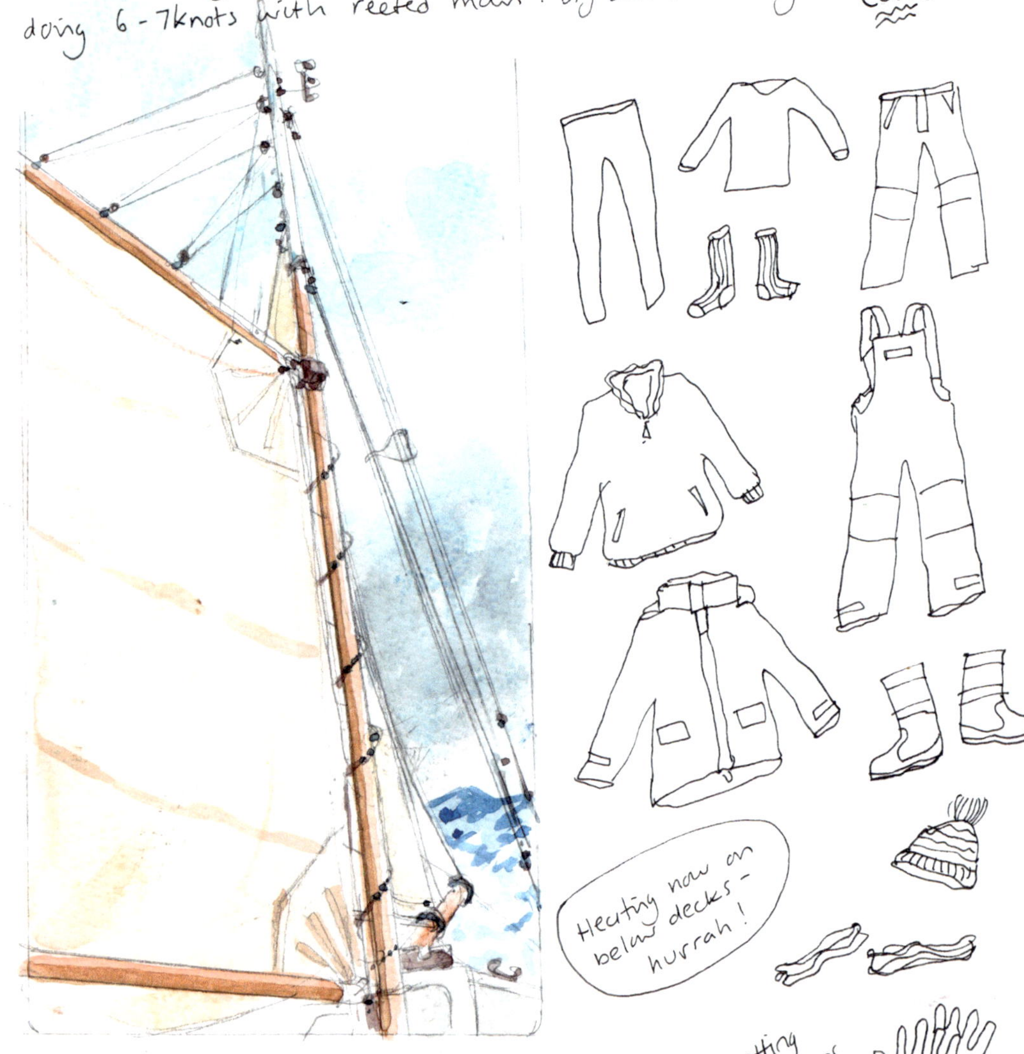

Quality of light is becoming more intense - sea a deep sapphire & sharp contrast between blue & white of the crests.

Clear blue sky for a while... no vapour trails here!

SATURDAY 14TH DECEMBER

DAY 9

Threading our way between storms & calms – heading east now after a frustrating time of calms and squalls

Odd sunset.. sun appearing through gaps in the cloud like orange discs

Krista makes oat & chocolate cookies out of leftover porridge – delicious!

Today's challenge is technical – Will says 'Teclacal'

the mizzen goose neck

about a third of the way there in distance

SUNDAY 15TH DECEMBER

DAY 10

Heading just south of east, port tack,
7-8 knots, overcast but dry. Steady
sailing.

DATA SHOWN:

SOG - speed over ground
COG - course over ground
BTW - bearing to waypoint
DTW - distance to waypoint
DTA - distance to arrival
TTA - time to arrival

also: position
mileage done so far

A visit to the chartroom ~ part one

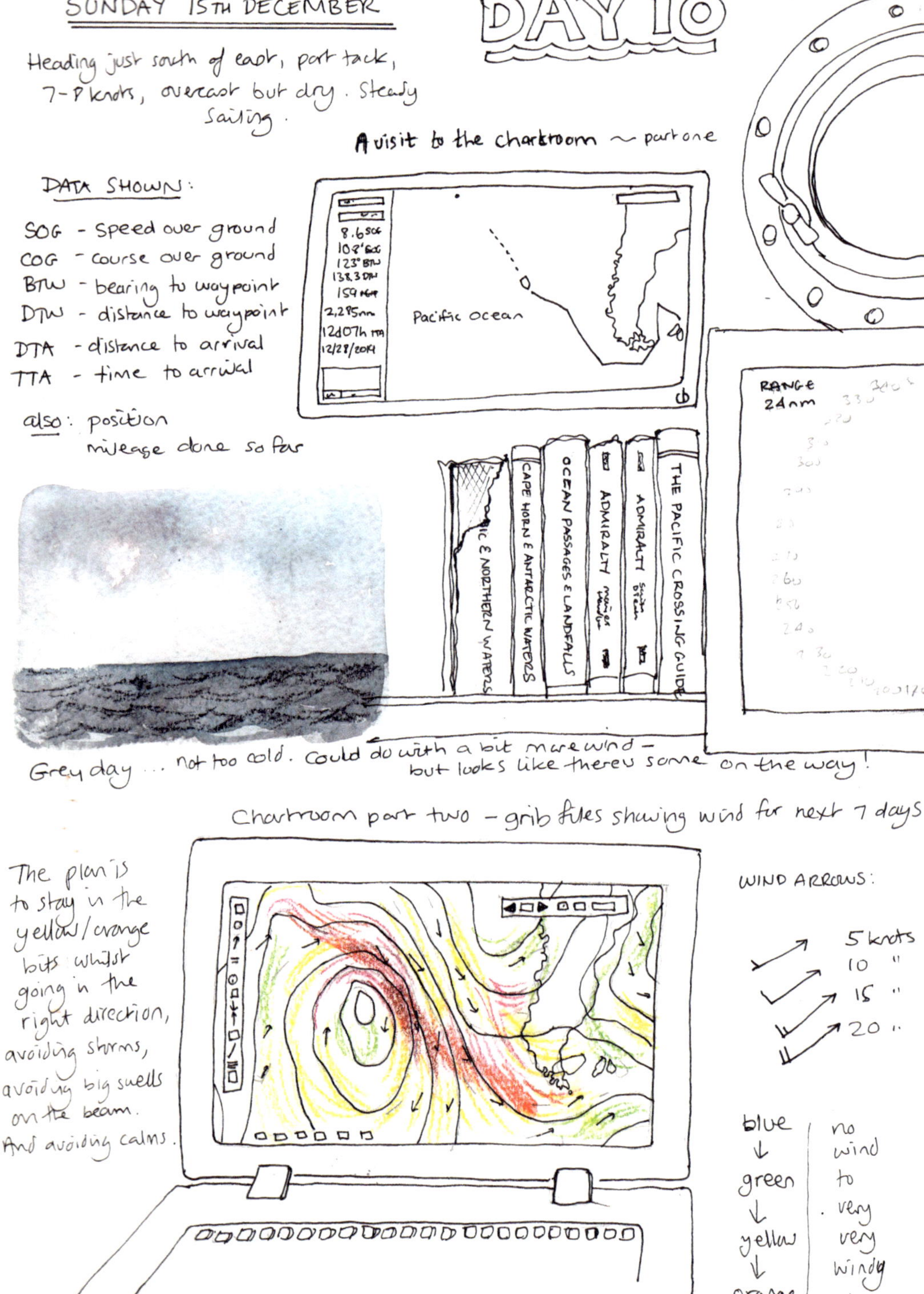

Grey day ... not too cold. Could do with a bit more wind — but looks like there's some on the way!

Chartroom part two — grib files showing wind for next 7 days

The plan is to stay in the yellow/orange bits whilst going in the right direction, avoiding storms, avoiding big swells on the beam. And avoiding calms.

MONDAY 16TH DECEMBER

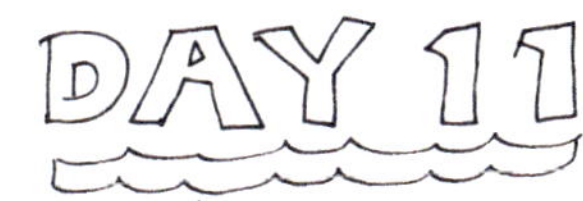

Above deck.. today's 'Technical' challenge,
the compass binnacle and entrance to chartroom

...below deck .. when Jet is not busy working out how to navigate us
to Cape Horn, threading our way through
complex weather systems,
she is cooking up a storm
in the galley

DAY 12

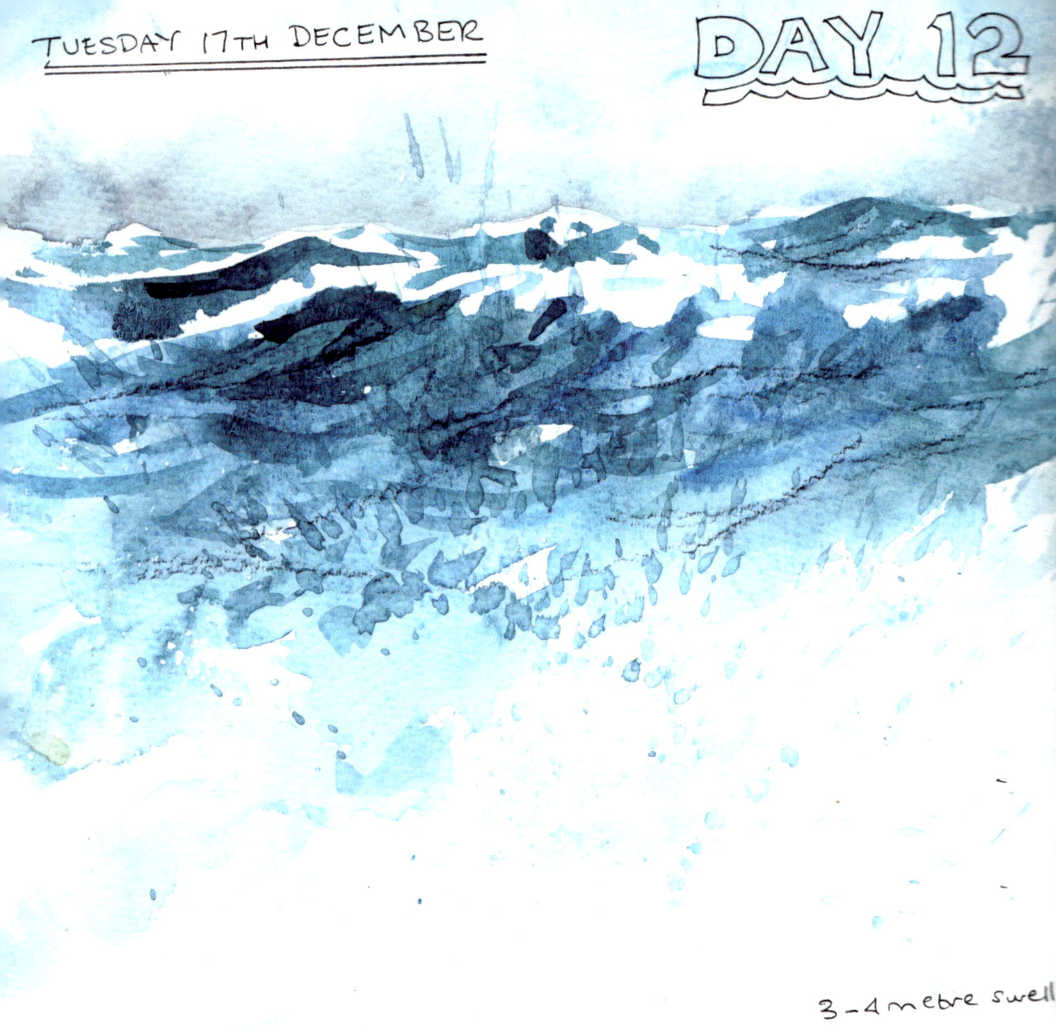

The roaring forties have started roaring. At 47°S we were becalmed when we went off watch last night. Sails down as they were slatting in the swell, just waiting in the rain & dark for a wind. Later in the night it arrived, plenty of it. Went on watch this morning to steep seas, clear cold sunlight and a fresh wind. 8-9 knots with only reefed mizzen & headsails.

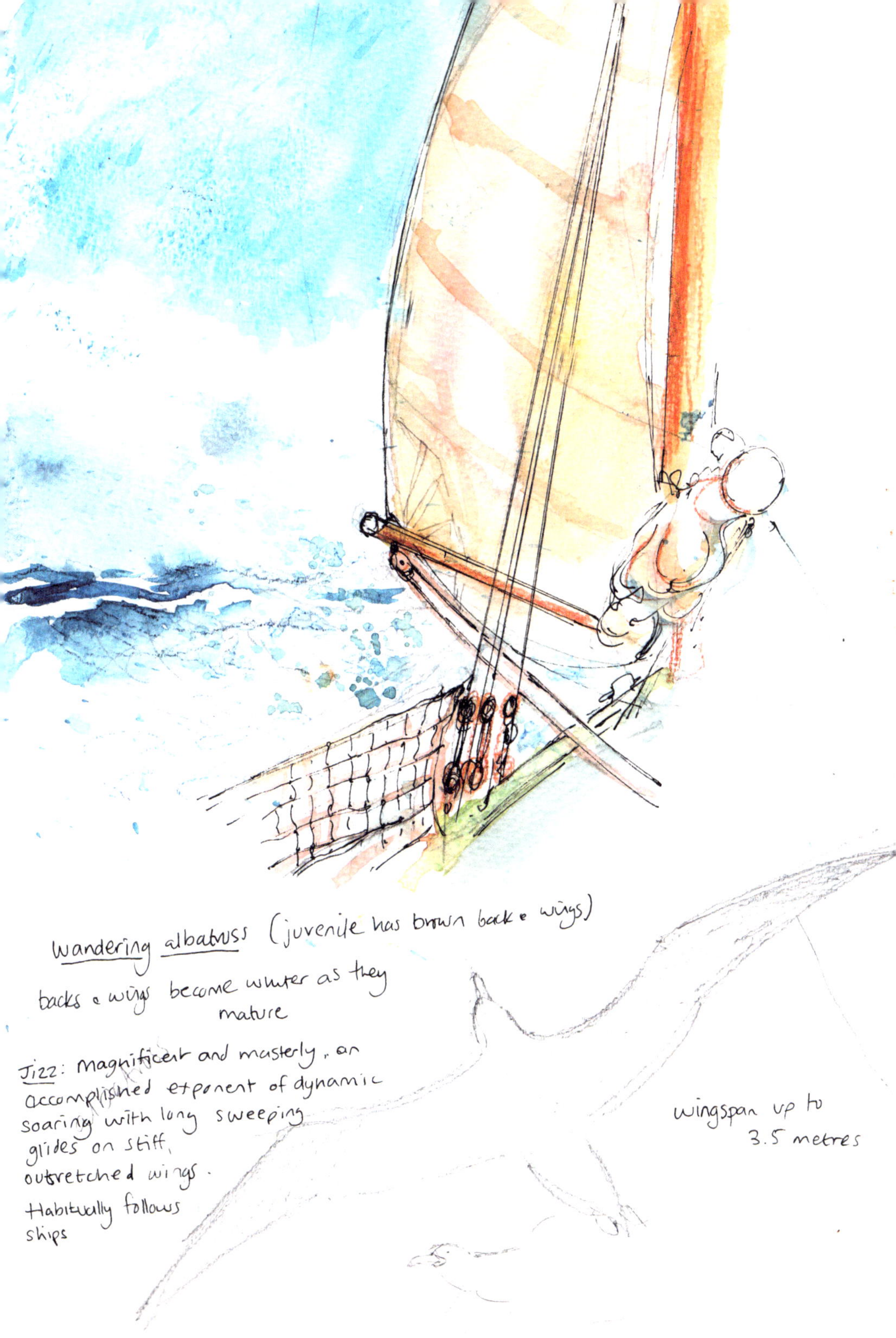

Wandering albatross (juvenile has brown back & wings)
backs & wings become whiter as they mature

Jizz: magnificent and masterly, an accomplished exponent of dynamic soaring with long sweeping glides on stiff, outstretched wings.
Habitually follows ships

wingspan up to 3.5 metres

WEDNESDAY 18TH DECEMBER — DAY 13

Cold & clear, lively sea, heading SE under reefed main & mizzen. Wind not as strong as yesterday. Albatross sightings more frequent but nothing else to see but the sea!

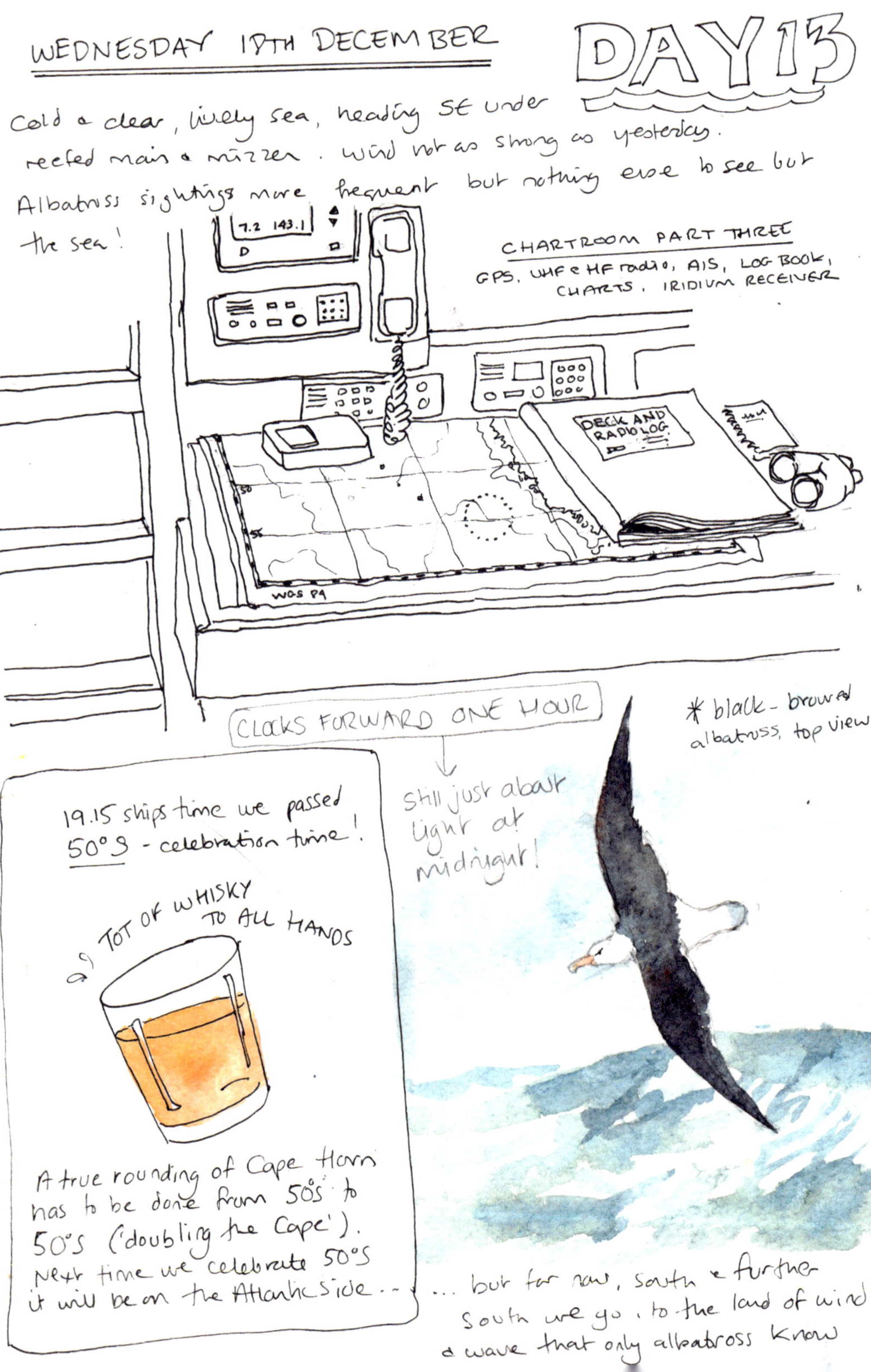

Company on our morning watch —
two albatross swooping and gliding
close by.

Probably black-browed albatross
* (black/dark brown wings on top,
white head, white/light tail)

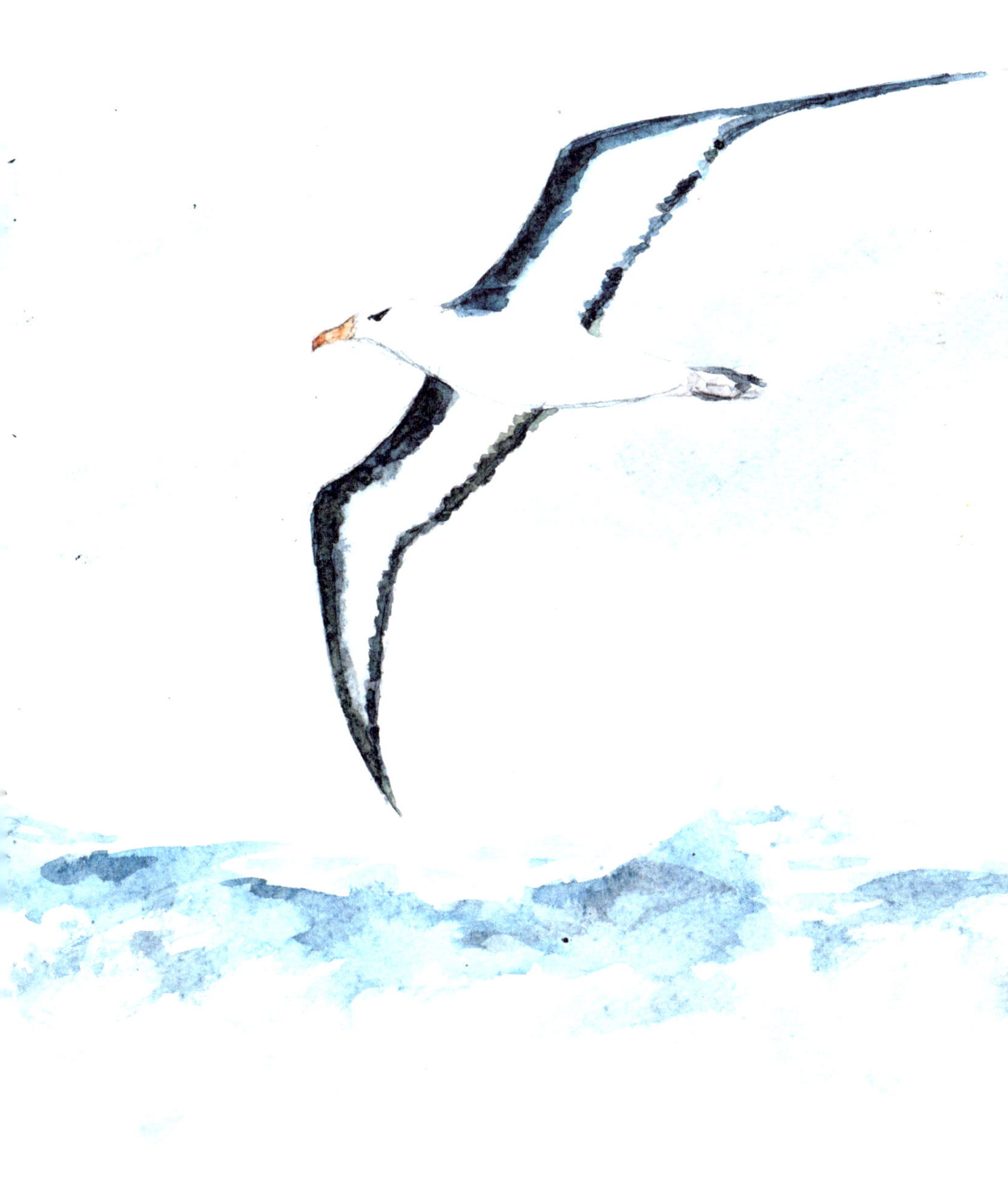

As we sailed south, the sea started to come alive – or at least, the sky did. Our first albatross were the smaller brown mollymauks; later the first sighting of the large wandering albatross caused great excitement. We consulted Peter Harrison's comprehensive book 'Seabirds' to try and identify each species that we saw – not easy when there is a bewildering number of sub-species all with subtle differences and all you can see from a moving ship is a moving bird gliding fast over the wave tops. Identification is made harder by the fact that like most birds the wings and markings change colour as they grow from juvenile to adult.

Getting dressed each morning was beginning to take a long time. Day 8 shows three layers but that soon increased to six. At coldest times I wore merino long sleeved vest, skinny poloneck, long sleeved thermal top, fleecy top, lightweight windproof jacket and oilskin jacket on top of everything. Round my neck several neck warmers, one pulled over my head, a woolly hat and the hood of one of the jackets pulled over everything. On the bottom half I had merino leggings, lined sailing trousers, oilskin trousers, enormous socks and waterproof sailing boots. I had two pairs of gloves which were always getting wet so one pair was always on the radiator to dry. Later, the thermals stayed on under pyjamas when I went to bed!

Words, pictures, conversations

My sketchbook was becoming more than a record of what I was seeing each day, it contained topics of conversation and ideas too. Chatting with Will on Day 9 about the fittings on the mizzen goose neck (where the boom joins the mast) gave me the idea of trying to draw it and yes, it was challenging! Drawing complex objects requires a great deal of concentration and has to be done slowly and with care, asking questions all the time: 'Where does that line join that one? How long is that bit compared to that bit? How big is that little space between the two blocks.....' and so on. It's not a process that can be hurried.

Later, I drew the discussion we were having about the horizon as a circle and our ship always in the centre of our world. This is a different kind of drawing – a bit of imagination, a splash of paint and a bit of playfulness.

There's nothing to see but this circle of ocean,
Where blue of the sky meets the blue of the sea

There's nowhere to be but the midst of the circle, our ship sailing steady and free

Being out of sight of land day after day is surprisingly soothing. The concerns of the shouty, overpopulated parts of the planet which occupy our everyday lives are nothing down here. Talking to my shipmates, we agreed that we didn't miss the internet or contact with the outside world; we knew it would all still be going on when we returned. Out here all was peace and the rhythm of the days, on watch or off watch. Instead of a myriad of concerns, we only had a few – What's the wind doing? Is it letting us sail in the right direction? Will our watch bring us joyful sailing at 8 knots with a fair breeze or will it be headwinds, calms, squalls and sail changes? How many layers do I need to put on? What's for dinner? Are my gloves dry?

Our main question of course was always 'Where are we?' On watch, Krista or Will took us through the latest weather forecast for the next few days which determined our course to steer, picking our way through the most favourable winds – in theory, at least. In practice, the weather had a habit of disobeying the forecast. 'It's supposed to be blowing 20 knots from the west right now!' Krista would howl, jabbing at the laptop screen as we wallowed in a fitful calm. But generally the forecast kept us out of trouble, avoiding the really nasty stuff. It also gave us the opportunity to escape the cold on deck to sit in a warm chartroom for a while whilst we discussed it. Drawing the chartroom on Day 10 gave me a good excuse to sit in the warm and dry for a bit longer; much nicer than trying to draw out on deck.

We couldn't help taking regular peeks at the chart plotter, which showed our ship as a tiny icon creeping oh so slowly across this huge ocean. When progress was good, we'd look at the estimated time to arrival (shown as TTA on the screen) with satisfaction. 'Hurrah, we'll be in Port Stanley by New Year's Eve!' But when we slowed to a crawl, or a contrary wind had us steering a different course to the one we wanted, it paid not to look. 'According to our current speed, we'll arrive in Port Stanley on 30th March!' When totally becalmed, looking at the TTA became a source of fun. '564 days to go..... do you think we'll run out of biscuits?'

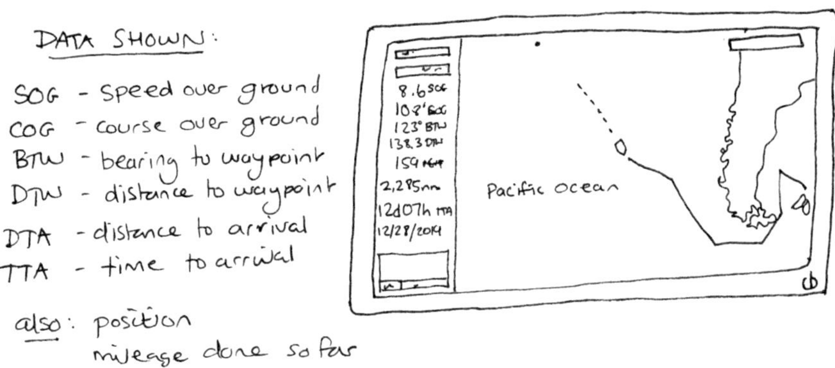

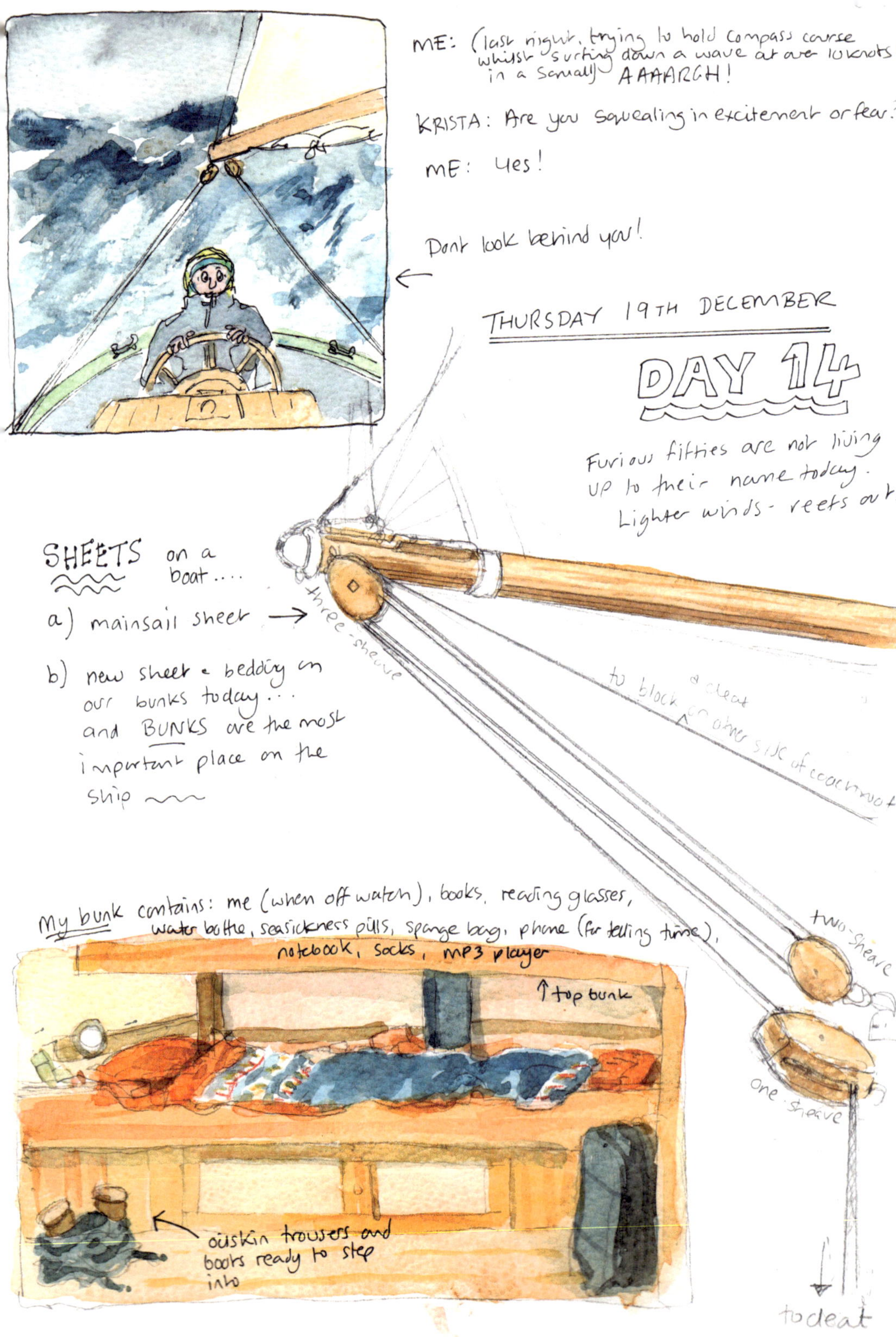

ME: (last night, trying to hold compass course whilst surfing down a wave at over 10 knots in a squall) AAAARGH!

KRISTA: Are you squealing in excitement or fear?

ME: Yes!

Dont look behind you!

THURSDAY 19TH DECEMBER

DAY 14

Furious fifties are not living up to their name today. Lighter winds - reefs out.

SHEETS on a boat....

a) mainsail sheet →

b) new sheet & bedding on our bunks today...
and BUNKS are the most important place on the ship

three-sheave

a cleat
to block on other side of coachroof

two-sheave

one-sheave

My bunk contains: me (when off watch), books, reading glasses, water bottle, seasickness pills, spange bag, phone (for telling time), notebook, socks, mp3 player

↑ top bunk

oilskin trousers and boots ready to step into

to deat

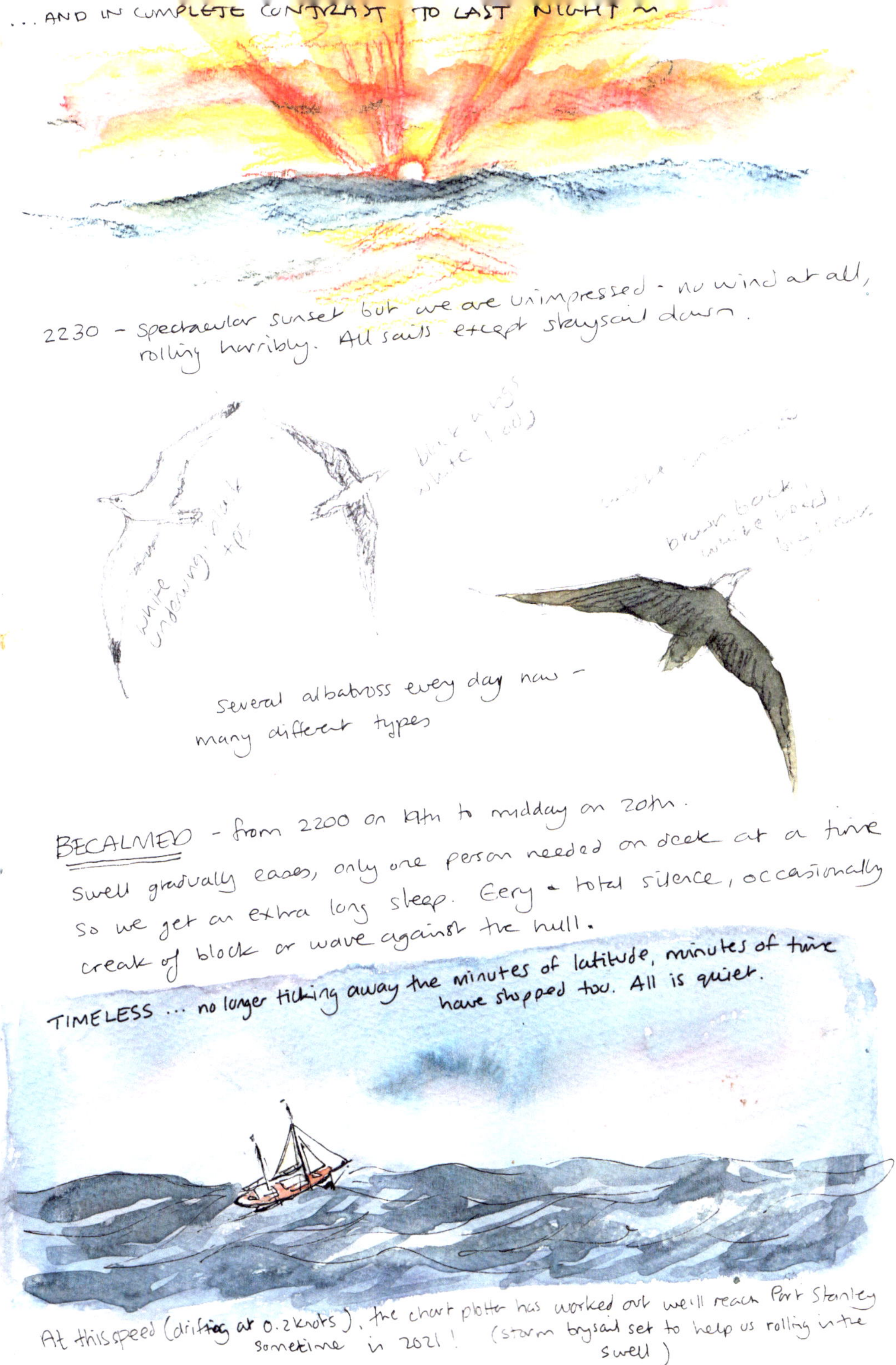

... AND IN COMPLETE CONTRAST TO LAST NIGHT ~

2230 - spectacular sunset but we are unimpressed - no wind at all, rolling horribly. All sails except staysail down.

Several albatross every day now — many different types

BECALMED - from 2200 on 19th to midday on 20th. Swell gradually eases, only one person needed on deck at a time so we get an extra long sleep. Eery & total silence, occasionally creak of block or wave against the hull.

TIMELESS ... no longer ticking away the minutes of latitude, minutes of time have stopped too. All is quiet.

At this speed (drifting at 0.2 knots), the chart plotter has worked out we'll reach Port Stanley sometime in 2021! (storm trysail set to help us rolling in the swell)

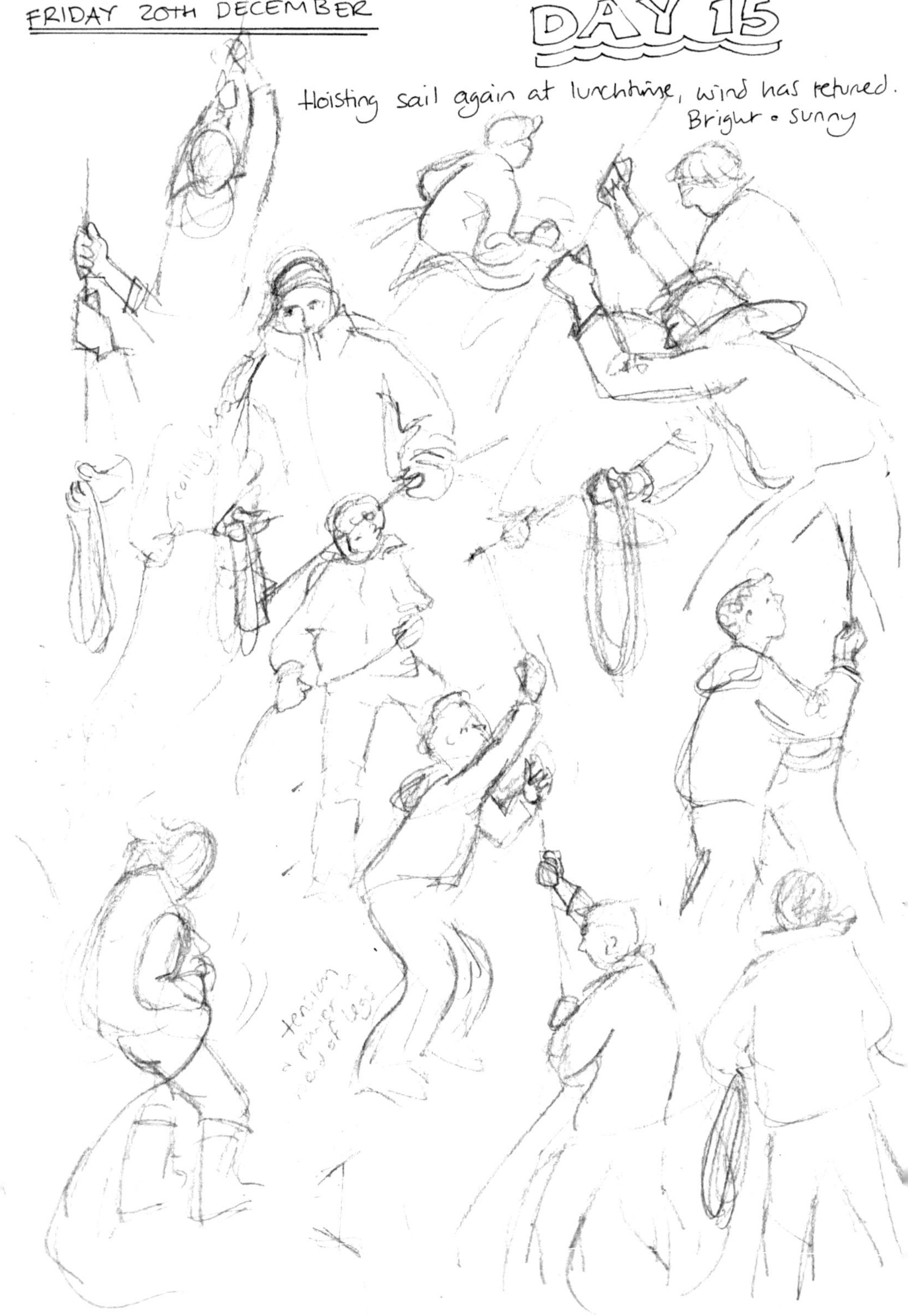

FRIDAY 20th DECEMBER
DAY 15
Hoisting sail again at lunchtime, wind has returned.
Bright & sunny

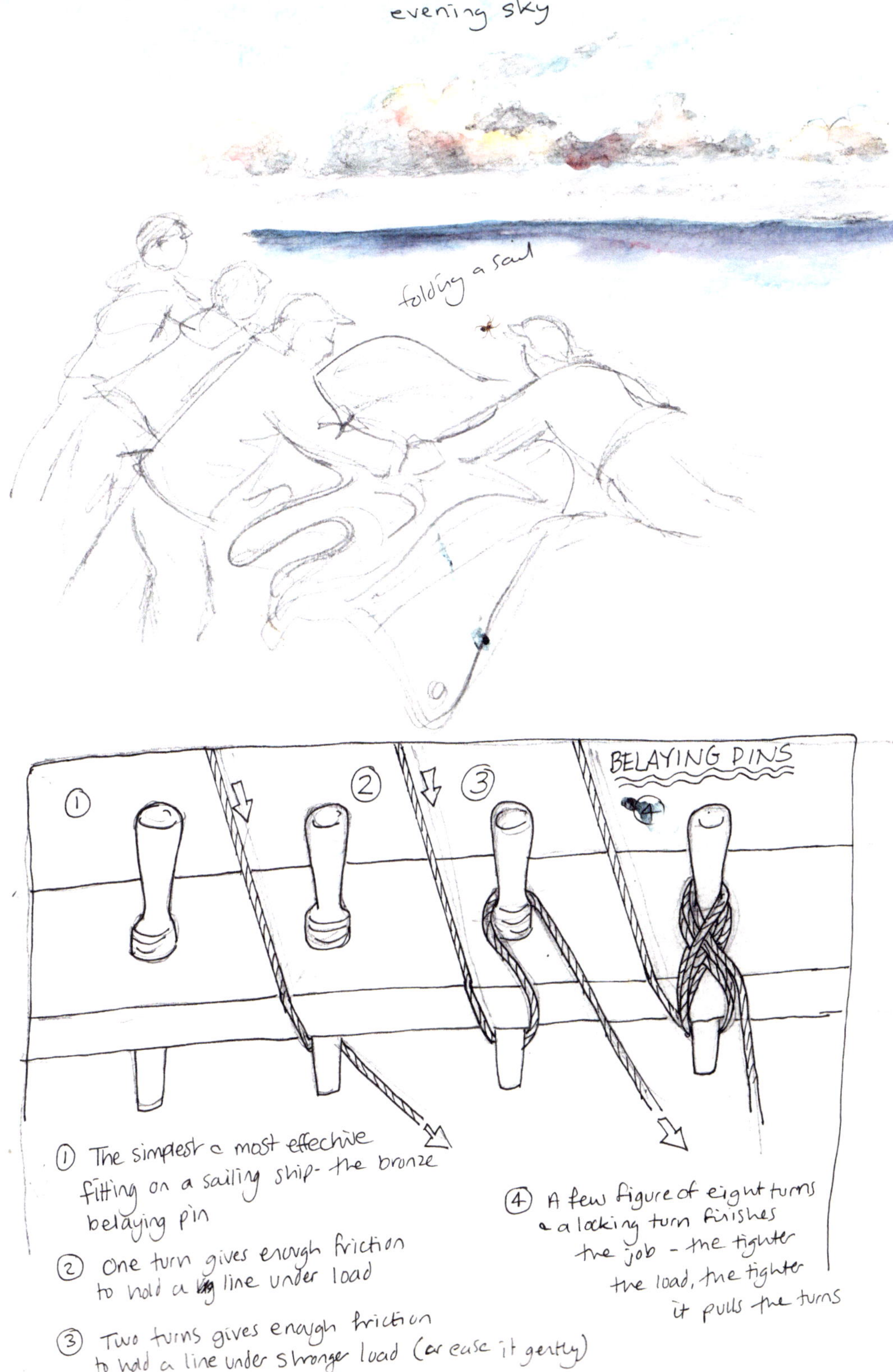

evening sky
folding a sail
BELAYING PINS
1
2
3
4
① The simplest & most effective
fitting on a sailing ship - the bronze
belaying pin
② One turn gives enough friction
to hold a line under load
③ Two turns gives enough friction
to hold a line under stronger load (or ease it gently)
④ A few figure of eight turns
& a locking turn finishes
the job - the tighter
the load, the tighter
it pulls the turns

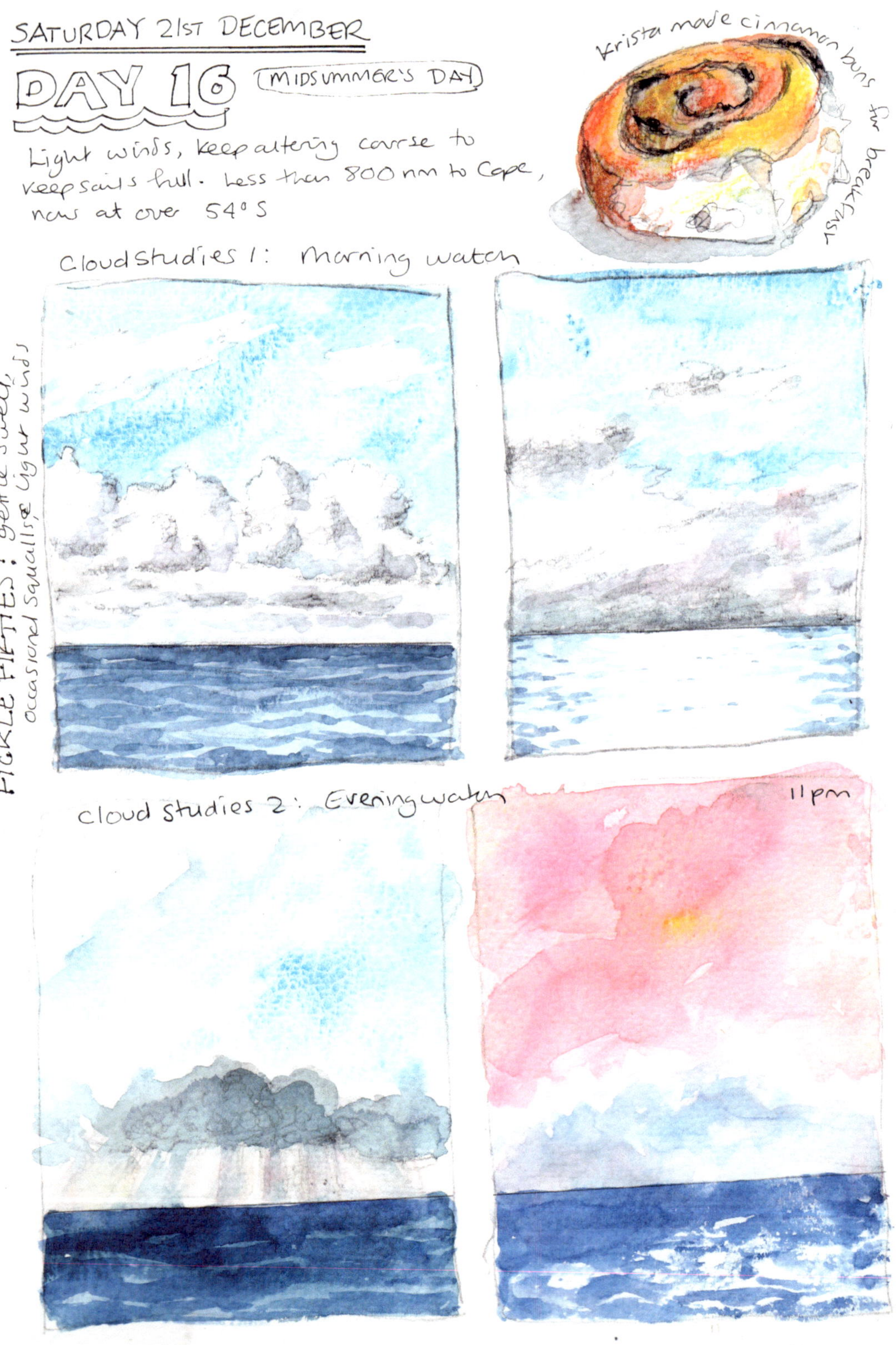

SATURDAY 21st DECEMBER

DAY 16 (MIDSUMMER'S DAY)

Light winds, keep altering course to keep sails full. Less than 800 nm to Cape, now at over 54°S

Cloud Studies 1: Morning watch

Cloud Studies 2: Evening watch   11pm

SHIP'S LIBRARY

Norse mythology
Books ... biographies   guide books   Origin of species
thrillers   cook books   sailing books   books about islands
books in Dutch   novels   books about explorers   books about Arctic waters
books in English
books about Franklin Rae

BECALMED AGAIN

all afternoon, rolling in the swell going nowhere. Christmas decorations now festoon the saloon.

About 9pm a southerly wind arrives, sails back up & sailing in the right direction at 6-7 knots. Very cold!

Accompanied all evening by various albatross who circled us & followed us, coming close at times. Several varieties including very large ones (wandering albatross?

Shipmates all

There were long periods doing nothing on watch when it's not your turn at the wheel. Conversations were far ranging, from profound (How did the Polynesians navigate the Pacific without a compass? Do you think there's life on any of those stars? What can be done about plastic in the oceans?) to trivial (OK, which country has the best pizza restaurant? Who was the worst person you ever sailed with? Can you touch your nose with your tongue? Look, everyone, I'm doing a wind dance!)

On the whole, we all got along well. Differences that would cause friction ashore were soothed by the ship's routine; opposing political views matter not a jot when you are all pulling on the same rope. When not on watch it was possible to spend plenty of time alone reading, listening to music or dozing in your bunk, your own small but private space.

Initially, my watch companions on this leg were two young men. Russ was an American vagabond sailor who crewed on cargo ships but wanted to work on sailing ships. Siyu was Chinese, lived in New York and was a rigger for a maritime museum. Like Russ, he wanted to spend his life working the oceans. These two were young and fit, courteous, good company and with a quiet sense of humour. Later, Siyu swapped his watch with Kate, an English woman the same age as me but made of a different metal altogether; practical and courageous she had driven helicopters, done part of the Clipper round the world yacht race and had a career as air traffic controller. She made a point of taking an interest in everyone and how they ticked, and could be relied upon to liven up flagging conversation.

We were supervised by Krista and Will, mate and bosun, who I'd got to know on the first leg of the voyage. Young and multi-skilled they worked their twelve hours in two shifts every day for months on end, with only occasional time off in harbour, if there was time once the boat had been provisioned and cleaned ready for the next voyage crew. Between them they could navigate, trim sails, mend anything that was broken, bake bread, splice rope and keep everything running smoothly. They both also worked on board the square- rigged ship *Europa*, which regularly sails the Antarctic and Southern Ocean route with charter guests. Siyu and Russ wanted to acquire the skills and the attitude to join this itinerant tribe of young professional sailors and I had no doubt that they would.

The routine of ship life was soothing; twenty minutes before due on watch, we were given a wake up call, or a reminder if already up and about. We were expected on deck at least five minutes before time. In cold weather I needed plenty of time to get all my layers on. Being on deck early was important at night to get night vision working, but in southern latitudes there were only a few hours of darkness. By the end of our 8-12 evening watch it was dark, but only just.

Change of watch was a time to chat to other crew members and there was also the official handover which we called story time, where the outgoing watch briefed the new arrivals about what had gone on – sail changes, weather state, course steered, any wildlife spotted. If there was nothing much to report we would often make something up - 'Ah yes, we were attacked by a giant squid but Russ wrestled with it and it slunk away.....' or 'We nearly saw a whale!' In a good breeze we would proudly hand over our four hour's run like a gift - 'We've done 34 miles! See if you can beat that.' All folly on the only form of transport where an outside force is controlling your speed. We would not be using the engine again until reaching 50 degrees of latitude in the Atlantic, unless we needed it in an emergency. After a frustrating slow watch of light winds and no progress we could only offer instead a promise of better things to come 'when the wind picks up', having analysed the forecast and come up with an optimistic interpretation. When the forecast was fair, we expected it to be accurate. When it was foul, we would say 'Ah well, it's bound to have changed its mind by then; perhaps that storm won't materialise'.

Painting the sea was my constant challenge and frustration. I brought five different blues with me but could never quite match the ever-changing shades, constantly moving and shifting from deep indigo to turquoise to ultramarine to white foam. I kept trying, not worrying about what kind of mess I was making on the page but hoping the act of looking and trying would be enough to capture something of what I was experiencing. Photographers who take photos of the sea have a hard time too. They may be more accurate in terms of colour and shape, but it's difficult to convey in any medium the feeling of a hill of water growing rapidly astern, higher and higher, beautiful and astonishing – the instinct is to duck. Surely we're in for a soaking?

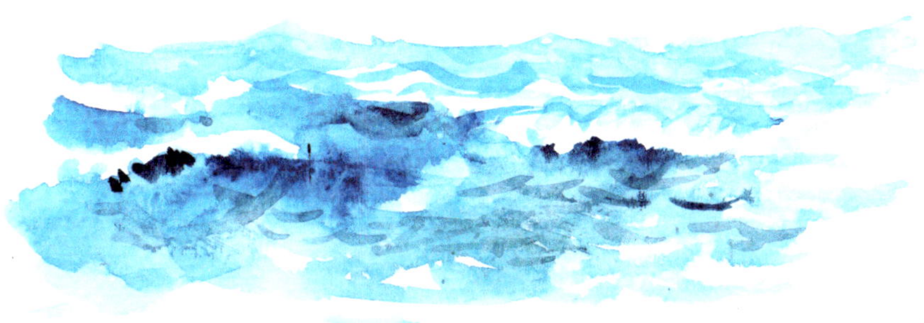

But no, the ship thinks nothing of it; at the last minute she lifts her buoyant stern and the wave slides harmlessly below us, out of sight. Occasionally a flick of spray over the deck reminds us who's in charge or a wave at an odd angle gives someone an unexpected soaking.

There is more contrast of light and dark on the sea out here than I have ever seen. I tried to leave plenty of white paper for the froth of foam at the bow and use plenty of indigo on that hard cold edge below the crest of a wave. It's not easy to get paints out on deck in a swell. My tactic was to wedge the water pot and paintbox into the coils of the mainsheet to stop them sliding off the coachroof. Bulldog clips on the sketchbook kept the pages in place. This plan worked well until a dollop of wave soaked everything or the mainsheet was needed in a hurry.

The albatross was our daily companion now, sometimes one solitary bird, sometimes several. We began to recognise the different types – the majestic wandering albatross with its 3 metre wingspan, and the similar royal albatross. Black-browed albatross were easy to identify. The rest were all designated 'albatross' if they were big and 'mollymauk' if they were smaller and brown-backed. I enjoyed the challenge of trying to sketch them. They never flapped their wings but they moved fast, soaring, gliding and continuously tilting which meant you saw their underside one minute and the top of their wings the next. For drawing detail of beak and head shapes I consulted the Peter Harrison book or looked at photographs taken by my shipmates. Siyu was a particularly skilled photographer and I used his clear close ups for the details of the lovely black-browed albatross on Day 13.

There is much sea-lore around these impressive birds. They were seen as bad luck, or good luck. They were killed for food by hungry sailors fed up of weevily biscuits, caught using a baited line with a wooden triangle on the end which caught the bird's hooked beak as it went for the bait. But it was also considered bad luck to harm an albatross (remember Rime of the Ancient Mariner?). In addition to all these contradictions, they are also supposed to embody the souls of sailors drowned and wrecked off Cape Horn:

'He's the ghost of a sailor, so I've heard say

Whose body sank and whose soul flew away

Down upon the Southern Ocean sailing, down below Cape Horn

And he's got no haven and he's got no home

Bound ever more to wheel and roam

Down upon the Southern Ocean sailing, down below Cape Horn

When I get too weary to sail no more

Let my bones sink better far away from shore

Down upon the Southern Ocean sailing, down below Cape Horn

You can cast me loose, leave me drifting free

And I'll keep that big bird company

Down upon the Southern Ocean sailing, down below Cape Horn'

(part of a song by Bob Watson; I sang this to my
watchmates and a nearby hovering albatross)

On Cape Horn island there is an inscription in Spanish by the poet Sara Vial beneath a memorial in the shape of an albatross. The translation reads as follows:

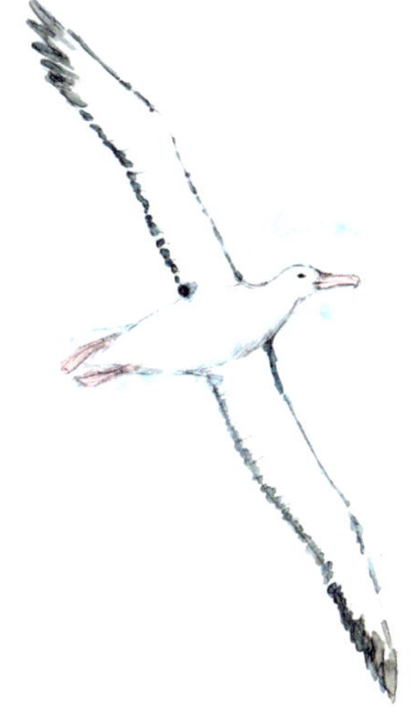

'I am the albatross that waits for you

at the end of the world.

I am the forgotten soul of the dead sailors

lost rounding the Horn

from all the seas in the world.

But they did not die

in the wild seas,

Today they fly on my wings,

towards eternity,

in the high cry

of the Antarctic winds'

The albatross's attraction for ships is causing its downfall, unfortunately, as they are drawn to the bait used by commercial longline fisherman, caught on the hooks and drown as they're dragged through the water. Campaigning is gradually changing this practice but there's a long way to go. Plastic is a more recent threat to albatross numbers. The albatross rear only a single egg at a time and chicks have been found dead of malnutrition with a stomach full of pieces of plastic, mistaken for small squid and fish by nurturing parents. It's sad to realise how far our messing up of the earth has gone; nowhere is untouched. I offered up a silent apology on behalf of our species to the many albatross who followed us every day, silently gracing our voyage.

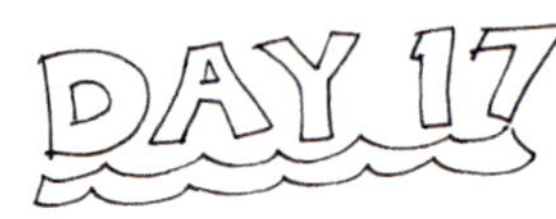

Sailing east in a cold southerly wind, sea a sharp indigo and hailstones in the squalls. Making good speed with all plain sail.

A rare sight of two albatross on the water close by. It takes them a while to fold their big wings - and a long time to get airborne again! (Detail taken from photo by Siyu Chen)

Rainbows amongst the squalls... this one a wide bar of colour that melted into th clouds

Evening watch - light winds & squalls, constant changes of course. This one gave us cause for concern, but swept in front of us with a flick of its tail and a cold shower.

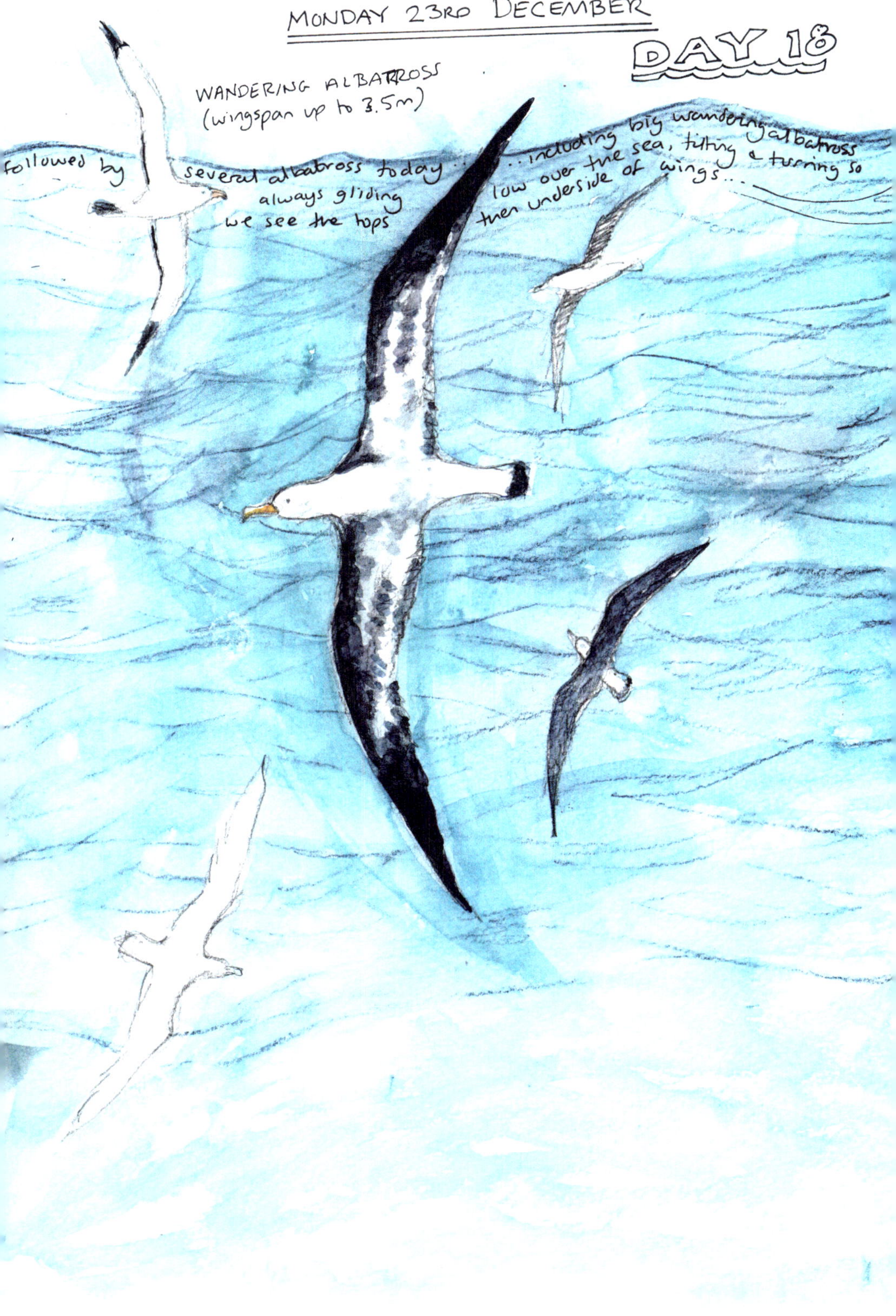

MONDAY 23RD DECEMBER
DAY 18
WANDERING ALBATROSS
(wingspan up to 3.5m)
followed by several albatross today...
always gliding
we see the tops
...including big wandering albatross
low over the sea, tilting & turning so
then underside of wings...

Good sailing today, heading in the right direction again, Steady wind from the north, occasional showers, 8-9 knots overground.

Coast of Chile now less than 150 miles away. Mood on deck is upbeat, New Years eve in Port Stanley looking possible again!

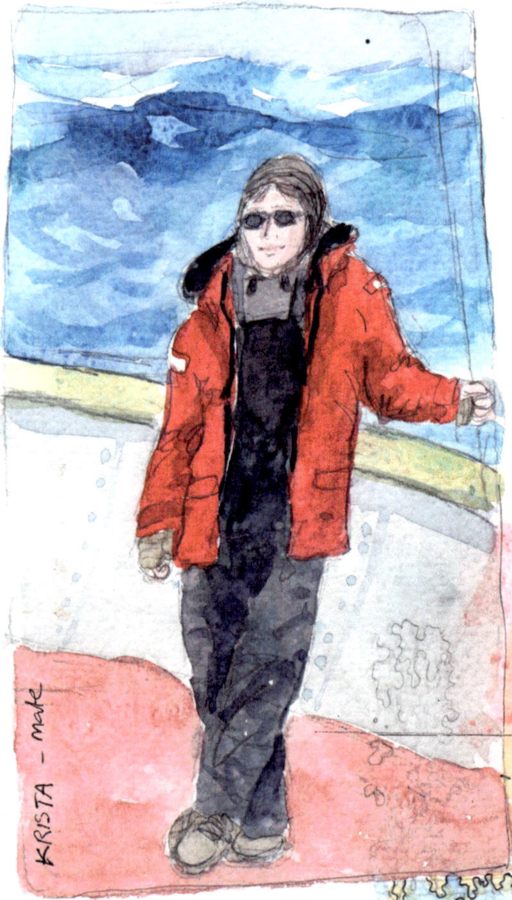

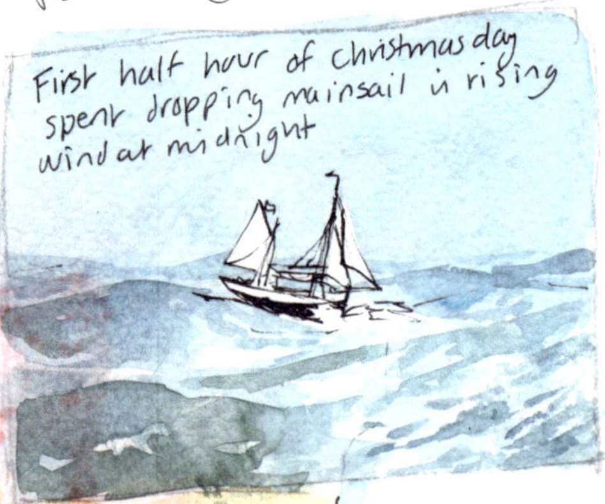

First half hour of christmas day spent dropping mainsail in rising wind at midnight

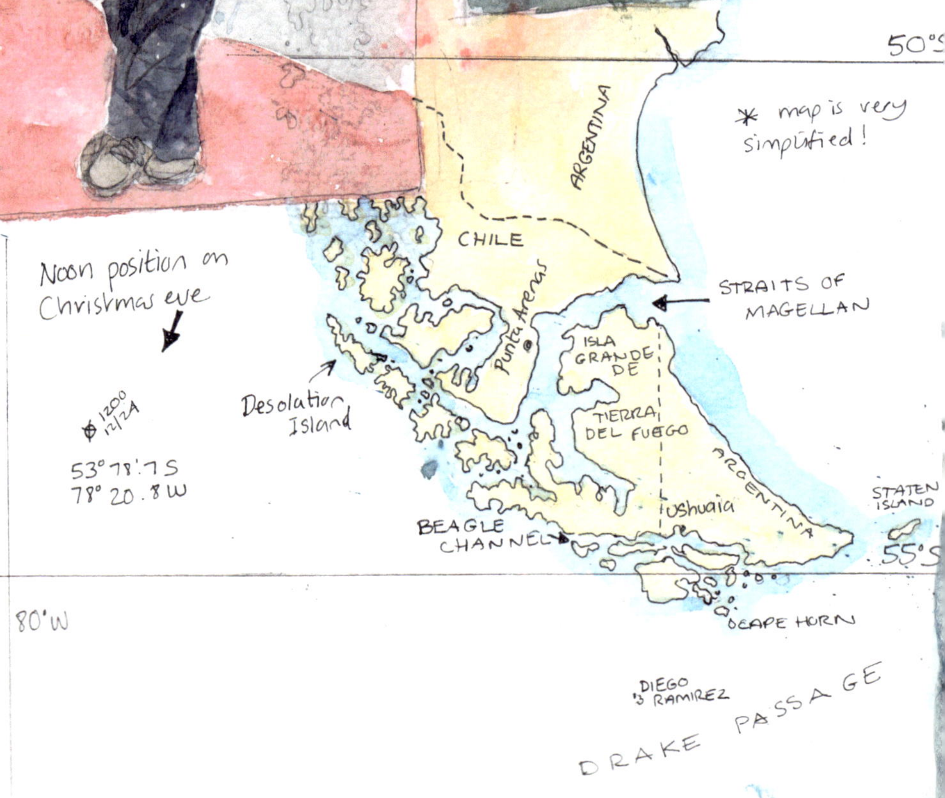

KRISTA — mate

50°S

* map is very simplified!

Noon position on Christmas eve

⊕ 1200
   12/24

53° 78'.7 S
78° 20.8 W

Desolation Island

ARGENTINA

CHILE

STRAITS OF MAGELLAN

Punta Arenas

ISLA GRANDE DE

TIERRA DEL FUEGO

ARGENTINA

Ushuaia

STATEN ISLAND

55°S

BEAGLE CHANNEL

CAPE HORN

80'W

DIEGO RAMIREZ

DRAKE PASSAGE

<u>WEDNESDAY 25TH DECEMBER</u>

DAY 20

55° 23.5'S 74 07.2'N

How do you like your morning tea on Christmas Day?

Happy Christmas!

– On deck, with Icy water sloshing round my ankles & an albatross hovering nearby.

Flocks of small birds flying fast close to the surface of the waves. Silver/grey backs so probably blue petrels...

... also prions (white underside, 'm' shape on wings)

Prion

Fast sailing, raining heavily by midnight when it's time to hoist the main as winds have eased.
Bed at 1.30 am, soaked!

Swell only 3–3.5 metres but very steep & rough, hard steering.
Depth has changed from 4,000 m to less than 1,000!

25th December 2019
55° 23.5'S
74° 07.2' W

South and further south

There was no doubt now that we were sailing in one of the most remote parts of the planet. There is no agreed definition as to where the Pacific Ocean ends and the Southern Ocean begins, but it is generally considered by the International Hydrographic Organisation to mean the waters below the seasonally fluctuating Antarctic Convergence zone. As far as sailors are concerned, the Southern Ocean is the cold ribbon of sea south of about 55 degrees latitude that encircles the bottom of the globe. For round the world racing sailors, the further south you go, the shorter the distance you have to travel but the more likely you are to bump into icebergs.

We had no need to venture into iceberg territory. We just needed to get below 56 degrees south, the latitude of Cape Horn. These waters have an evil reputation which is well deserved. Wind and waves travel round the globe unhindered by land and both can cause chaotic conditions in the relatively narrow gap between Antarctica and Cape Horn where the water shallows from 6,000 to less than 1,000 metres. We were sailing west to east, which is downwind (or should be) and at the most benign time of year, mid summer. Nevertheless the weather is prone to sudden changes at any time and there is no room for complacency. In rough weather steering *Tecla* was challenging and I was always a little nervous taking the helm when there was a big swell running. Steering 120 tons of steel at 11 knots down the face of a wave is the kind of white knuckle ride you don't get in a fairground. There's no time to work out whether it's thrilling or terrifying – you're too busy focussing on the compass to make sure you don't go too far off course. My shoulders ached after even a short spell at the wheel in a big swell but it's an experience I wouldn't have wanted to miss.

In spite of the fearsome reputation of this ocean for rough weather, we experienced several frustrating periods of calm. There was always a swell running even when there was no wind, so 'calm' is a relative term as we rocked and swayed, blocks and booms rattling and banging. We tried to keep some sail up to steady the ship and stop her rolling, but often the regular crack of a slatting sail was too much to bear – and bad for the canvas, so we took it down again. As modern day sailors we are so used to being able to reach for the ignition key when the wind dies that it was a revelation having to do as seaman throughout the centuries have had to do – just sit and wait.

When not engaged in bursts of intense activity there was plenty of time to stand and stare. Or, as the weather got colder, jiggle around with hands in pockets. In spite of layers, thick socks and leather boots it was too cold to stand still for long. Will and Russ initiated keep fit challenges and started doing press ups or dangling off the rigging just using their hands. I responded with balance challenges but I have to report that standing on one leg for more than a second or two on a moving deck is virtually impossible. (I was reminded of a time when I was art tutor on a cruise ship that hit rough weather. That evening's entertainment was a juggler.... I'm sure he was excellent on dry land. Now which entertainment officer had thought that was a good idea?)

We soon warmed up when sail handling was needed. As I'm a lightweight, it was usually sensible for me to leave the heaving to those with muscle so that I could focus on tailing and belaying. This meant taking up the slack on a rope and using the friction of the belaying pins to hold the rope in place whilst those pulling paused to move their hands up the rope. As soon as the tension came onto the rope I could hold it easily with one turn, later two turns, around the pin, and then when the job was done, quickly finish it off with a few figure of eight turns (that's the 'belaying' bit). With such simple but effective technology huge loads could be handled and held in place. At the end of every sail handling bout the decks would be a sea of rope spaghetti, all needing coiling and stowing. I could hardly lift some of the heavy and longer coils.

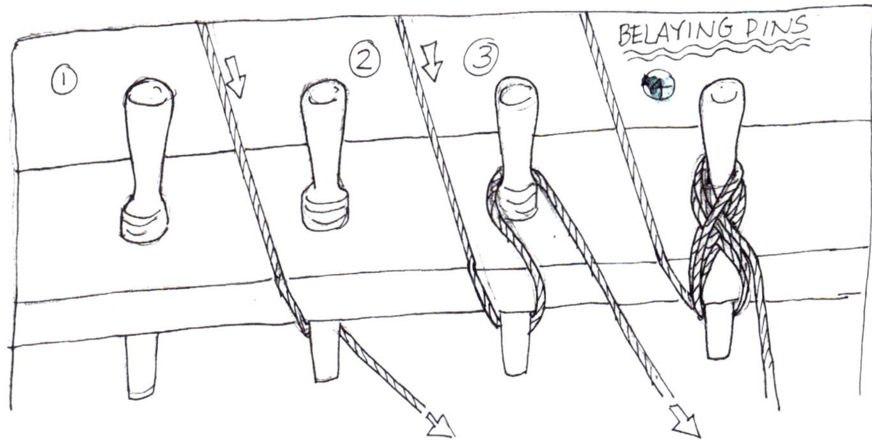

We were very much in squall territory now. These menacing lumps of black cloud made us work hard as they travelled fast and usually contained not just heavy rain or hail but strong winds. It kept Krista and Will on their toes – is this one coming our way? Will we need to reef the sails? Do we need to wake the captain, who has only just got back to sleep after the last squall, or will it miss us altogether? Krista's dilemma as mate was whether to err on the side of caution and wake Jet just in case we were in for a drama, or to hold tight and hope it passed us by. Usually the squalls were fierce but short lived and we could manage by easing the sheets to reduce pressure on the sails until it had passed, but the most important thing was to avoid any damage to the sails or rigging. I was glad in so many ways that on this voyage I was not a decision maker but simply crew, tucked safely under the wings of those more confident and experienced in such waters than me.

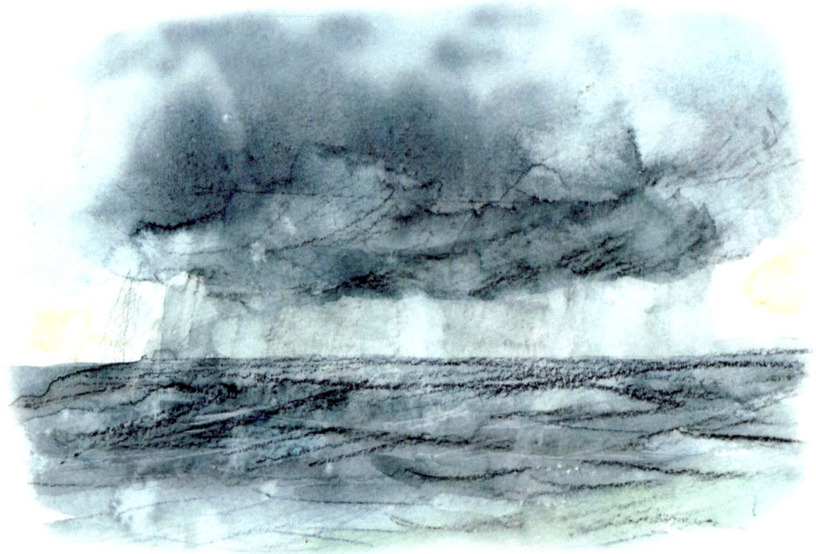

Are we nearly there yet?

Day 19 was Christmas Eve but all thoughts of Christmas Day were overshadowed by the bigger event – rounding the Horn. The tip of South America was now appearing on the chart plotter in more detail and who could resist zooming in and looking in wonder at the maze of islands and channels with their historic and evocative names – Magellan Straits, Beagle Channel, Desolation Island? I traced the map from the chart (I always carry tracing paper in my sketching gear when I think there's a map opportunity as they are so difficult to draw freehand). Even with the help of tracing paper my version (Day 19) is a very tame copy of the original which was much more intricate than I could manage to reproduce.

Christmas Day was spent sailing fast through a beautiful wild sea somewhere south west of Chile. The cabin was strung with fairy lights and Jet had cooked a special meal on Christmas Eve with mulled wine and Krista's Christmas cookies to follow. Those of us not on watch made an attempt to dress for dinner; I pulled out a slightly crumpled but colourful sarong I'd bought on Easter Island to wear as a shawl and found some earrings and lipstick. After wearing nothing but thermals and oilskins for several weeks and not worrying about appearances, it made a change to look in a mirror.

The weather was too boisterous to give us much opportunity to relax on Christmas Day. It rained heavily on our evening watch and we were sailing fast with reefed sails, heading into the Drake Channel where the ocean floor rises from over 4 kilometres to less than 1,000 metres, kicking up a rough sea. Approaching midnight I was cold, wet and would really rather have been somewhere else – a nice warm bunk would do. I was beginning to understand why so many sea songs and shanties refer to the sailor's desire to come off watch promptly without having to stay on deck and help with sail changes. These usually take place at watch handover when there is more manpower available: *'Strike the bell, second mate and let us go below, look out to windward you can see it's going to blow....'* (In this song, 'Strike the Bell', the sailor is resigned to disappointment. *'He's thinking more of shortening sail than striking the bell!'*) On a square-rigged ship this could be a dangerous and lengthy procedure in rough weather. At least on *Tecla* we had no square sails, so all our activity was at deck level.

Just before midnight, Jet popped her head out of chartroom, a shawl round her shoulders, strands of dark hair blowing loose from her plait. She tilted her face to the wind. 'I think that wind has eased, eh? Maybe we'll shake out that reef, give us a steadier speed over this sea....' The next watch came on deck and all together we scrambled around on the dark, wet deck, untying reef points and listening for the sequence of commands to hoist the mainsail and mizzen back to full size. Something went wrong in the rigging at some point and Will shinned up with head torch and harness on to sort it out. We stood by with coils of rope in hand and the rain trickling down our faces, waiting for the command to heave. By 1 am I was finally below deck, stripping off sodden oilskins and feeling strangely exuberant. What a Christmas!

Cape Horn at last

On Boxing Day morning the 4-8 watch were proud to hand over their gift to us – the snow capped mountains of Chile on the horizon. We were sailing fast so the excitement grew as we watched the land reveal itself. How far now to the Horn? 40 miles..... 20 miles..... a grey shape slowly came into focus, the southern tip of Horn Island.

Francis Drake gave his name to Drake Passage, the 600 mile wide stretch of water that links the Pacific and Atlantic oceans, but it was a Dutchman called Schouten who gave the Cape its name in 1616, not for its shape but after his home town of Hoorn in the Netherlands. The Cape quickly gained a reputation as a nasty but necessary landmark for ships travelling between Atlantic and Pacific, particularly for those heading east to west against prevailing winds. For a square-rigged ship, not able to sail more than 60 degrees into the wind (less in heavy weather), rounding the Horn could take months and often did and many were lost in the attempt. But there was no choice; cargo needed carrying regardless of how many sailors died in the process. Several shanties take advantage of the rhyme: *'We had to sail around Cape Horn / where you wished to God you'd never been born.'*

Reading a book about the history of sea trade in the ship's library* I came across a map showing the track of the sailing ship *Edward Sewell* which had taken two months in 1914 to get through this short stretch of water. She was heading east to west against the prevailing winds in March and April, which is the end of summer. That jagged line on the map represents an unimaginable amount of tenacity and endurance.

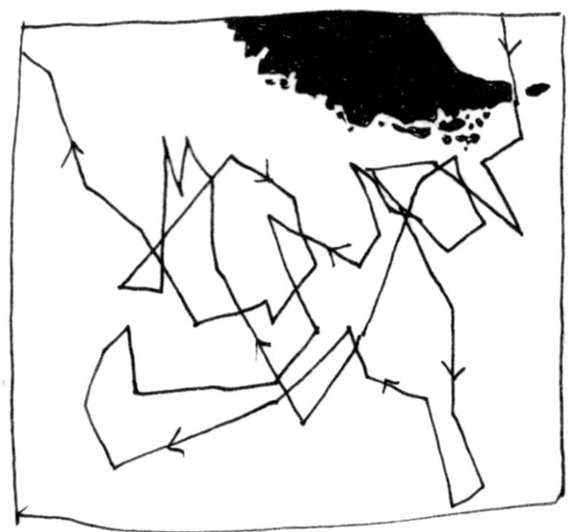

*From *Men and Ships around Cape Horn 1616-1939* by Jean Randier

Three miles forward, ten miles back
Then running south on the starboard tack
Calms tomorrow, storms today
The wind won't always blow your way

The wheels of commerce will not wait
For fair winds to arrive
Though the waves are high and the sky is black
We're close hauled on the starboard tack
And we know that there's no turning back
Through icy seas we'll drive

On a sailing ship it's a mistake to anticipate an arrival time based on your current speed. Ten miles west of the Cape, now clearly visible ahead, we were becalmed. Rolling in the swell, the cliffs of Chile looking close on our port side, we regretted saying with such confidence 'We'll be heading north east again by 4pm'. If the calm spell had continued longer and we had drifted dangerously close to the cliffs Jet would have started the engine. Luckily by evening a breeze had come back, strengthening rapidly. The wind nearly always blows from the west here, but this one was from the north east, the direction we wanted to go. By the time I came on watch at 8pm we were sailing fast with reefed sails south towards Antarctica. It was 30 hours later that we could finally say that we were 'Round the Horn'.

It was during our unplanned detour south that I experienced one of the high points of the trip (Day 23). Nothing dramatic, but a morning of liquid beauty. The wind had eased and although it was still cold it was a cloudless day. There was something about the light here that is so different to a sunny day in lower latitudes. It gives everything a transparent glow. My painting that day may not be photographically accurate but it reconnects me to that feeling of wonder and clarity. *Tecla* was sailing as perfectly as a ship knows how and my albatross-eye viewpoint that day was purely from the imagination – the sweet curve of sails and pattern of the seas. Half an hour at the helm in rough weather usually left me with sore shoulders and the feeling of having had a good workout, but on this day she moved smoothly through the gentle swell, needing barely a hand on the wheel.

Land-ho!

Came on watch at 8am to find the
snow-capped mountains of Chile to port
— and about 80 miles to Cape Horn.
Fast sailing under reefed main & mizzen

Later

4pm, becalmed & rolling.
Cape Horn in sight, 30m ahead.
V. frustrating!

DAY 21

Dolphins playing in our bow wave

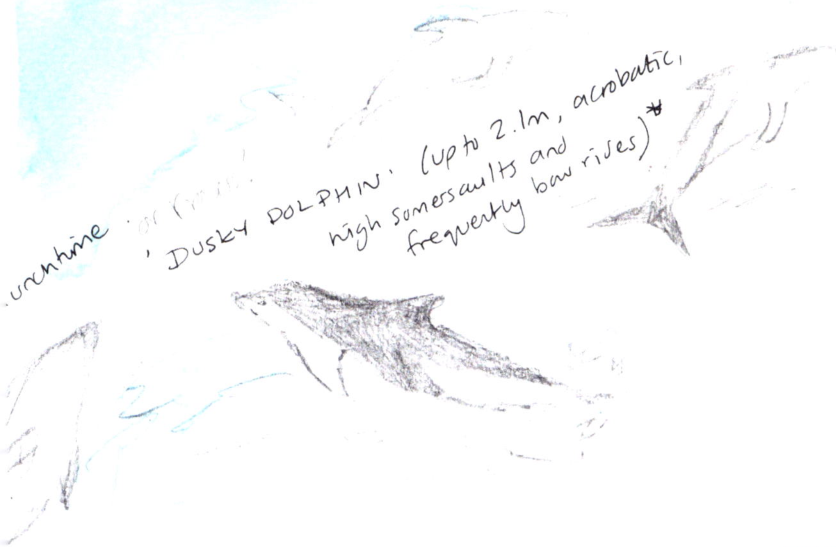

...urchine...or (...)!

'DUSKY DOLPHIN'. (up to 2.1m, acrobatic, high somersaults and frequently bow rises)*

Cape Horn - named by Dutch explorer Schouten in 1616 after his home town, Hoorn

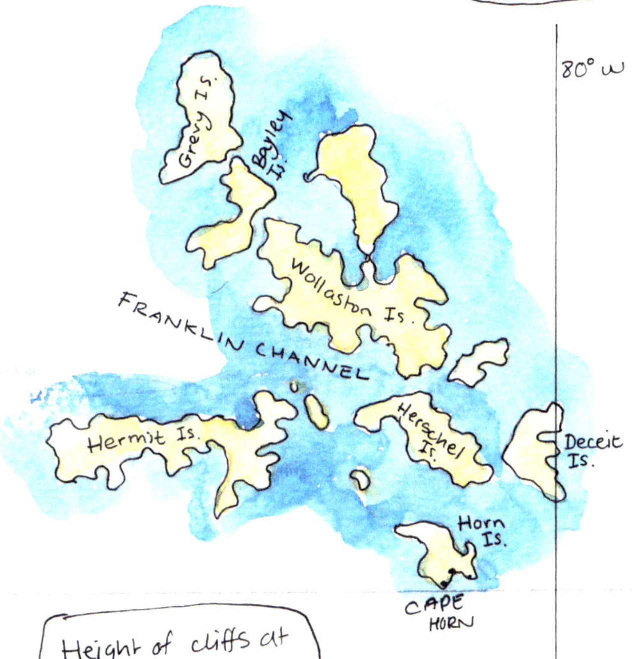

80° W

56°S

Height of cliffs at Cape Horn - 424m

FRIDAY 27TH DECEMBER

DAY 22

Morning watch - heading north east again,
took reefs out, but we're still 40 miles south east of the Cape. So close
but so far, yesterday!

If we think we're having a
frustrating time, this was
the track of the four-masted
barque 'Edward Sewell' in 1914. *

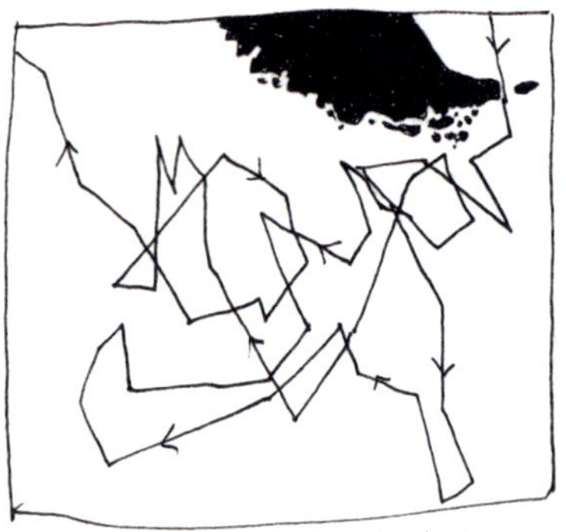

The passage here took two
months!
(March - May - a difficult
time of year a going east -
west the hardest way)

AFTERNOON - BECALMED AGAIN!
Rolling, rolling, rolling ......

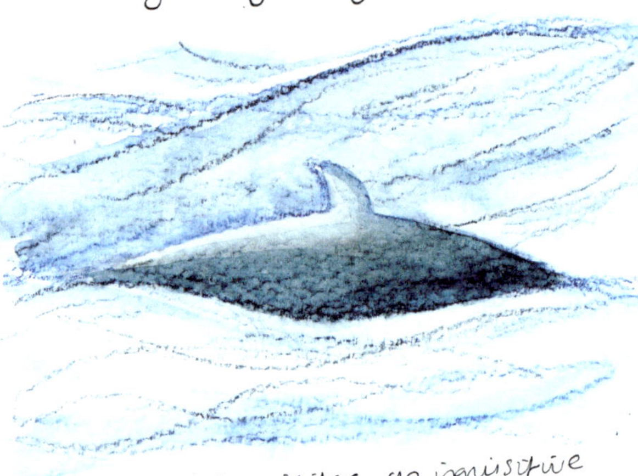

early evening visitor - an inquisitive
minke whale circles the ship

ship sighted during the evening -
small cruise ship heading to
Ushuaia

Pathway to the sun .... clear yellow sunset, gentle swell

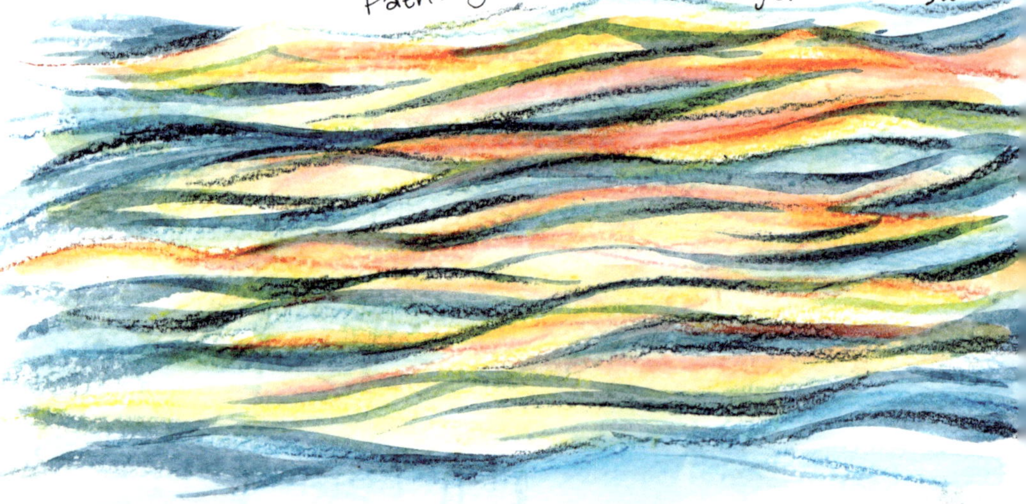

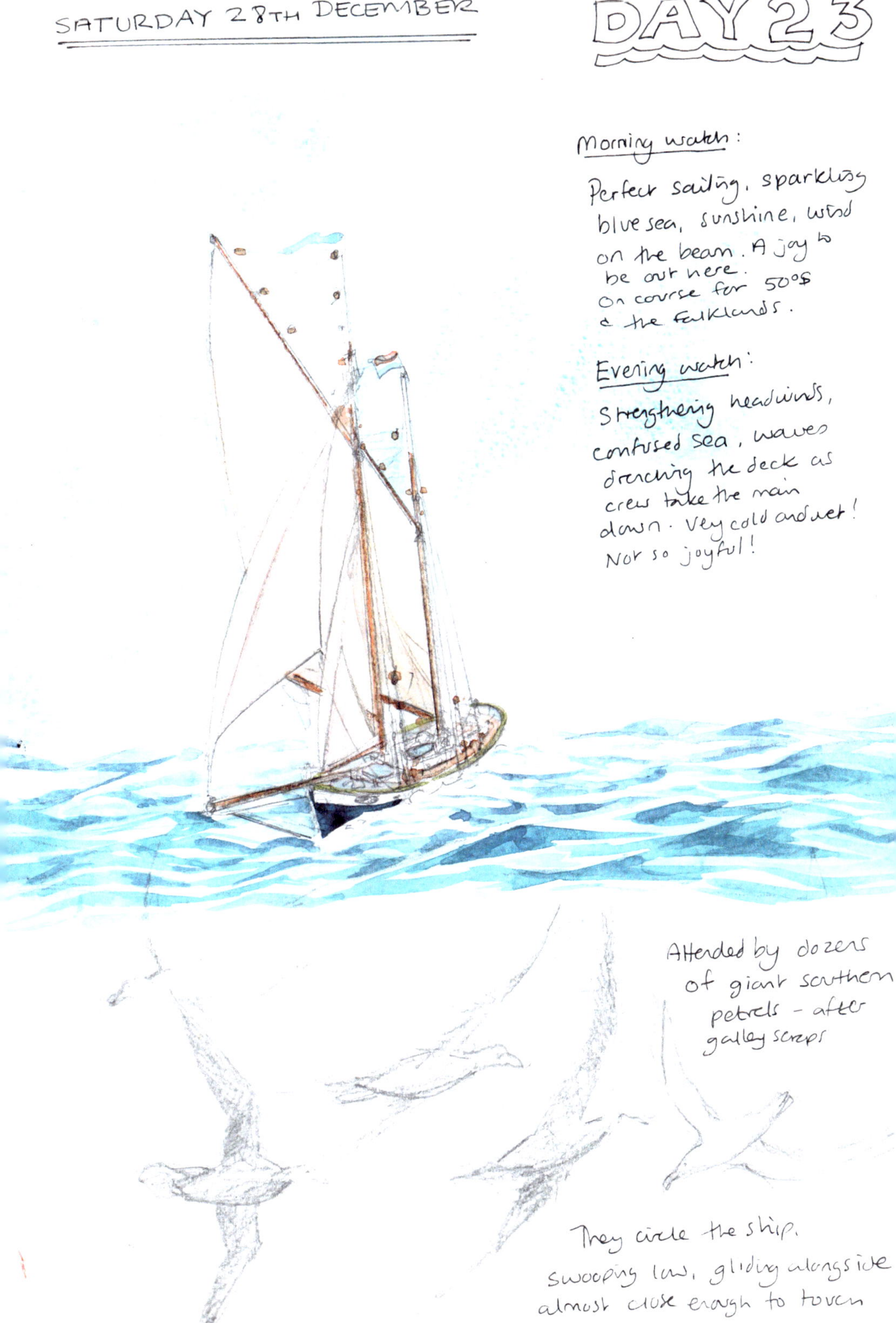

Morning watch:

Perfect sailing, sparkling blue sea, sunshine, wind on the beam. A joy to be out here. On course for 50°S & the Falklands.

Evening watch:

Strengthening headwinds, confused sea, waves drenching the deck as crew take the main down. Very cold and wet! Not so joyful!

Attended by dozens of giant southern petrels - after galley scraps

They circle the ship, swooping low, gliding alongside almost close enough to touch

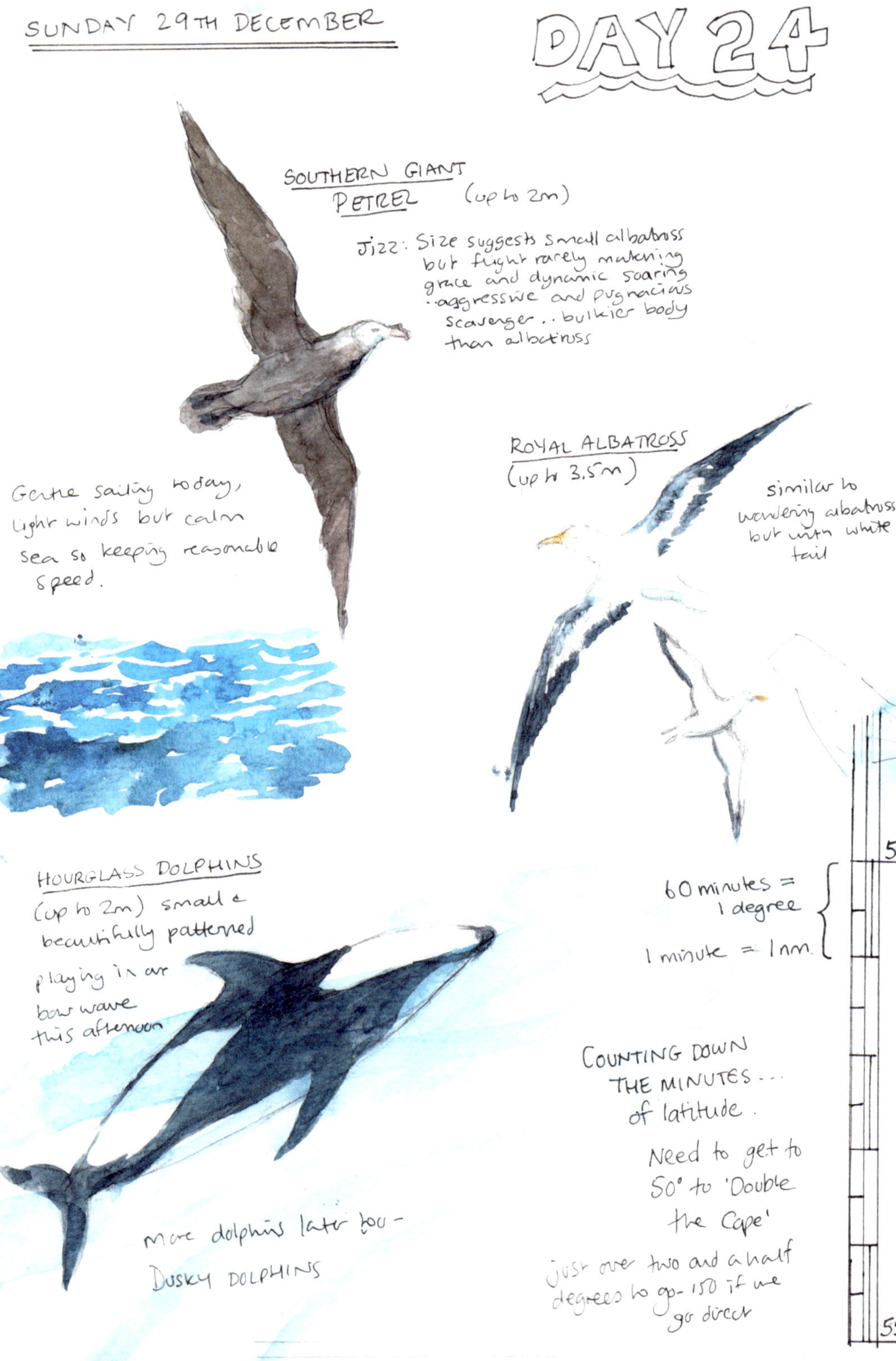

SUNDAY 29TH DECEMBER

DAY 24

SOUTHERN GIANT PETREL (up to 2m)

Jizz: Size suggests small albatross but flight rarely matching grace and dynamic soaring ..aggressive and pugnacious scavenger.. bulkier body than albatross

Gentle sailing today, light winds but calm sea so keeping reasonable speed.

ROYAL ALBATROSS (up to 3.5m)

similar to wandering albatross but with white tail

HOURGLASS DOLPHINS (up to 2m) small & beautifully patterned playing in our bow wave this afternoon

More dolphins later too - DUSKY DOLPHINS

60 minutes = 1 degree

1 minute = 1 nm.

50°

COUNTING DOWN THE MINUTES... of latitude.

Need to get to 50° to 'Double the Cape'

just over two and a half degrees to go - 150 if we go direct

55°

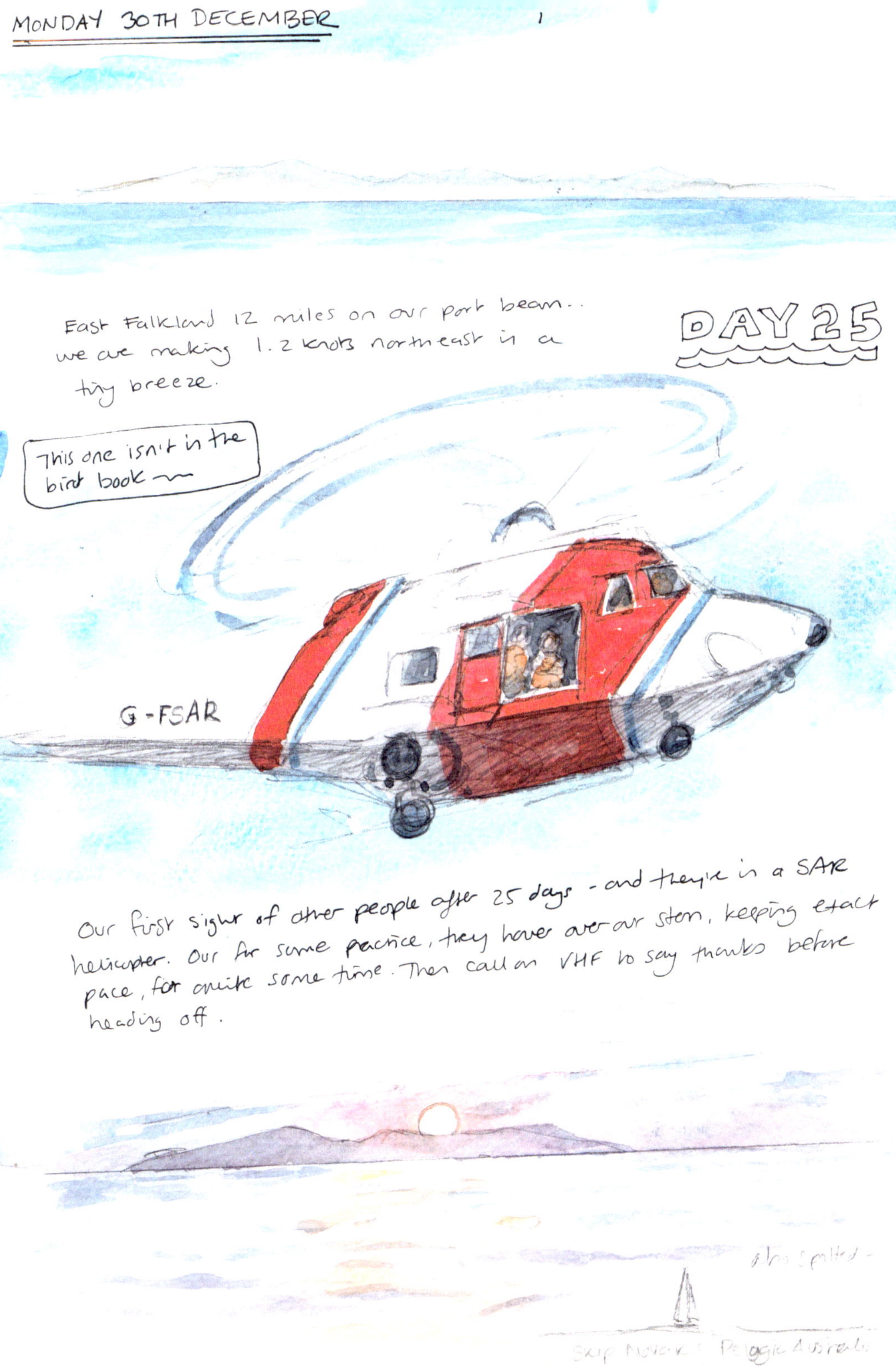

DAY 25
East Falkland 12 miles on our port beam..
we are making 1.2 knots northeast in a
tiny breeze.
This one isn't in the bird book ~
G - FSAR
Our first sight of other people after 25 days - and they're in a SAR helicopter. Our for some practice, they hover over our stern, keeping exact pace, for quite some time. Then call on VHF to say thanks before heading off.

TUESDAY 31st DECEMBER

Frustrating morning, becalmed again, so close but so far with no wind. Late morning, wind picks up, all sails set including ones we inverted (like Russ's hammock as a water sail). A gentle breeze from astern finally does it.

We made it!

50°S at 1631

Captain issues tot of whisky to all hands. Huge relief all round as the timing was so close — another calm settled as we turned back under engine to get to Port Stanley as quickly as possible.

New Years Eve celebrations on deck with fairy lights, music, food. drink

2020

Wednesday morning 11am, Cape Pembroke

Heading north once more

Somehow we hadn't expected the last part of the voyage to be the most challenging of all. We thought that once we'd rounded the Horn that was the tricky bit over. Then it was just a matter of nipping round the corner to 50 degrees north and before you could say 'old sea dog' we'd be sipping beer in a bar in Port Stanley. It wasn't quite like that. The wind blew from every direction at every strength; there were times when we were reefing sail with waves tumbling over us and times when we were becalmed on a flat sea and going nowhere. The unexpected calms of the final few days were the hardest to bear as we were still sailing without engine to complete our Cape Horn challenge and it looked as if we were going to fail at the last hurdle. We would have sailed over 3,000 miles and rounded the Horn but failed to become true 'Cape Horners' because there wasn't enough wind in this windy ocean to get us to 50 degrees south in time.

The tension mounted as we crept so slowly over those last hundred miles. We could have covered that distance easily with a good wind, but now we had only 24 hours left and it seemed impossible as we rolled in the swell with the hills of West Falkland a few miles to port.

Happy New Year!

We made it to 50 degrees late afternoon on New Year's Eve. If we hadn't been in a hurry, it would have been a beautiful day for a gentle sail, with clear blue skies and a soft breeze flicking the sea into wavelets. I wasn't much in the mood for drawing! We set every sail we had (and some we didn't, like Russ's hammock tied to the mizzen boom as a water sail), and the breeze held out as Krista counted down the degrees of latitude from the chartroom. Five... four.... Three... two...one... 49 degrees 59.9 minutes!

We were lucky. By time we'd enjoyed our second 50 degree celebratory tot of whisky, taken down the sails and turned to motor back to Stanley, the wind had vanished. It returned as we were approaching harbour, whipping up the wave crests and stinging our eyes as we watched East Falkland grow into a wild and colourful landscape of rocky shores, beaches and hills. The voyage was nearly over.

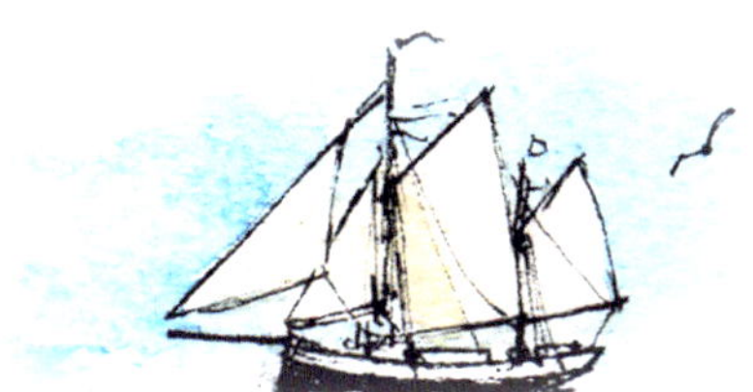

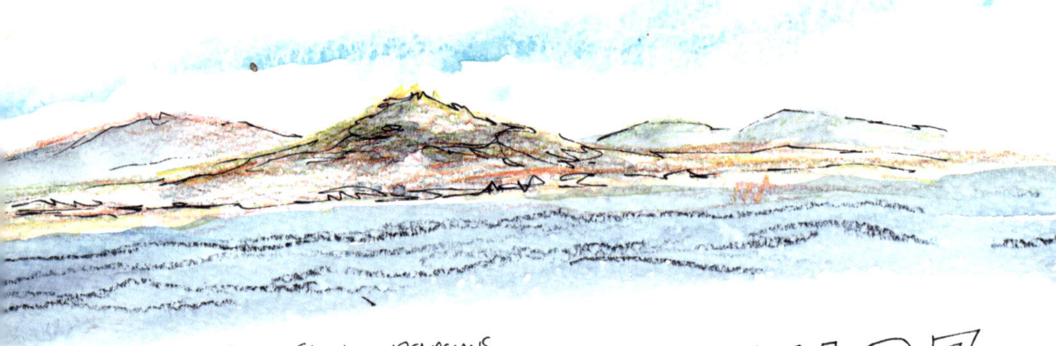

Approaching Port Stanley narrows

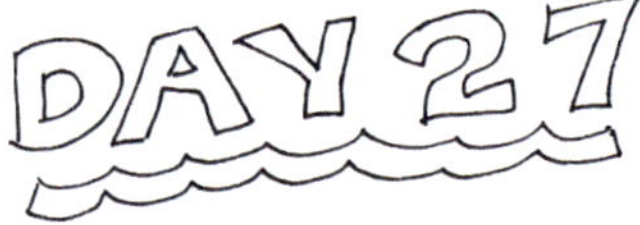

Dropped anchor Port Stanley 11.48.

First impressions ....

very cold & windy. All the
winds we didn't get in the
last few days are
                    blowing now

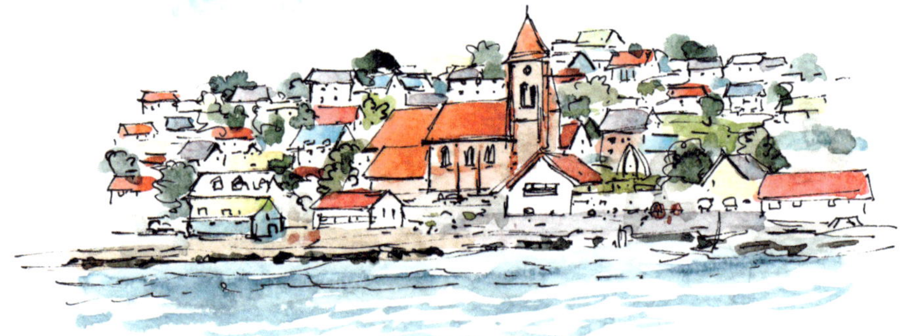

...AND HELLO FALKLANDS

Dropped anchor off Port Stanley 1st January 2020, came ashore 5pm on 2nd (50 knots of wind prevented us leaving the ship sooner).

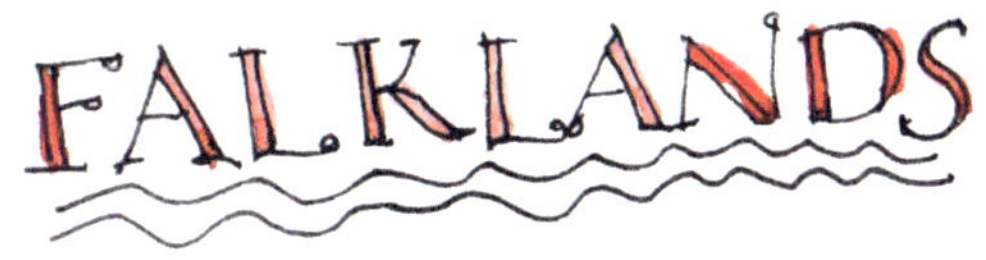

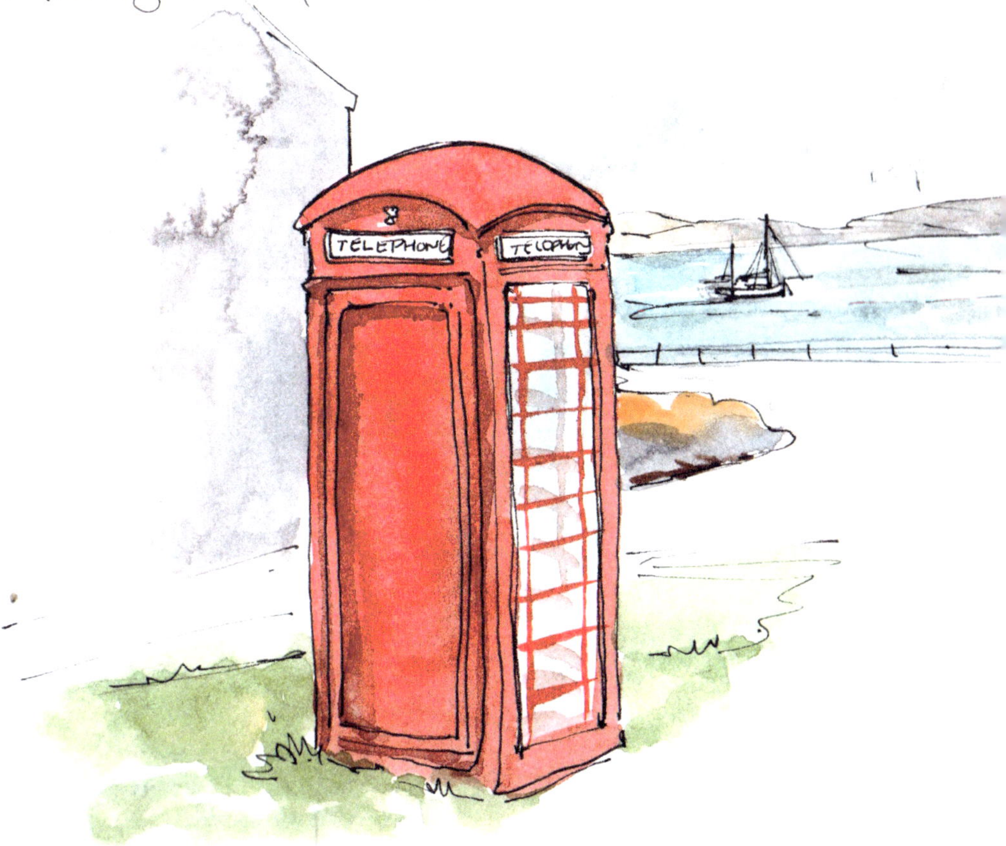

No taxis around, visitor centre closed. Crewmate Dave goes to nearby cafe in search of help: a lovely lady called Linda takes us up to Shorty's motel on the edge of town. It is not a long walk without luggage — but would have been very difficult with all my stuff!

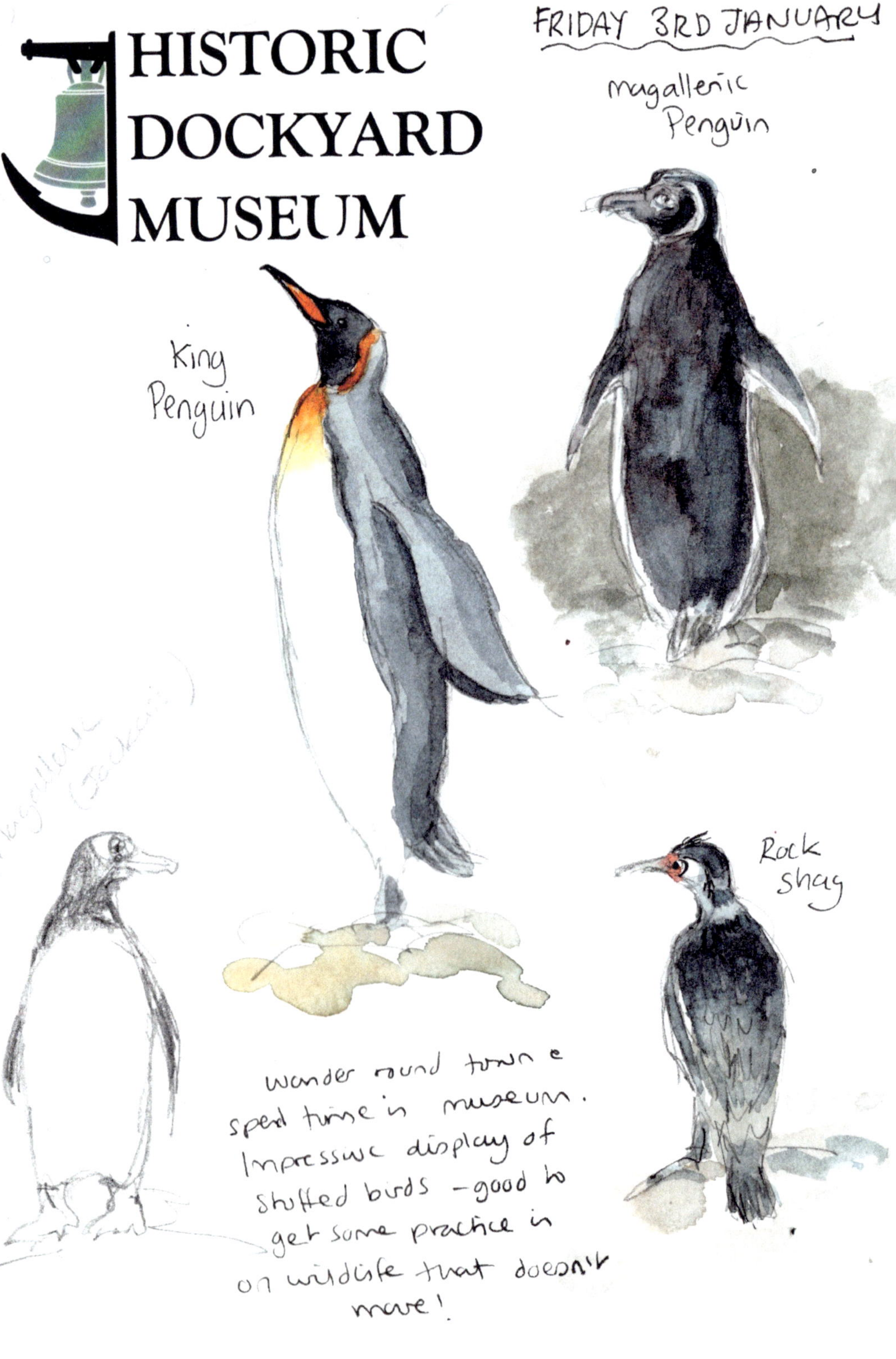

HISTORIC DOCKYARD MUSEUM
FRIDAY 3RD JANUARY
magallenic Penguin
King Penguin
Rock shag
wander round town &
spent time in museum.
Impressive display of
stuffed birds — good to
get some practice in
on wildlife that doesn't
move!

Port Stanley

On 2nd January 2020, the morning after our arrival in Port Stanley, it was time to leave *Tecla*. But the wind had one final trick to play on us. Having left us becalmed when we needed it, it now returned with a vengeance. Whilst we were packing up, exchanging emails and promising to share photographs, the wind had been rising and the sheltered waters of Port Stanley were flecked with whitecaps. Our anchor dragged so the crew re-anchored further across the harbour. With gusts of over 50 knots, using the dinghy to get us ashore was now out of the question. All we could do was wait. Several people had booked an afternoon tour and had to cancel, but luckily I had no plans and was happy to sit and finish the novel I had borrowed from the ship's library. It was 5pm before we were ferried ashore, dressed in full oilskins with tarpaulin over our luggage to protect it from the spray. It was finally goodbye.

It was strange being alone again, sleeping in a hotel room with central heating, proper beds and bathroom. I had arranged to spend 12 days in Port Stanley before flying home and so began to get used to a new daily routine.

I began my exploration with the Historic Dockyard Museum which gave me a gentle introduction to drawing the wildlife – always easier when they don't move! - and plenty of maritime history. Museums are great places to sketch; they're usually quiet, stuffed full of the quirky and interesting, and there's a story to go with each artefact that catches your eye. There were a few chairs but most of the time I had to sit on the floor, trying to keep coat, bag and water pot out of the way of tourists' feet. I have said that museums are usually quiet, but I soon discovered that when a cruise ship came into harbour (which was most days), the town and museum were busy with visitors in their matching waterproof jackets issued by the cruise line. If the weather was bad, the small number of bars and cafes quickly filled up.

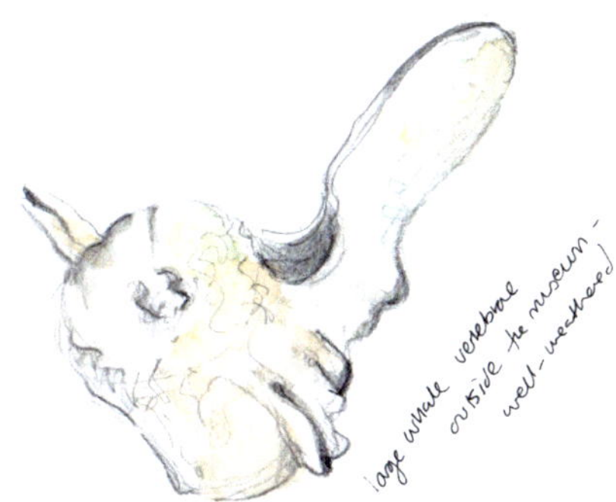

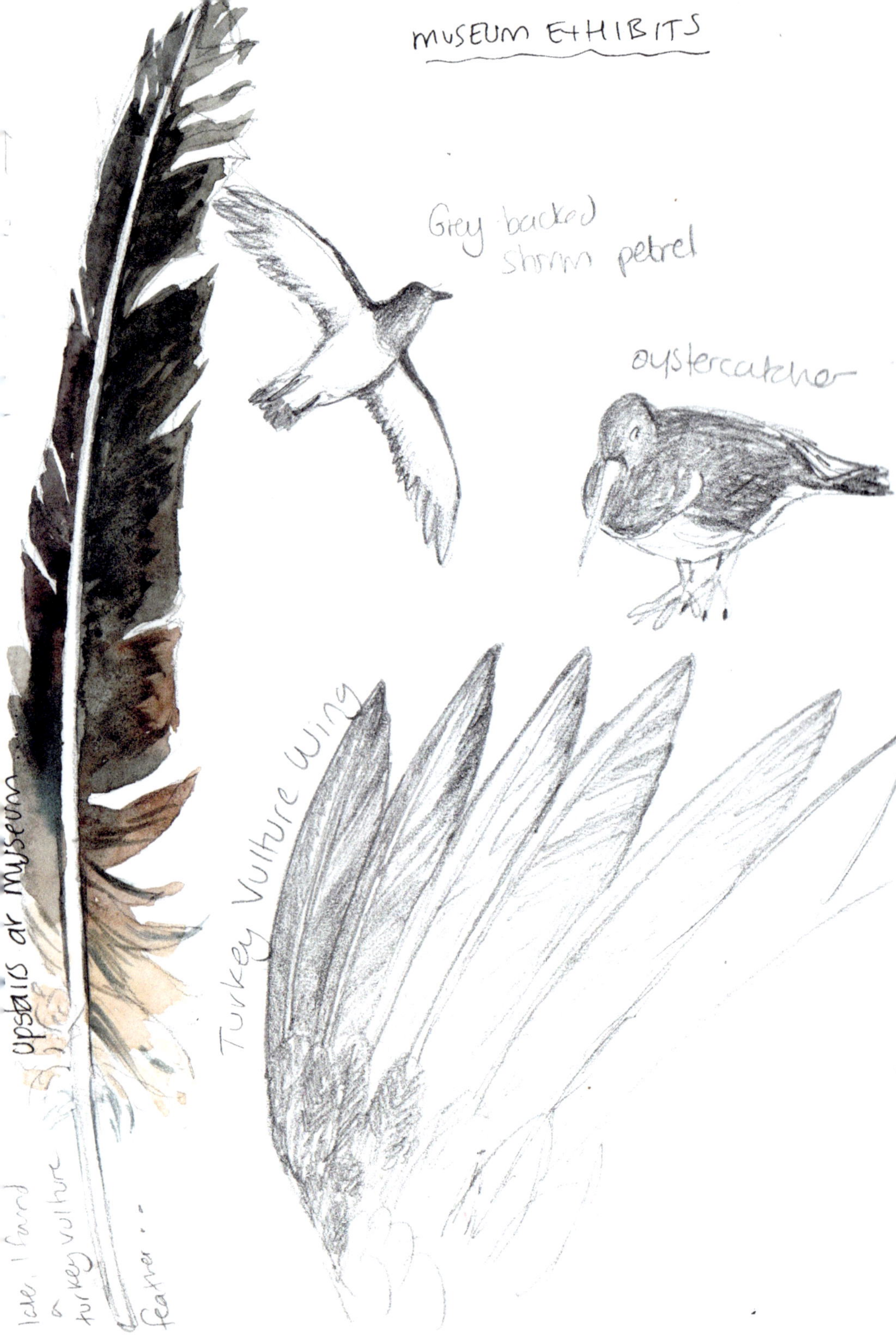
MUSEUM EXHIBITS

Grey backed
storm petrel

oystercatcher

Turkey Vulture Wing

upstairs at Museum

late. I found
a turkey vulture
feather . . .

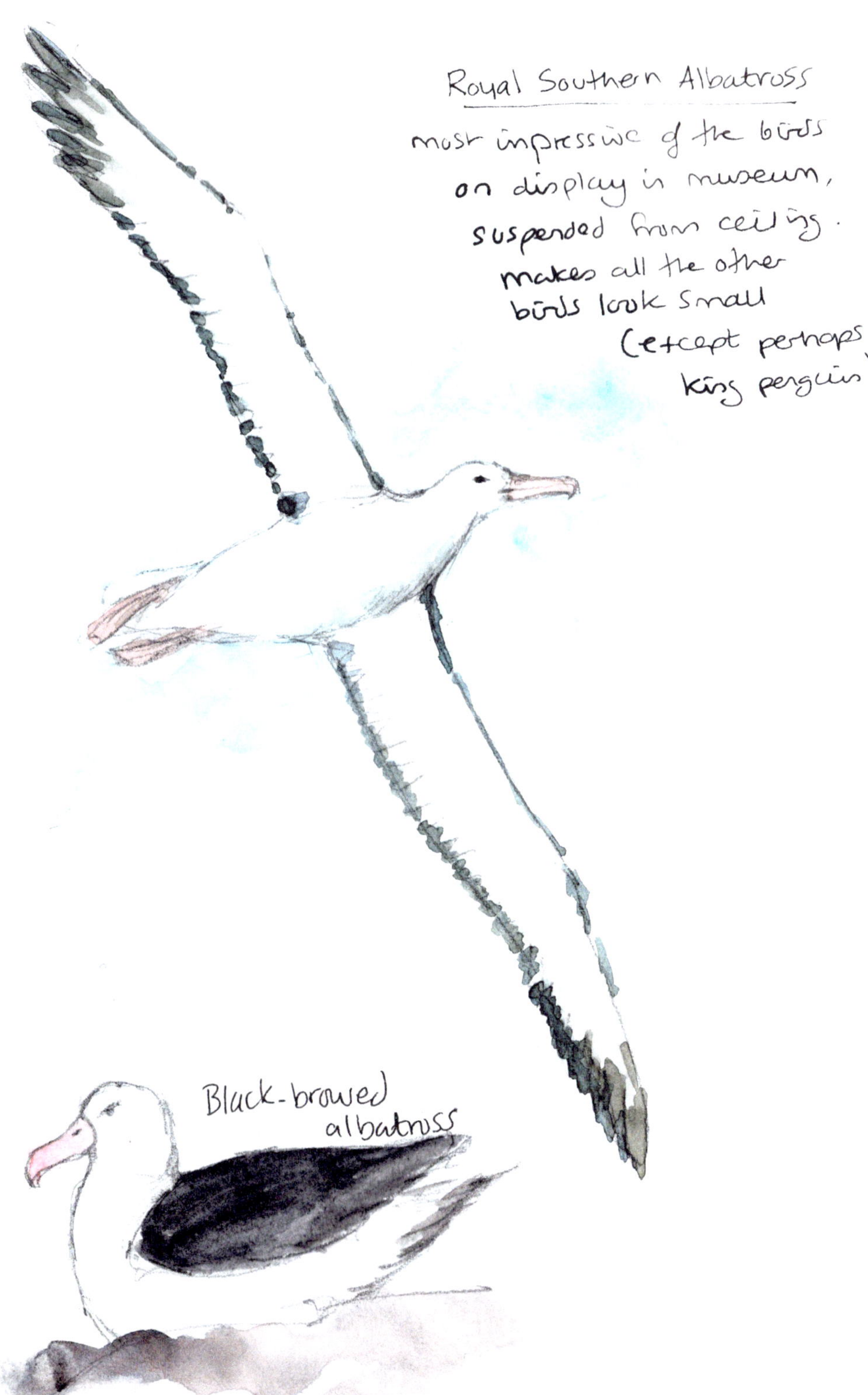

Royal Southern Albatross
most impressive of the birds
on display in museum,
suspended from ceiling.
makes all the other
birds look small
(except perhaps
king penguins)
Black-browed
albatross

After all the real things are the impressions we have.
Tangible things are not so essential as we suppose. To be
pleased at a flower, or a song, or a cloud, is better than to
be satisfied with rich food and clothing. It is nearly six
months since I left home. I have lost much. I have
gained more. I am content."

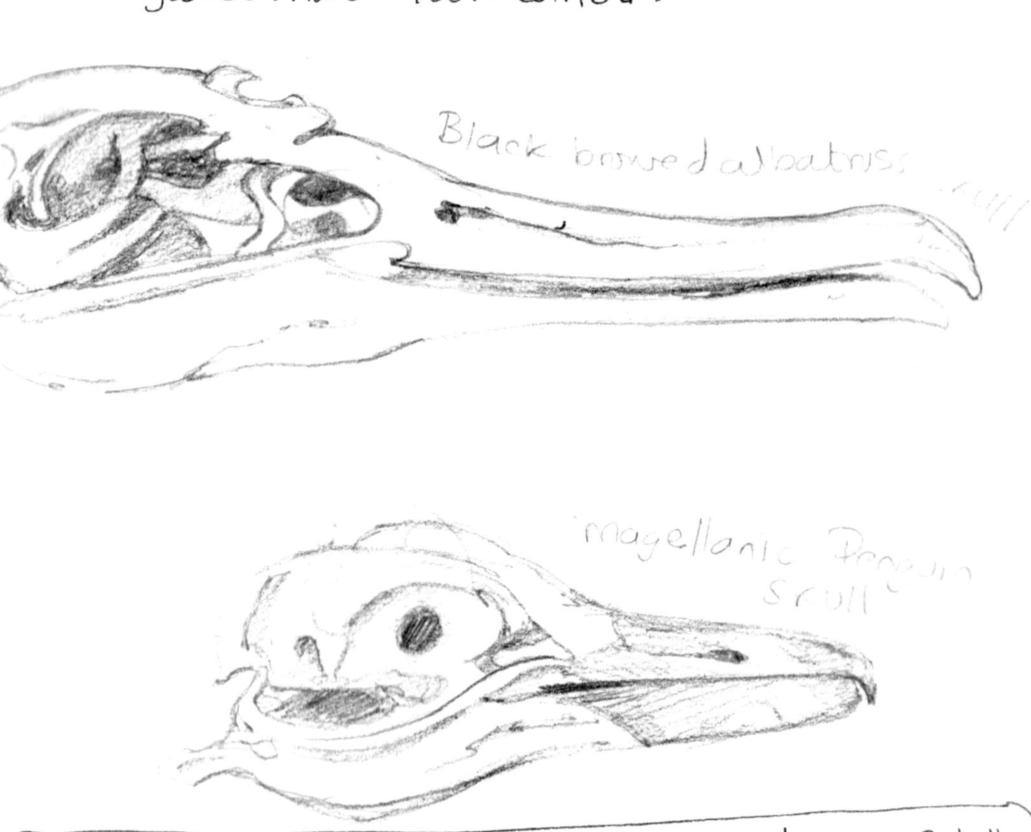

American schoolteacher Lydia Keen was on the John R. Kelley
during its final voyage. She was 28, the daughter of a
sea captain who had died. The ship foundered on the rocks
whilst at anchor in Port William. Lydia survived along
with her diary

"For 10 years I have been prudent. I have tried to be
good. Now I have lost everything. I have no more
than when I began, save experience and faith. These
things I thank God I can never lose

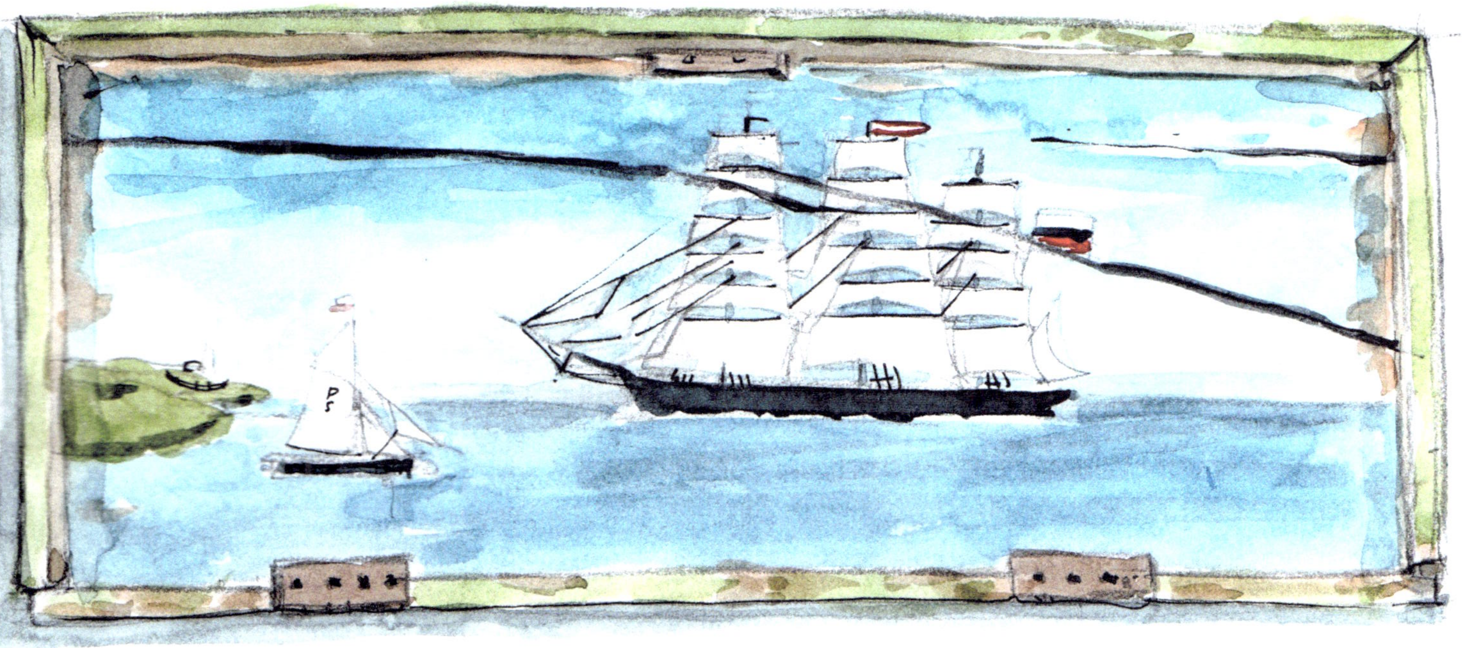

DECORATED LID FROM A SEAMAN'S CHEST. Sailors frequently painted portraits of their favourite ships on the inside of their chest lids.

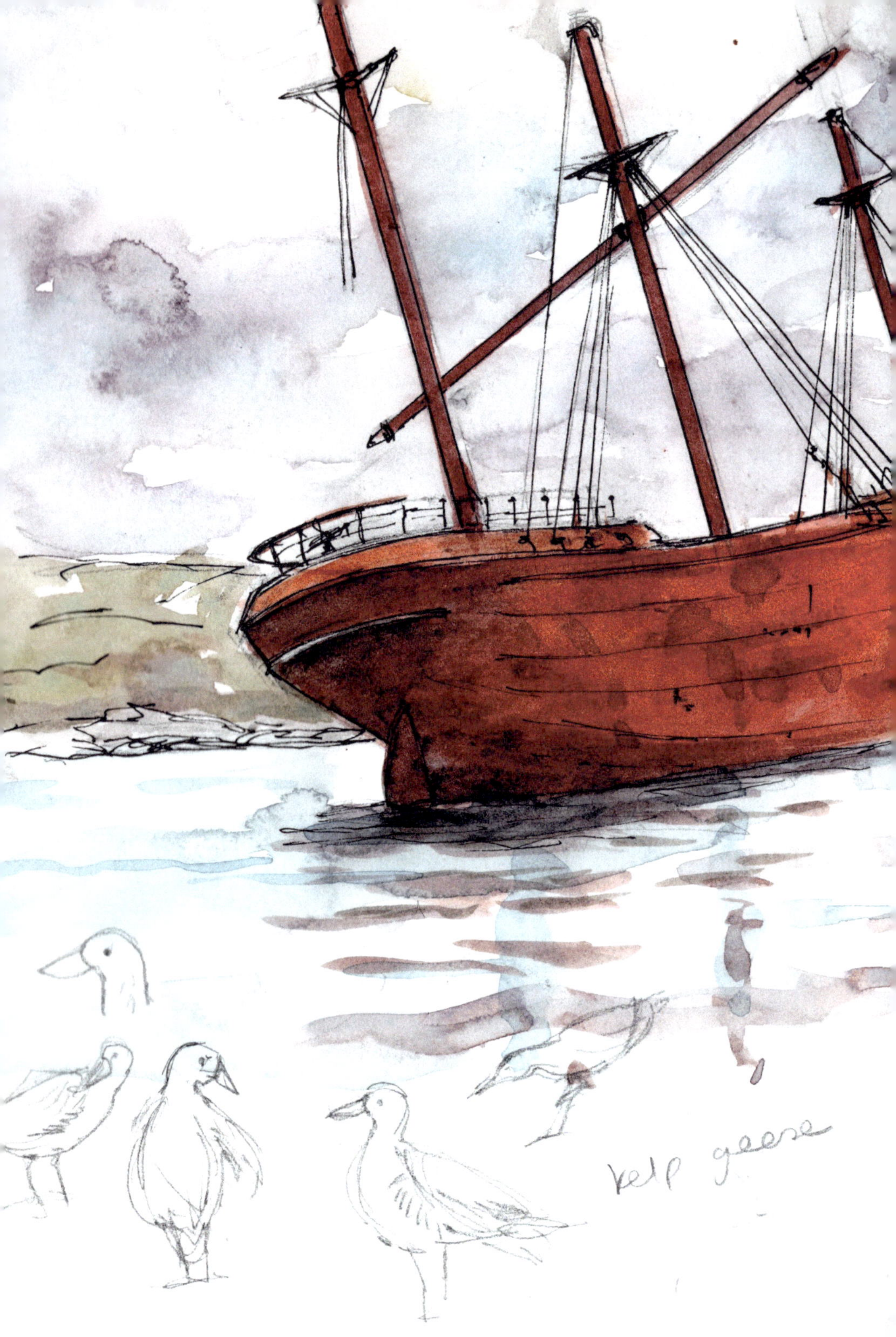
kelp geese

SATURDAY 4th JANUARY

Rain cleared after lunch, walked to
whalebone Cove

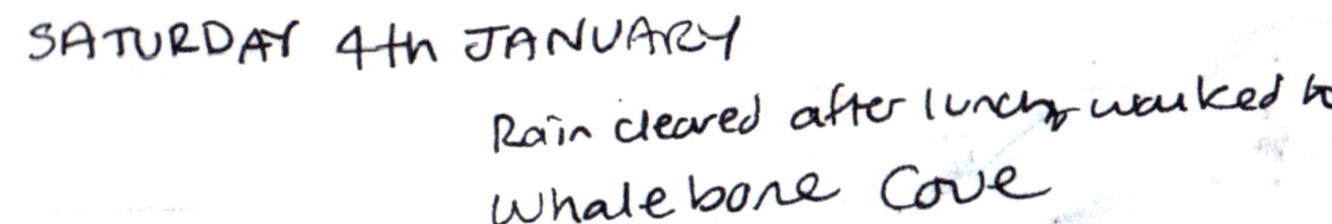

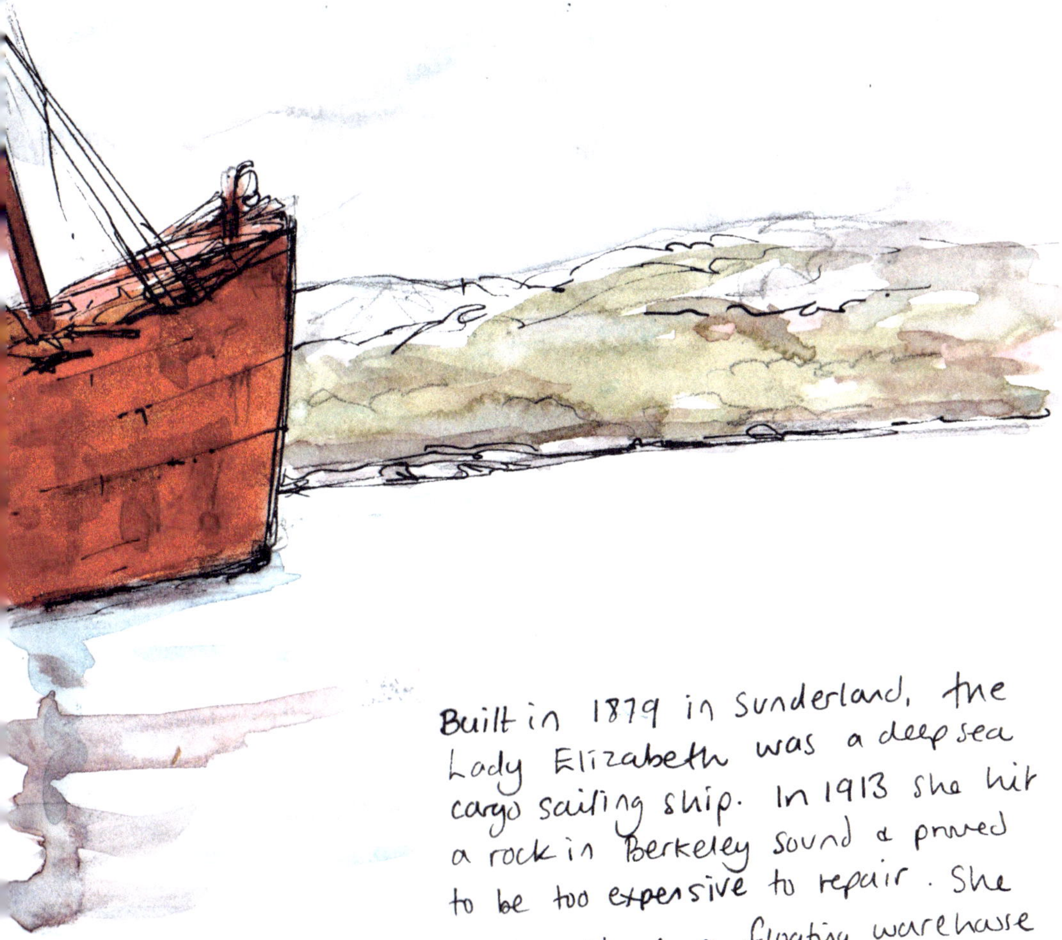

Built in 1879 in Sunderland, the
Lady Elizabeth was a deep sea
cargo sailing ship. In 1913 she hit
a rock in Berkeley Sound & proved
to be too expensive to repair. She
was sold as a floating warehouse
and sunk in whalebone Cove in
1936.

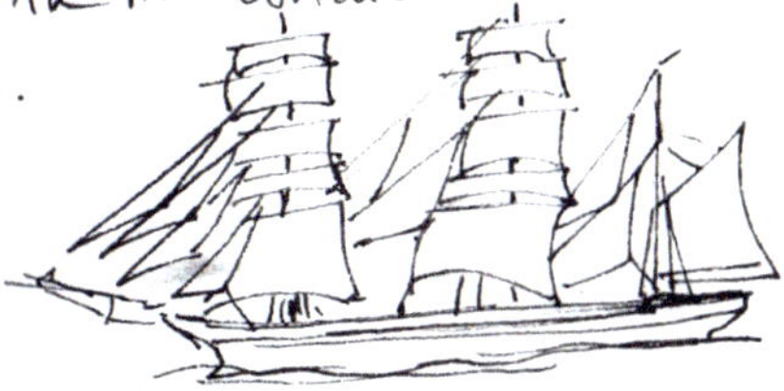

I find it impossible to walk along a shoreline without beachcombing, putting an assortment of pebbles, shells and feathers in my bag. Back at the hotel I spread my treasures out on the table. If the size is right, I often just lay them on the page and draw round them to get the basic shape. Drawing 'found' objects is a good way to finish off the pages and savour the day's experiences.

Painting pebbles, shells and feathers is a good contrast to scenic sketches, zooming in on detail instead of trying to summarise several miles of landscape in a few inches of page. It can help to establish the palette I need for a new place, as the colours for the detailed studies are the same as those of the broader landscape. It's useful to look at each place afresh rather than dip into the same habitual colours for each new location.

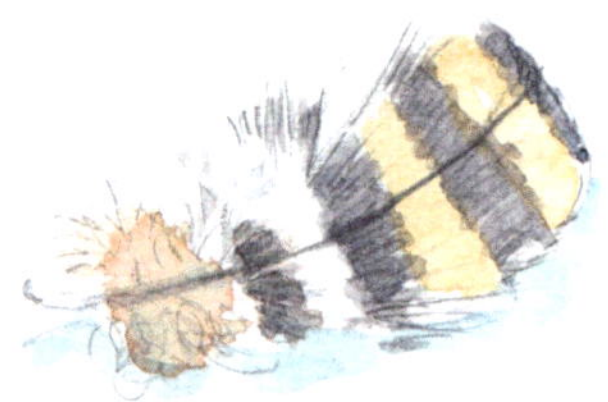

Travel in the Falklands is difficult. There are few roads, mostly unsurfaced, and all the places worth visiting involve a great deal of off-road driving on private land. So you really need a guide with a 4x4 which as a solo traveller is expensive unless you can team up with others. Most days the town is swarming with cruise ship visitors who get taken on pre-arranged tours; I took to hanging around the Visitor Centre each morning to find out if there were any excursions that I could join.

I was fortunate that one of my shipmates had given me an introduction to a friend of his who worked in the Conservation office, and it was Mike and his family who made my time on the island so worthwhile. The day after I walked into Mike's office to introduce myself he took me out to nearby Cape Pembroke and then we joined his family for a breezy but sunny picnic lunch on a local beach.

What a great place to bring up a family. Mike's wife Jo teaches nursery education and their young children Emily and Jacob have clean air and wide open spaces. Our picnic beach was only couple of miles out of town but we were alone at this windy but beautiful cove. I clambered up some rocks with 9 year old Jacob. 'Race you to the top!' he shouted and we stood looking at a pod of dolphins playing in the tumbling waves. 'Commerson's dolphins,' said Jacob. 'We get loads of those here. And we had a King penguin in Surf Bay the other weekend.'

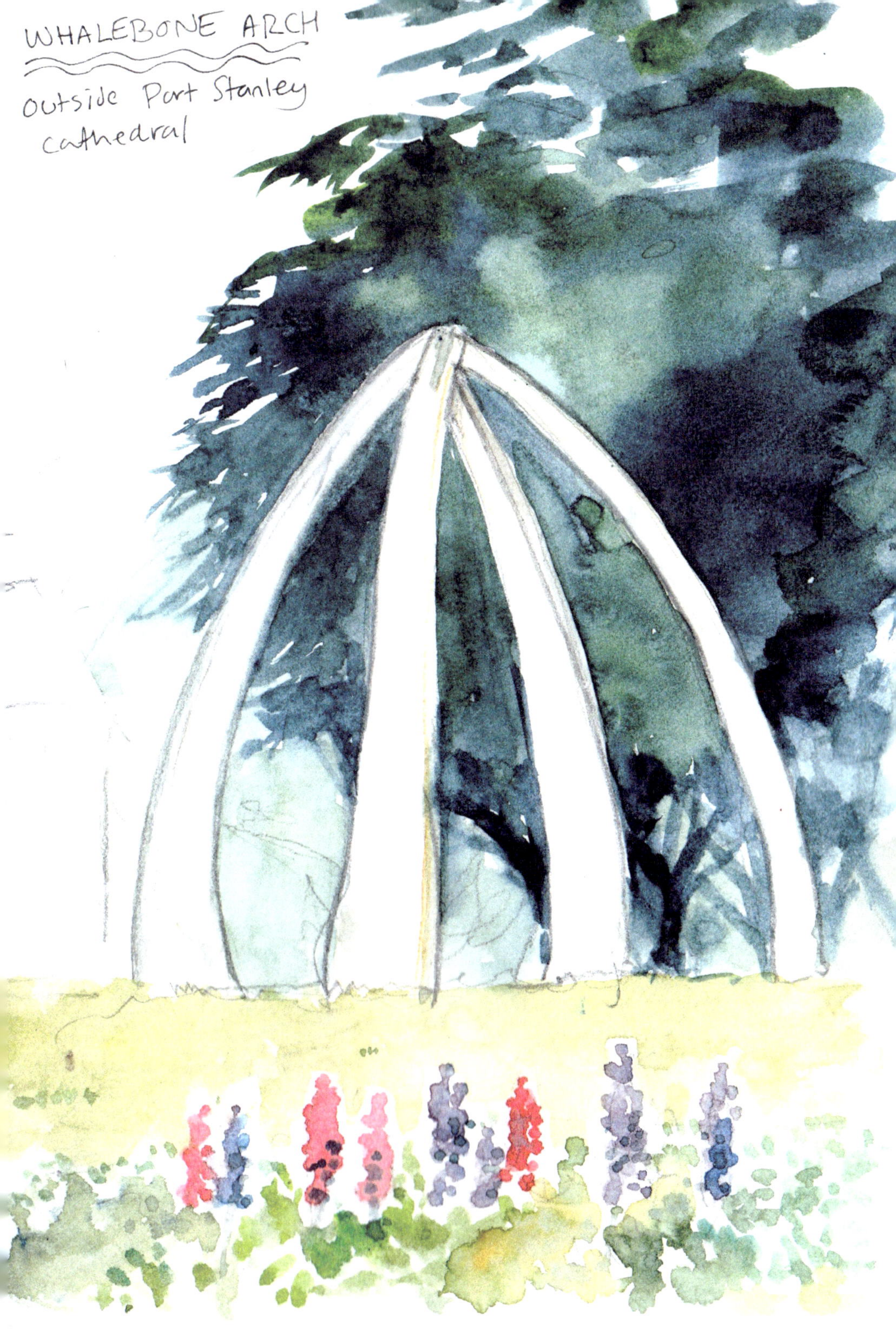
WHALEBONE ARCH
Outside Port Stanley
Cathedral

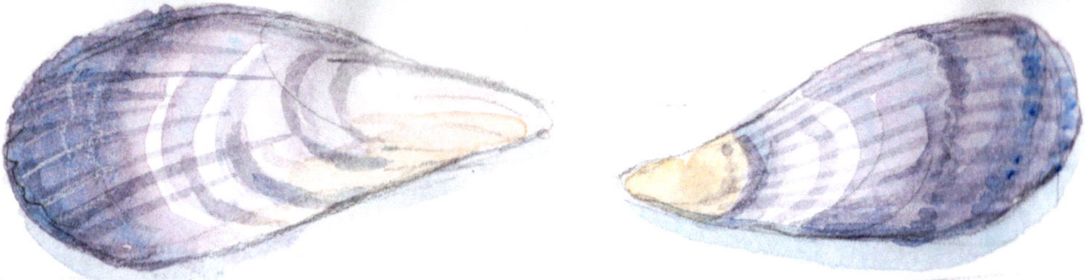

Old trawler at La Canache Boatyard, Port Stanley
Beauty in decay

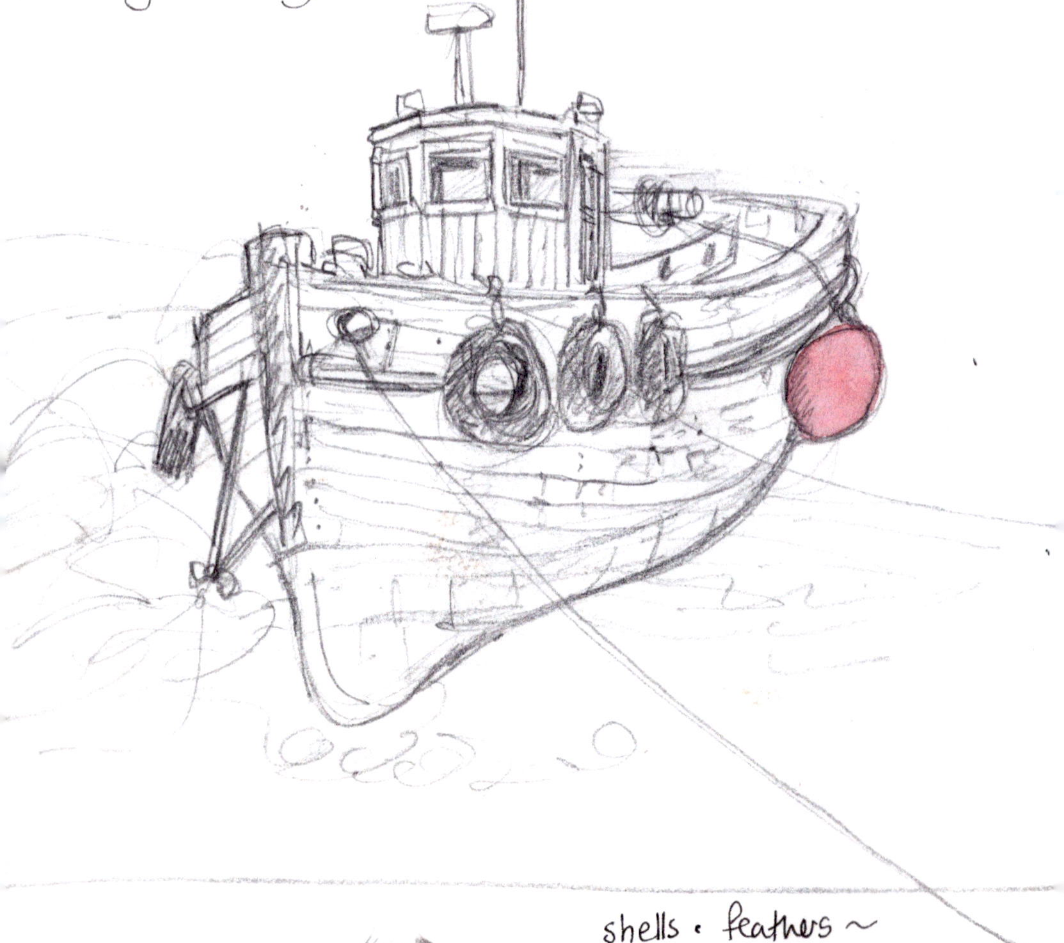

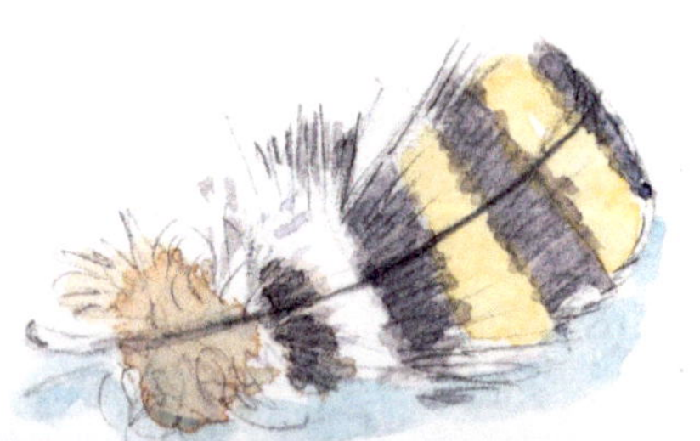

shells • feathers ~
beachcombing on the
way back from
Whalebone Cove

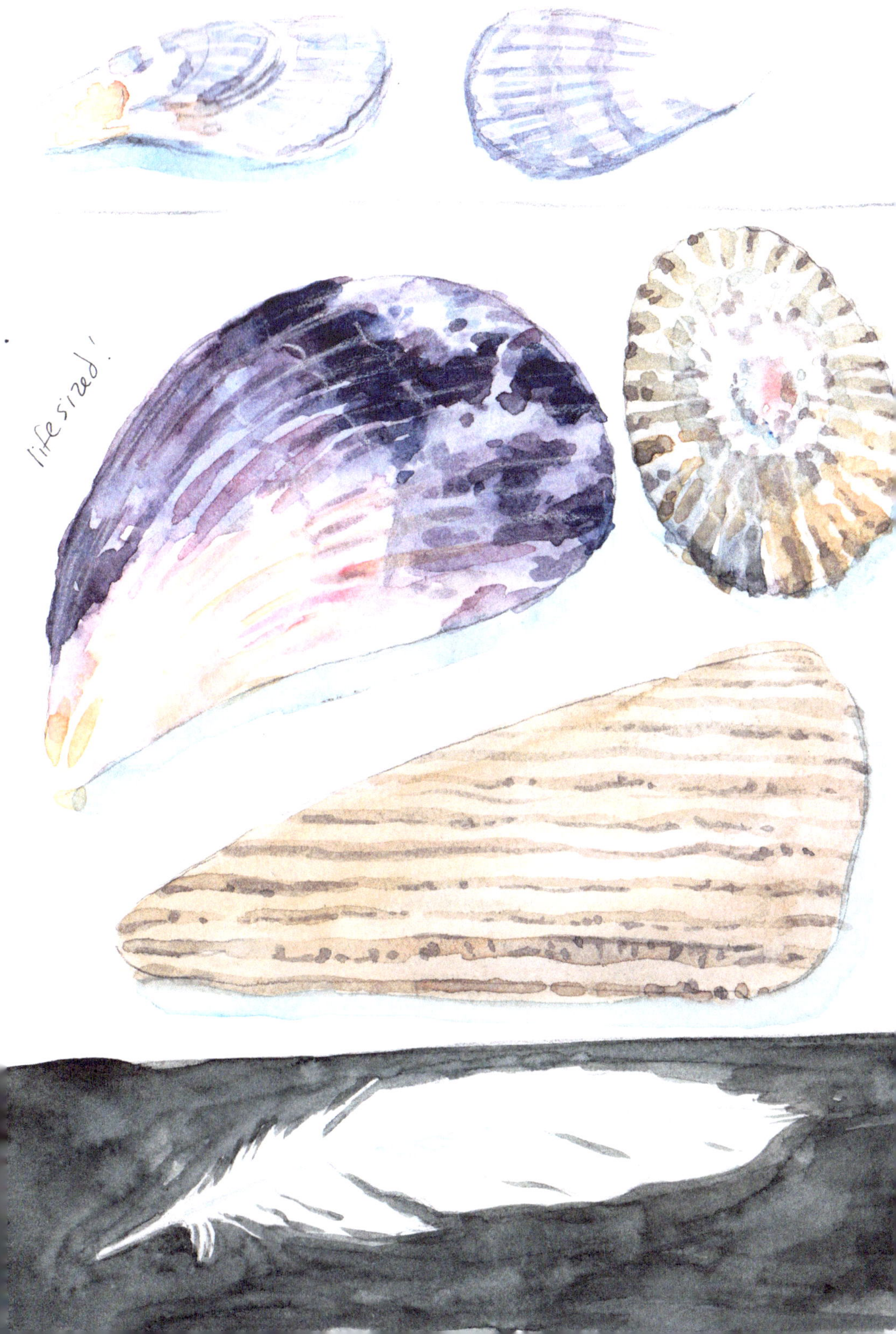
life sized !

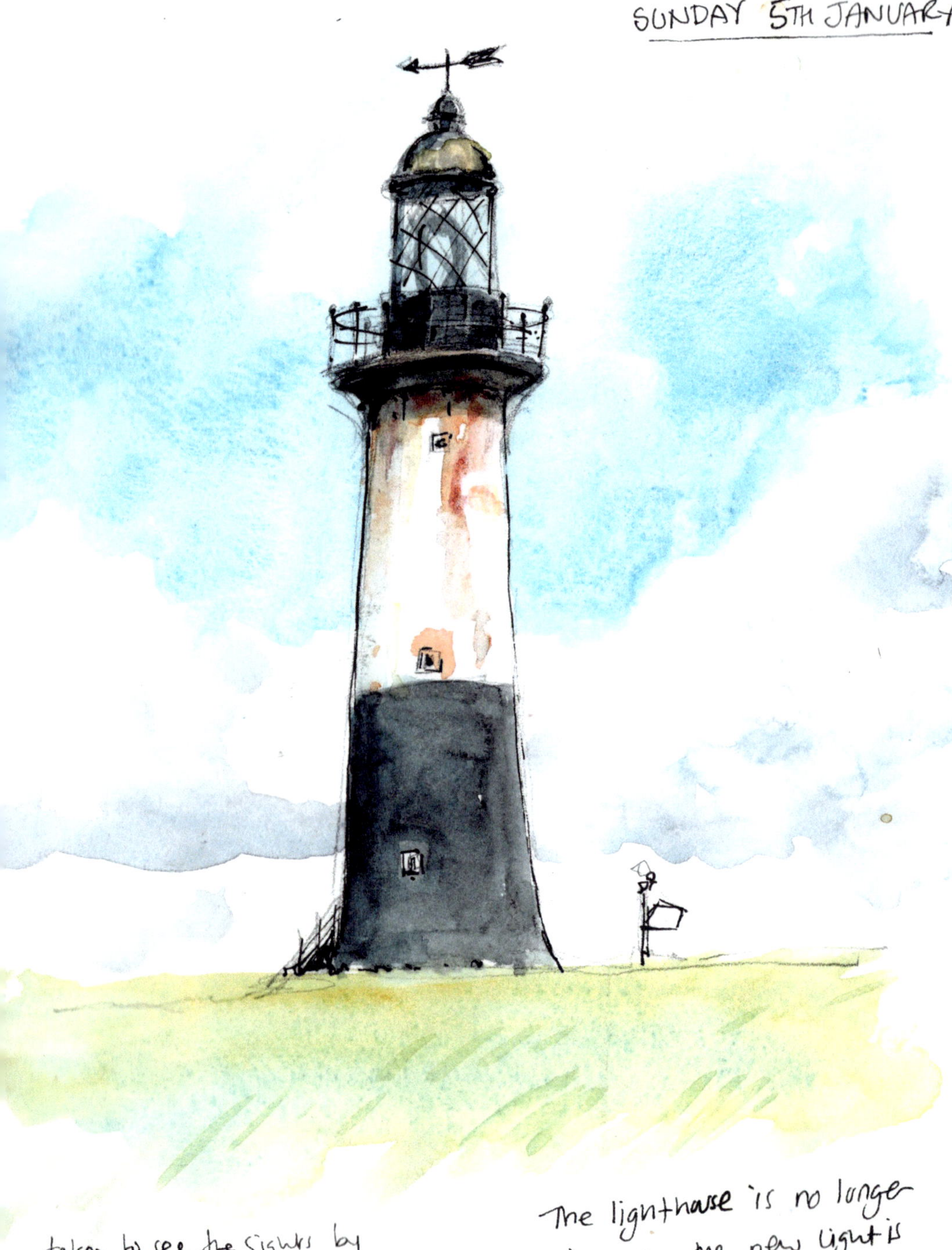

taken to see the sights by
michael Ford from
Conservation office

CAPE PEMBROKE LIGHT

The lighthouse is no longer
in use — the new light is
the small structure
alongside, with a small
solar panel.

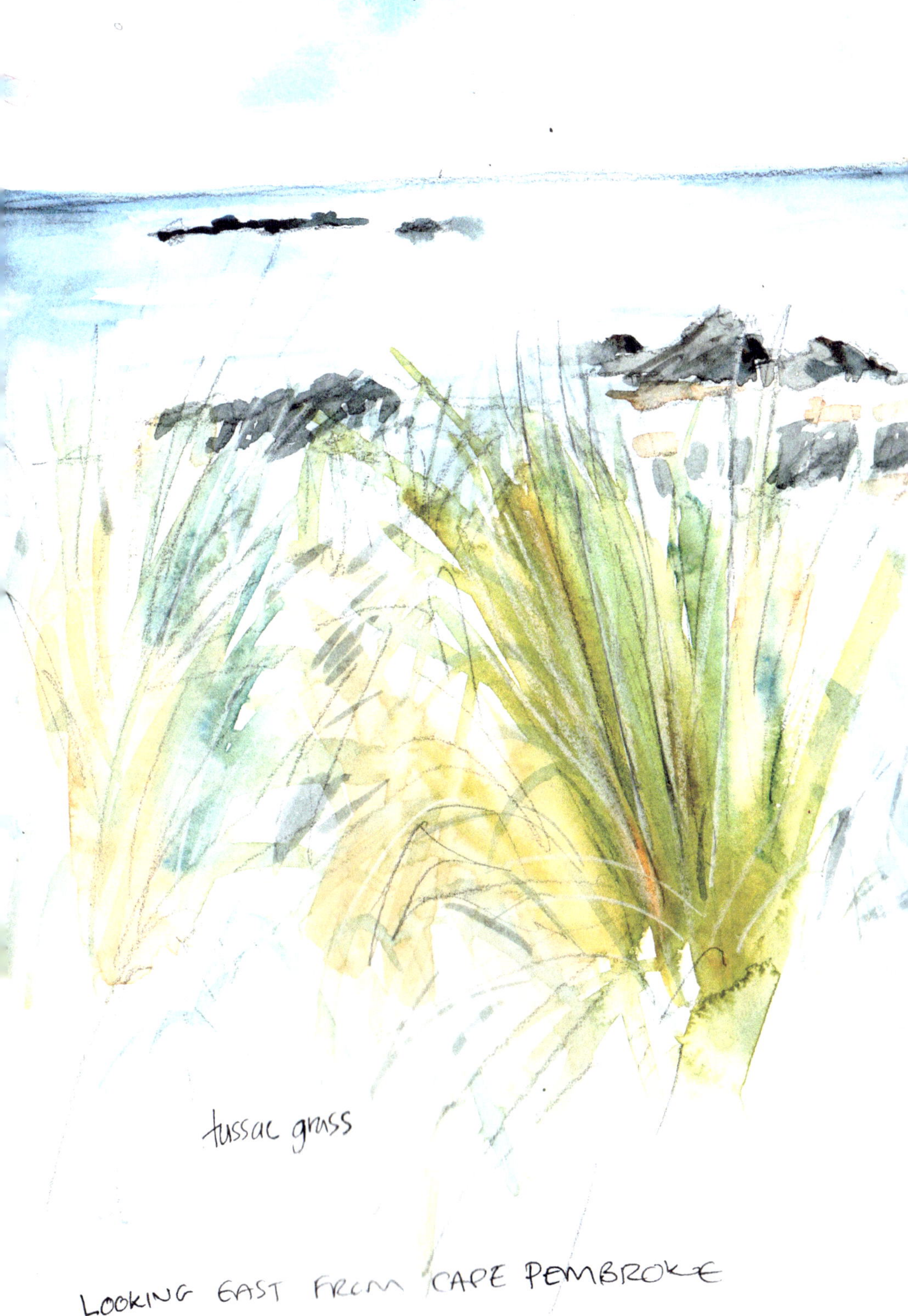

tussac grass
LOOKING EAST FROM CAPE PEMBROKE

Drive out to Gipsy Cove & see 'Tecla' sailing past
on her next adventure. Sunshine & calm sea.
Wish I was still on board & going with her!

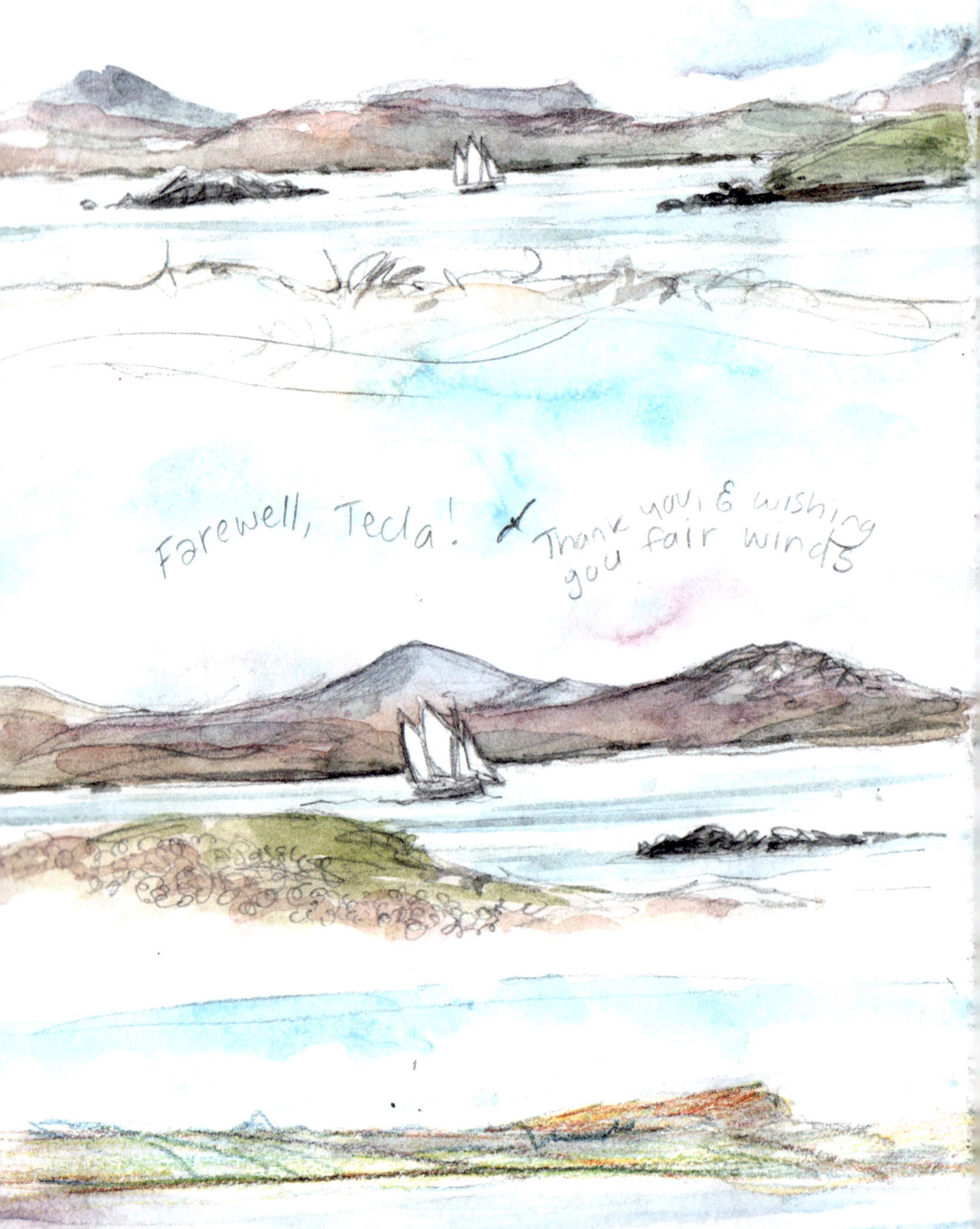

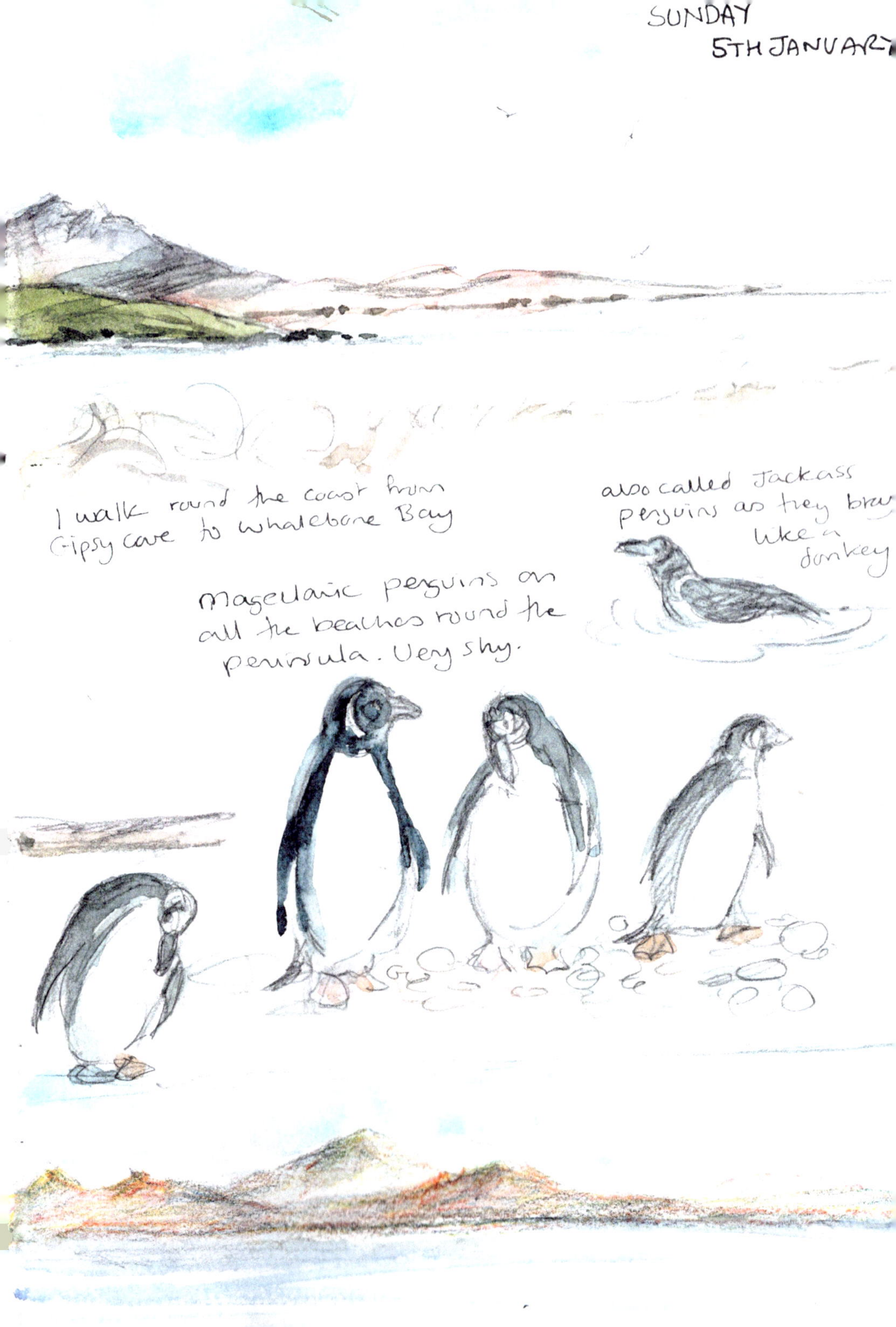

I walk round the coast from Gipsy Cove to Whalebone Bay

also called Jackass penguins as they bray like a donkey

Magellanic penguins on all the beaches round the peninsula. Very shy.

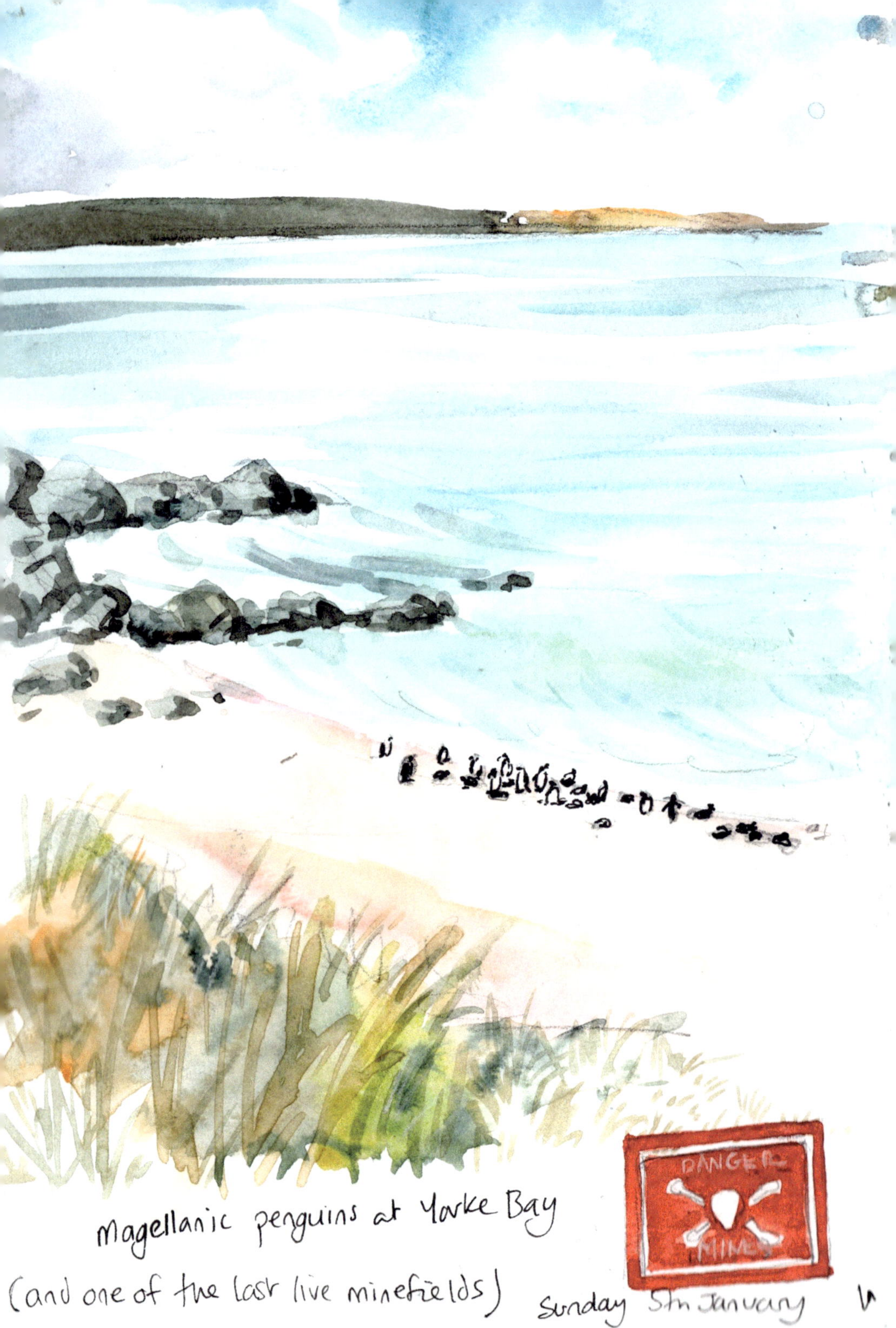

Magellanic penguins at Yorke Bay
(and one of the last live minefields)

Sunday 5th January

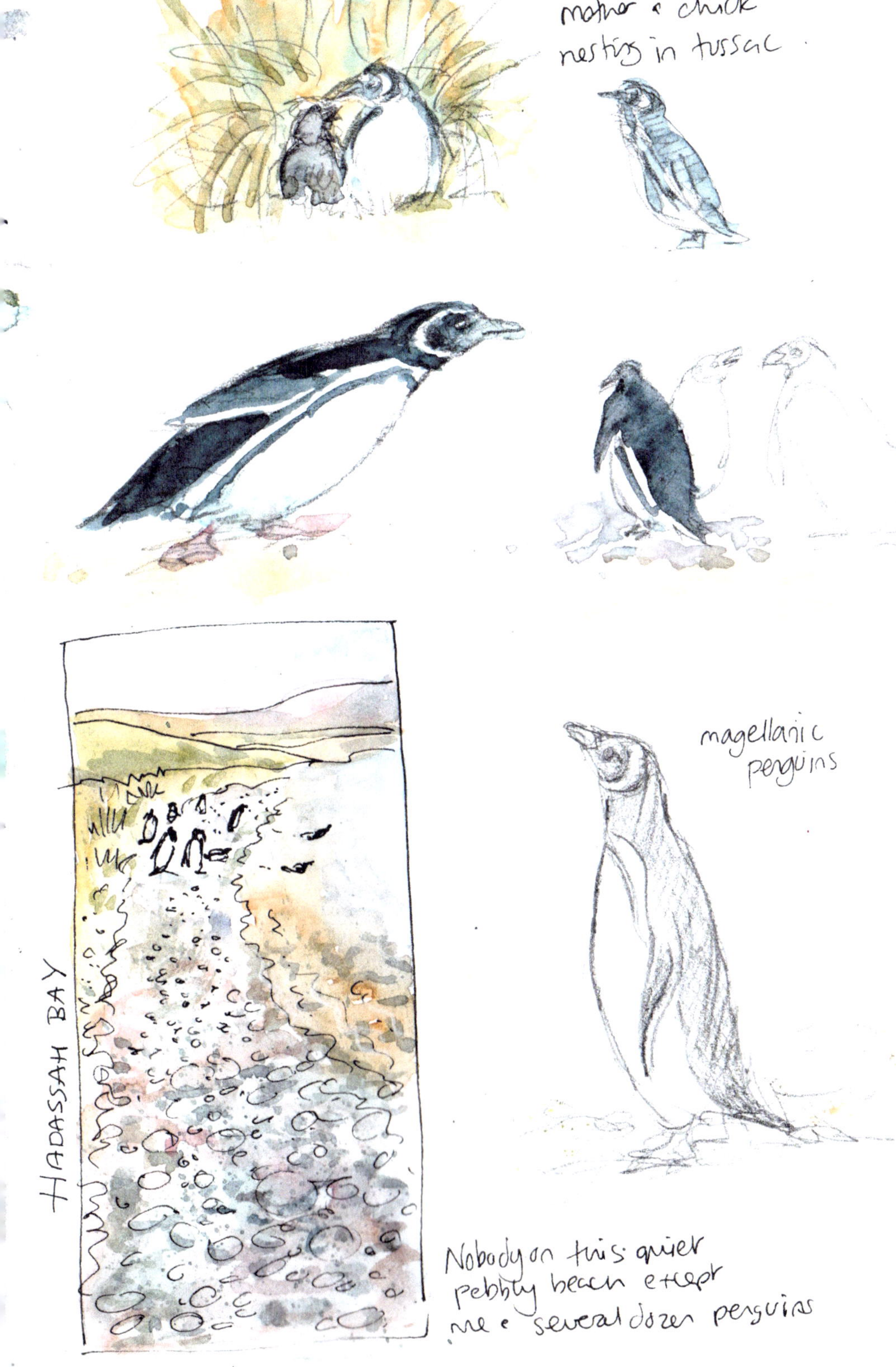

mother & chick
nesting in tussac
magellanic
penguins
Hadassah Bay
Nobody on this quiet
pebbly beach except
me & several dozen penguins

SUNDAY EVENING - BOAT TRIP OUT TO KIDNEY ISLAND.

several dozen adults & chicks perched on ledges at the edge of the tussac...

...very noisy chicks calling adults squawking

WE PUSH THROUGH TALL TUSSAC GRASS IN SINGLE
FILE TO THE NORTH SHORE AND GET CLOSE TO
ROCKHOPPER PENGUINS

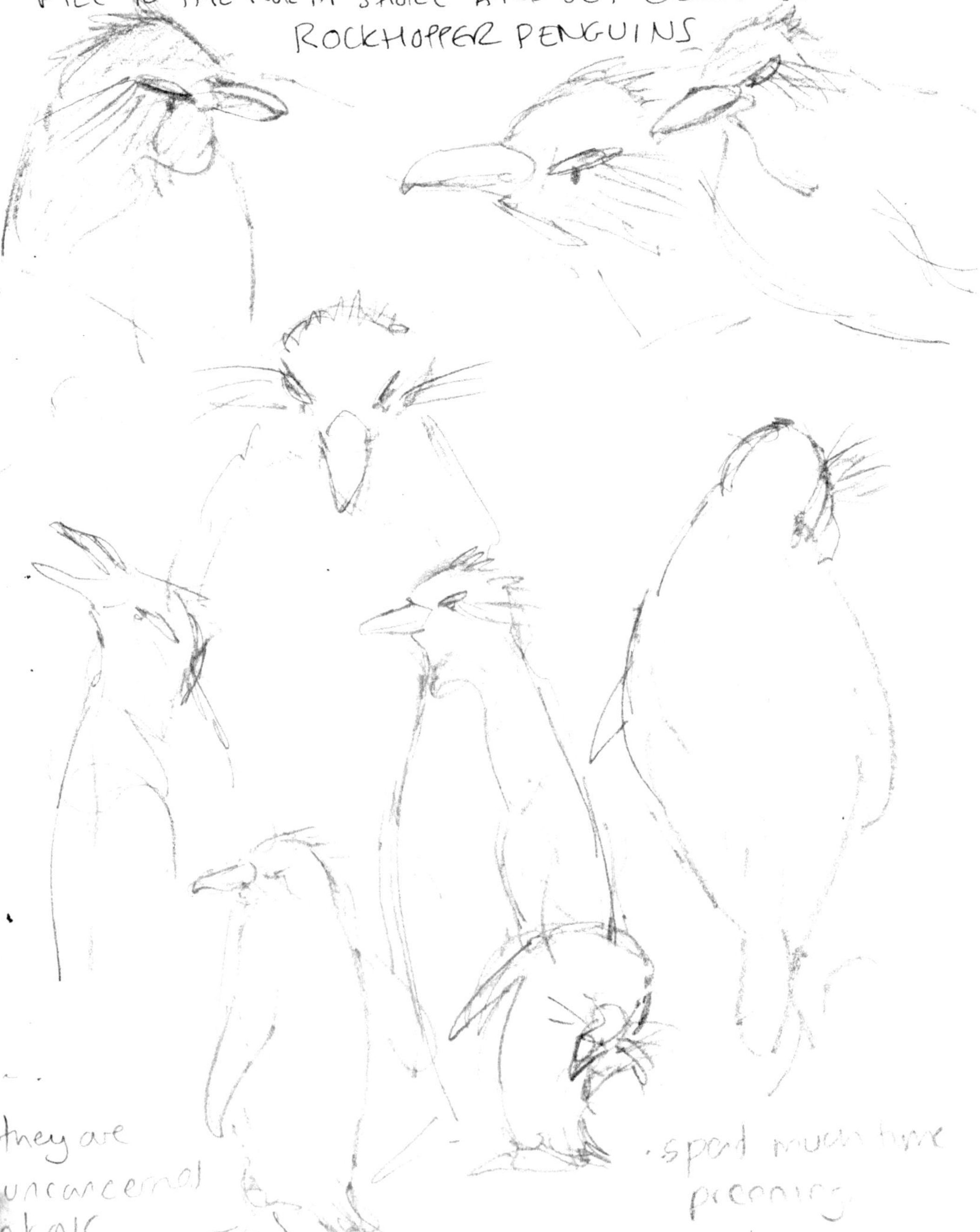

they are
unconcerned
at our
presence

spend much time
preening

plenty of smell!

Rockhoppers on the north side of Kidney Island

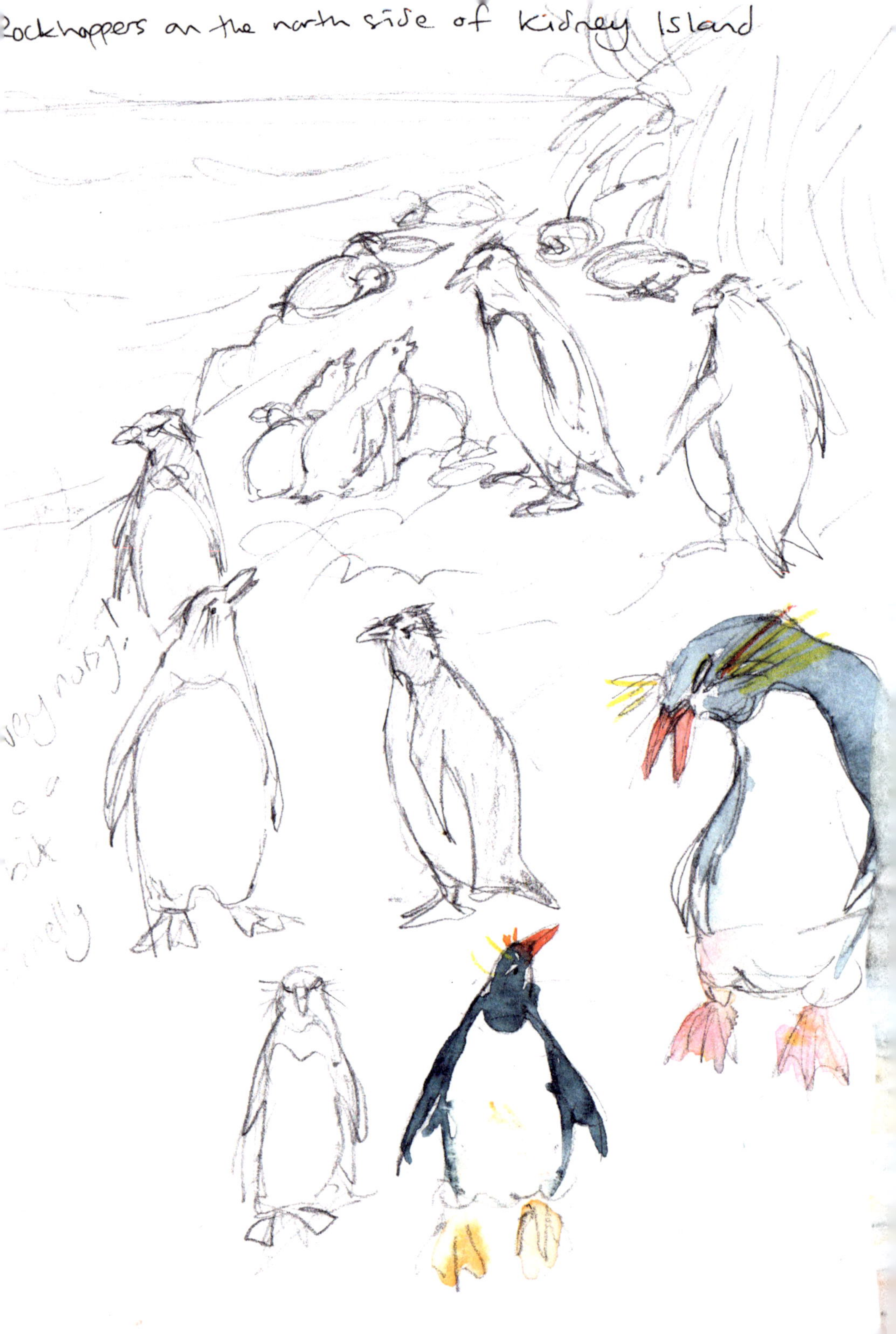

at dusk, we wait on the beach. Tens of thousands
of sooty shearwaters fill the sky, returning to their nests
in the tussac. For half an hour or so the
sky is full of them. How do they
find their nest again?
They crash land in the tussac,
there is no elegant way to
do it!

TUSSAC GRASS COVERS KIDNEY ISLAND ...
... and it grows to head height

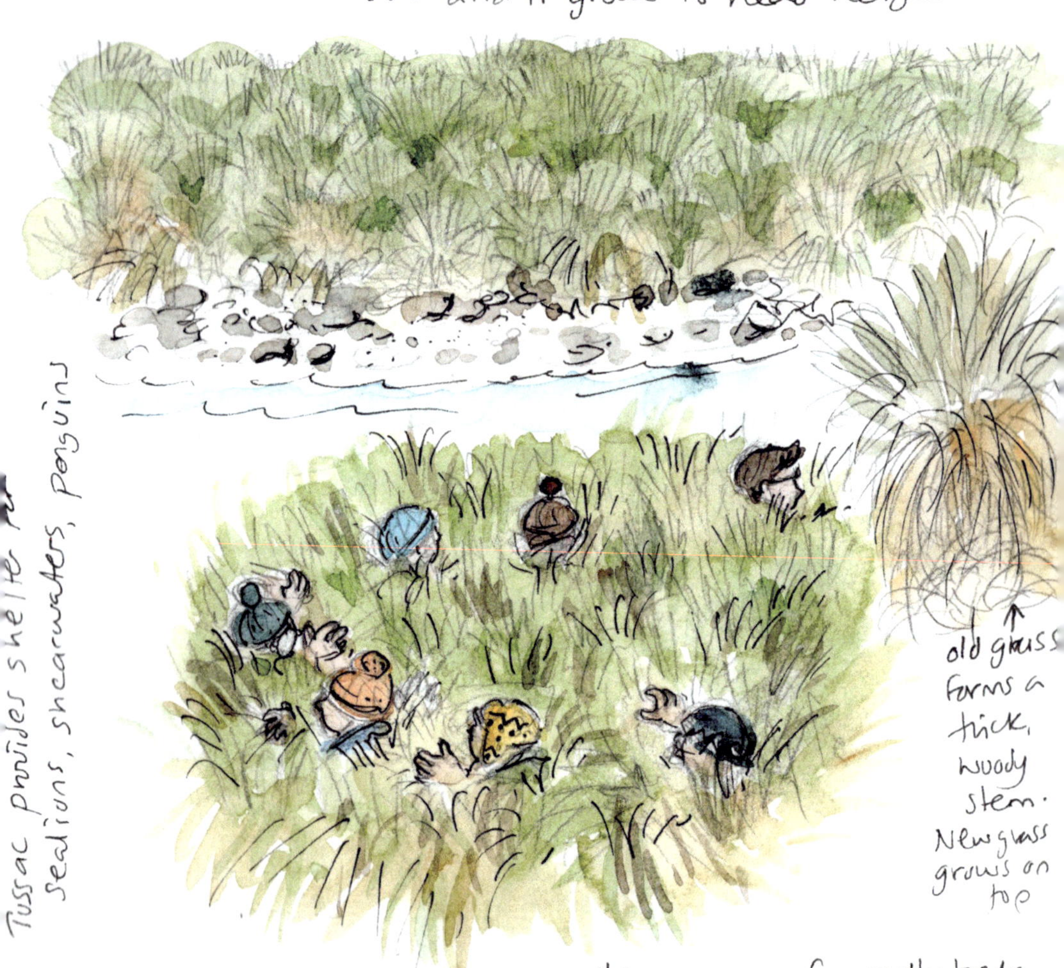

We follow our guide, Michelle, a row of woolly hats
bobbing single file through the thick clumps of tussac.
A shepherd's hut near the shore is where farmers used
to come & harvest tussac for their livestock.
Overgrazing on the main islands is the reason tussac is
rarer there, & dunes prone to erosion.

Our journey takes us to the rockhopper
penguin colonies on the other side of
the island.

My first view of penguins was at Yorke Bay, close to Port Stanley. Mike drove me there and I walked back round the headland, stopping to sketch along the way. There are still a few minefields left after the 1982 war, well fenced off. Luckily, penguins aren't heavy enough to detonate them! (Later in the week I was rescued from a torrential rain storm by a couple of mine clearers in a landrover who picked me up and kindly gave me a lift all the way back to my hotel.) Whilst on my walk around the headland I saw *Tecla* sailing out of the narrows on the next stage of her journey, towards South Georgia, Antarctica and Tierra del Fuego. Part of my heart went with her.

I was lucky enough to join an evening boat trip to nearby Kidney Island to see Rockhopper penguins. We had to thread our way through clumps of head high tussac grass to reach the busy colony but it was well worth it. The rockhoppers are small but noisy, completely unconcerned at our presence as they chattered, preened and squabbled. My sketches were very hasty—it wasn't easy trying to manage sketchbook and pencils whilst wedged into the spiky grass in the fading light and cold wind.

The more excited I get about a place, the more I want to draw. You'll see that my picnic at Whale Point with Mike and the children made an impression I will never forget, and so did the King Penguin colony at Volunteer Point. Both trips were well worth several hours of bouncing in land rovers across seemingly impossible terrain.

Back in the hotel each evening I had time to finish the day's sketches. If a cool wind had been blowing during the day – and it usually had – it was difficult to complete a sketch on location as there was no time to let one colour dry before adding another. Most of these pages were finished off from memory later.

Not every day was full of penguins. I spent plenty of rainy days in cafes, reading second hand novels from the Visitor Centre, or wandering round the streets of Port Stanley thinking I ought to be sketching but not always feeling in the mood if it was raining or I'd not managed to make any travel plans. But I did draw every day; the unfinished sketches reflect my mood as much as the busy colourful pages.

The legacy of the 1982 war remains very much in evidence. The adult population of Port Stanley remember all too well the shock of armed soldiers bursting into their schoolrooms and the sight of troops marching down the main road. The landscape shows its scars. The hillside outside Port Stanley is full of small round ponds caused by mortar holes. At the top of Sapper Hill one of the saddest sights is a few ragged scraps of tarpaulin between a stack of boulders. That was a makeshift shelter and lookout post for Argentinian soldiers who may have wondered what on earth they were doing there.

Down on the waterfront

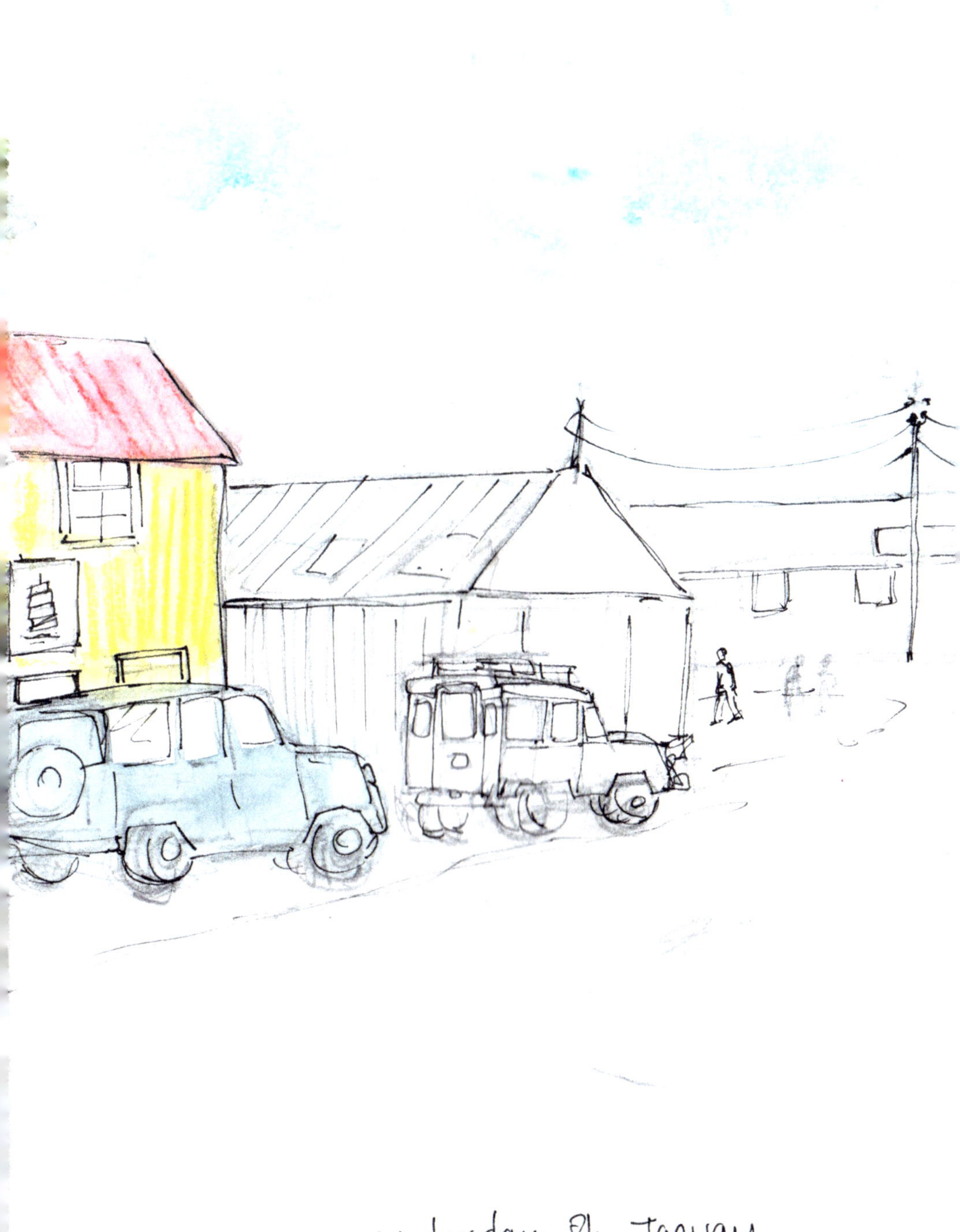

Wednesday 8th January
Port Stanley

The emptiest, fullest place I have ever been.

Much of the trip to Whale Point with Mike & his children is over Fitzroy farm. Two hours of rough terrain, boggy bits, moorland & occasionally a track. The children are unconcerned — I'm holding on to my seat very tightly. Mike is an expert off-road driver — I am astonished at what an old landrover can do!

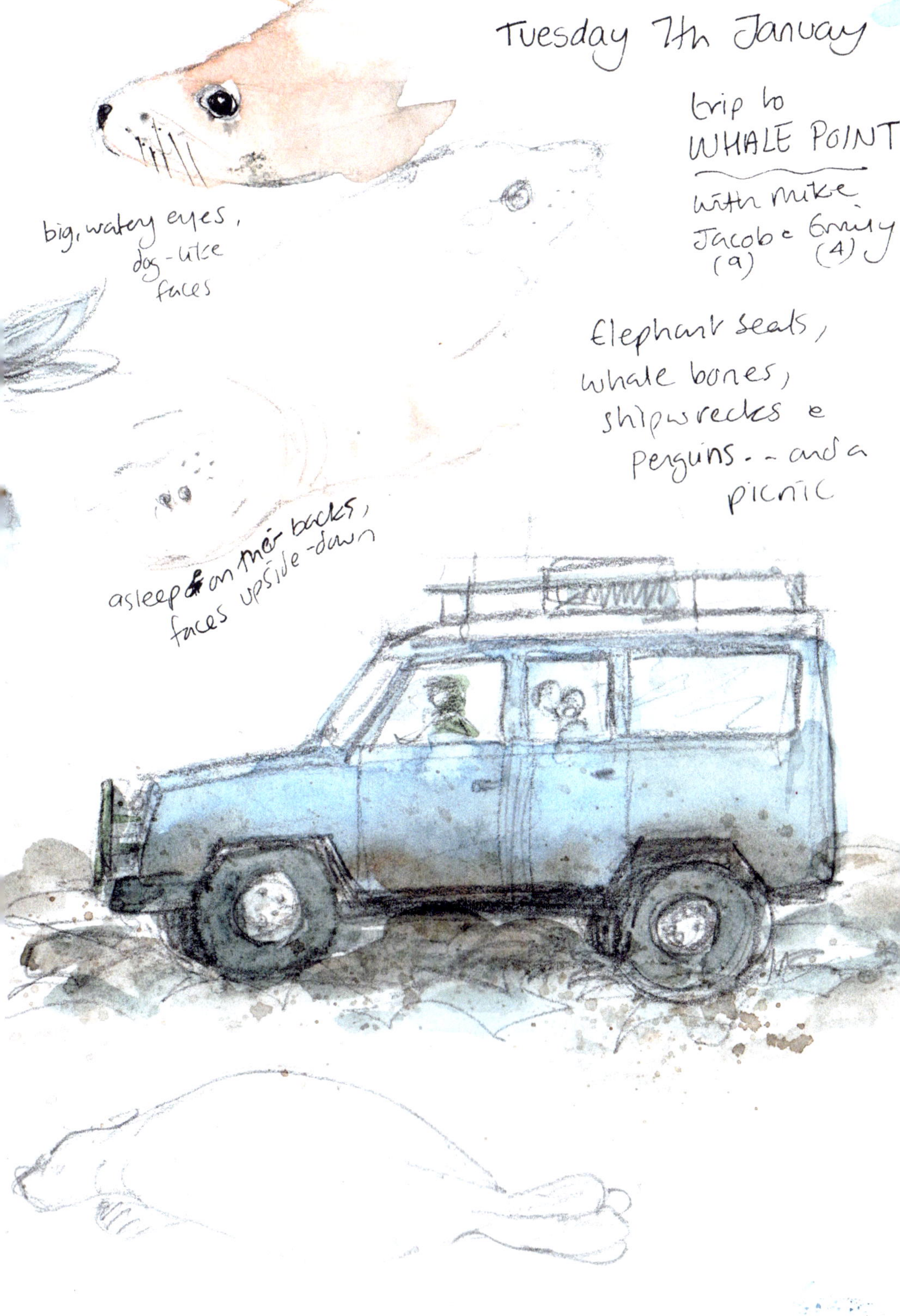

Tuesday 7th January

trip to
WHALE POINT

with Mike
Jacob & Emily
(9)   (4)

Elephant seals,
whale bones,
shipwrecks &
penguins... and a
picnic

big, watery eyes,
dog-like
faces

asleep on their backs,
faces upside-down

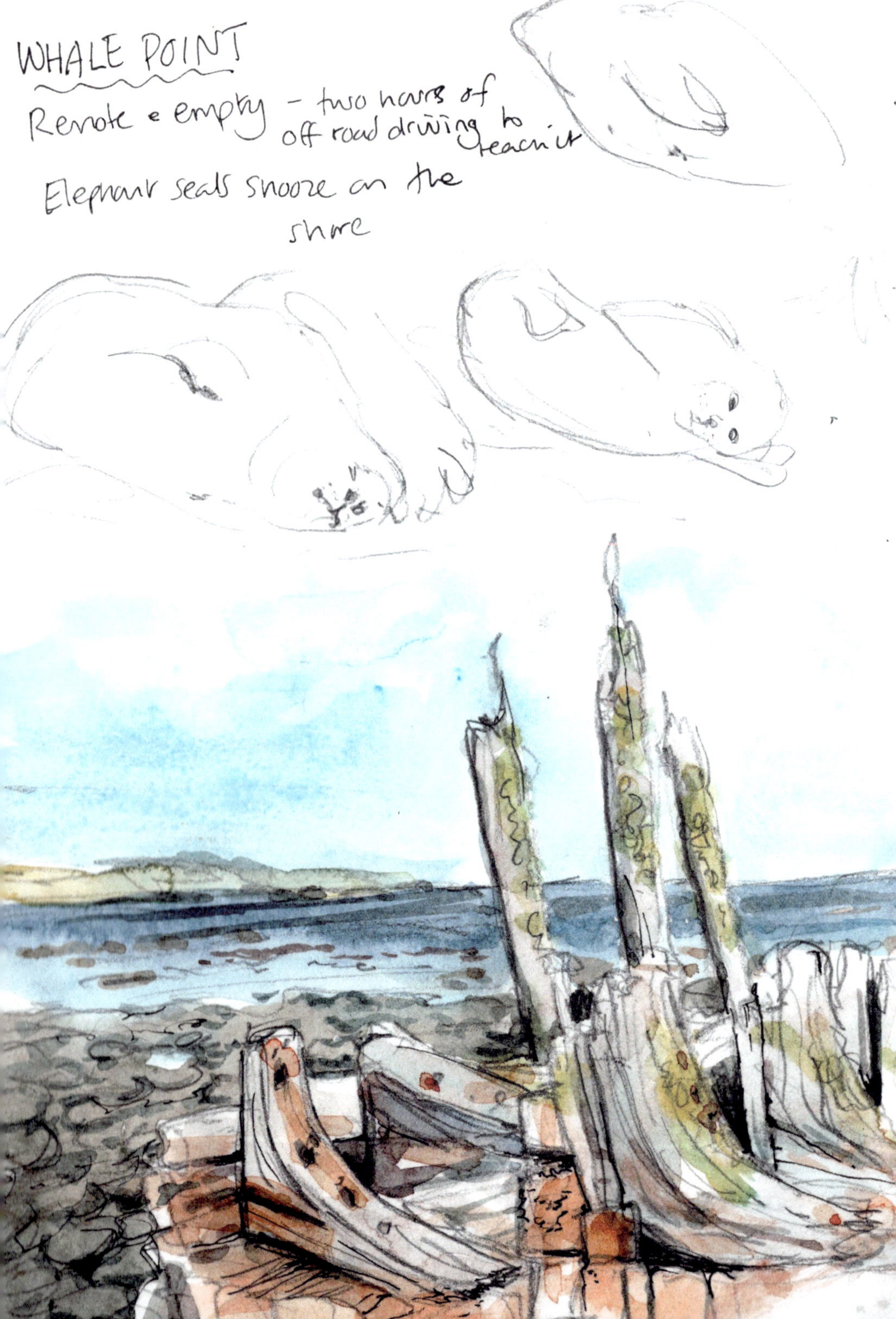

WHALE POINT
Remote & empty – two hours of
off road driving to reach it
Elephant seals snooze on the
shore

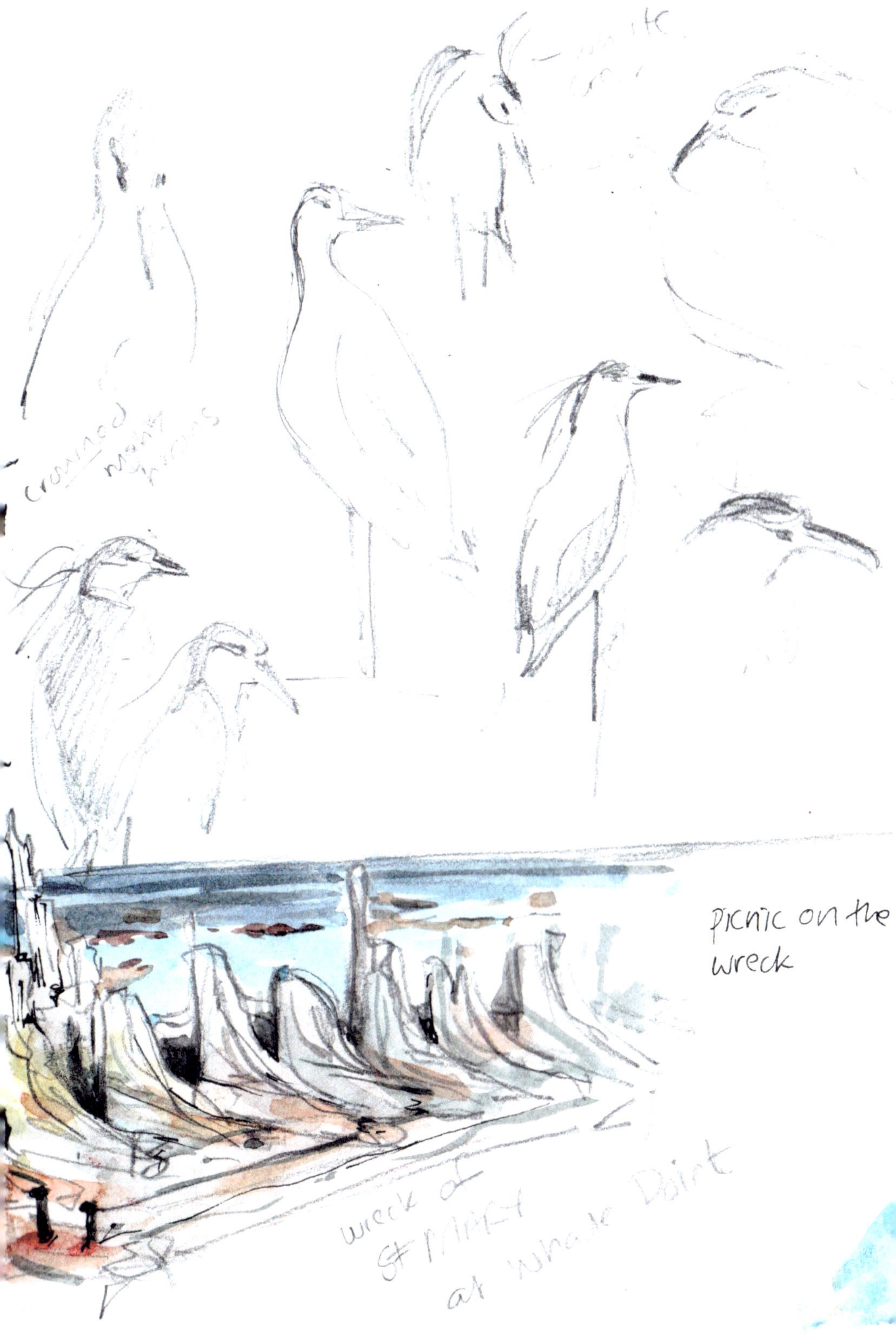

crossed many forms
picnic on the wreck
wreck of St MARY at Whale Point

ELEPHANT SEALS AT WHALE POINT

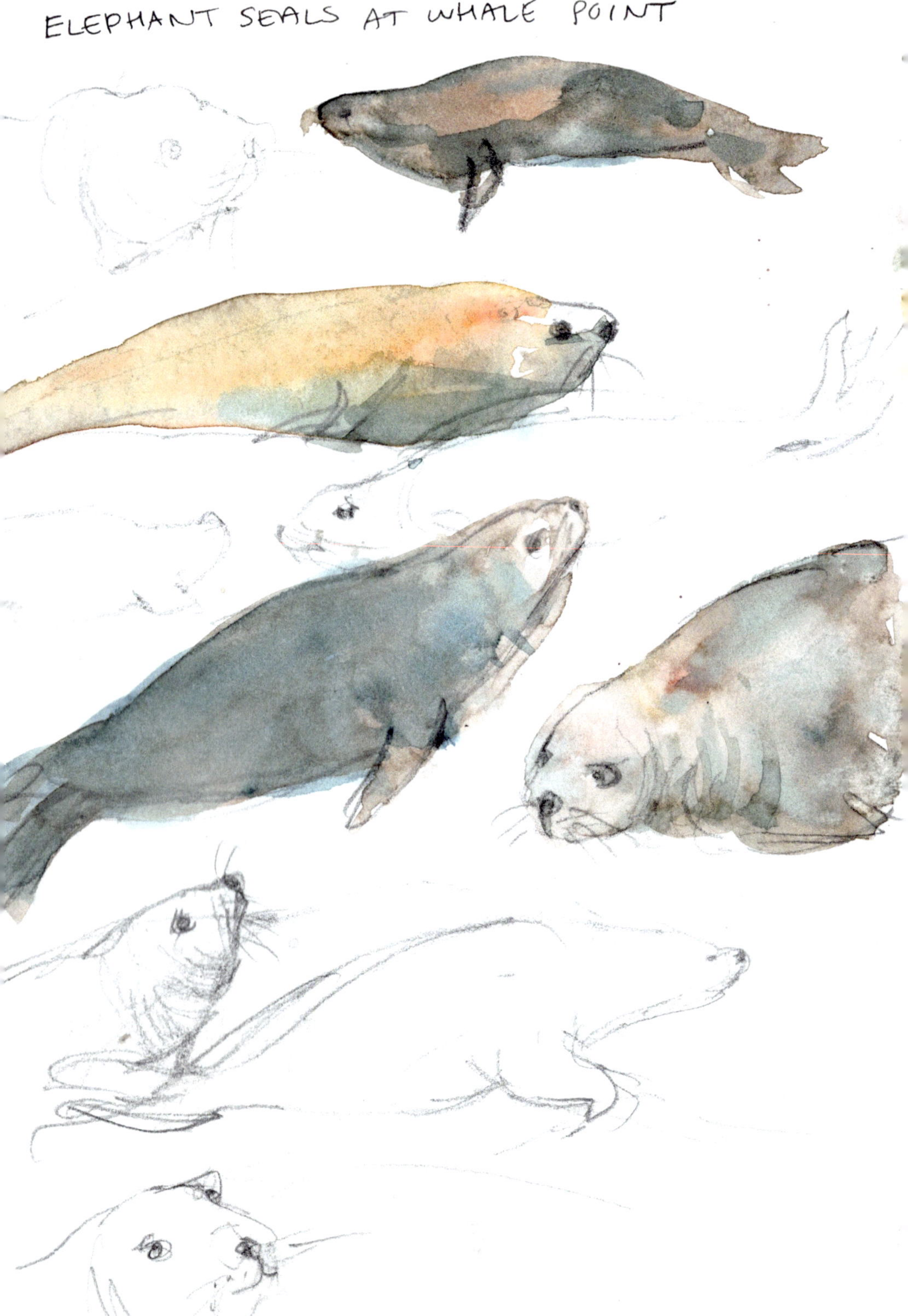

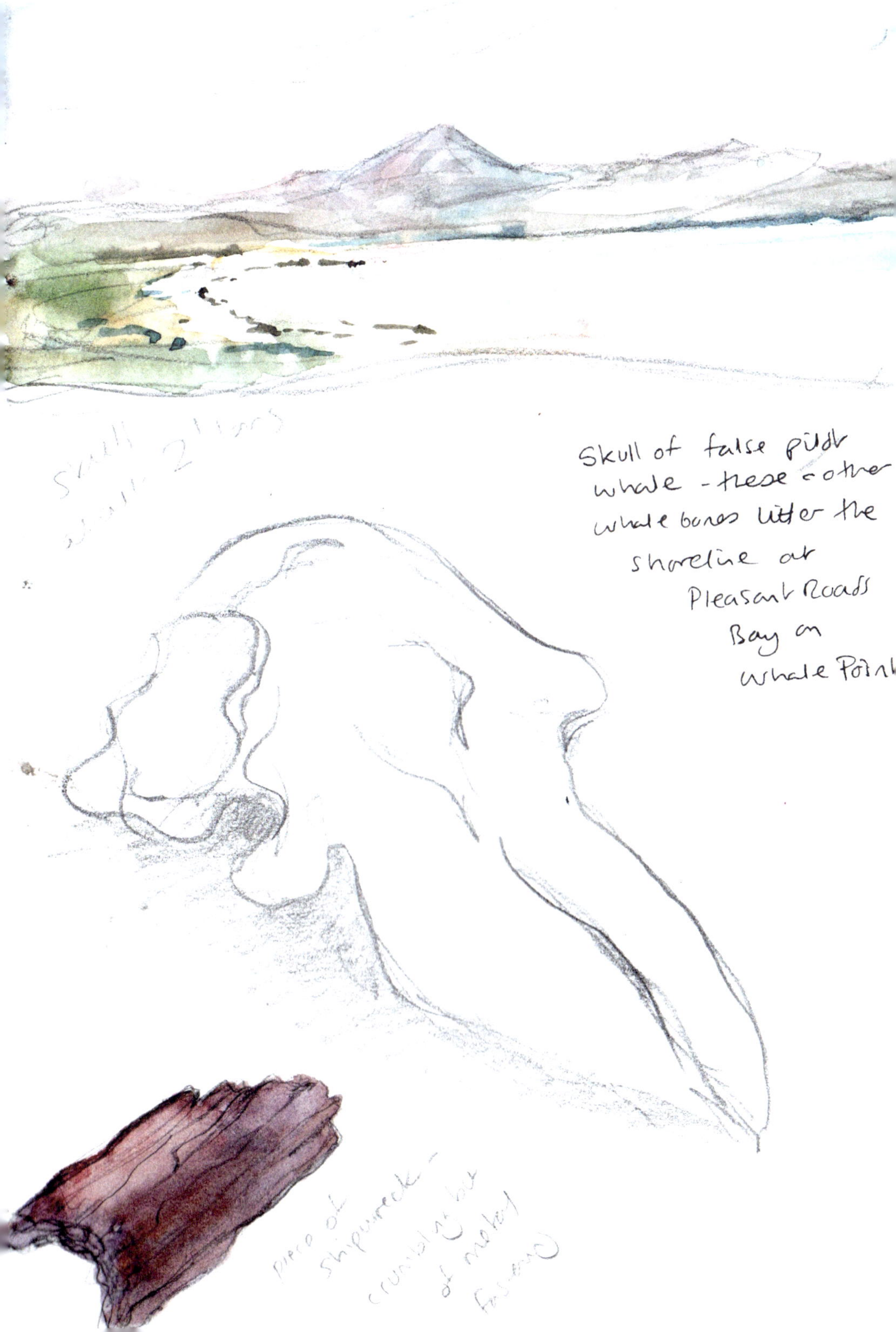

Skull of false pilot
whale - these & other
whale bones litter the
shoreline at
Pleasant Roads
Bay on
Whale Point
piece of
shipwreck -
crumbling bit
of metal
Fastening

GENTOO PENGUINS AT PLEASANT ROADS BAY, WHALE POINT

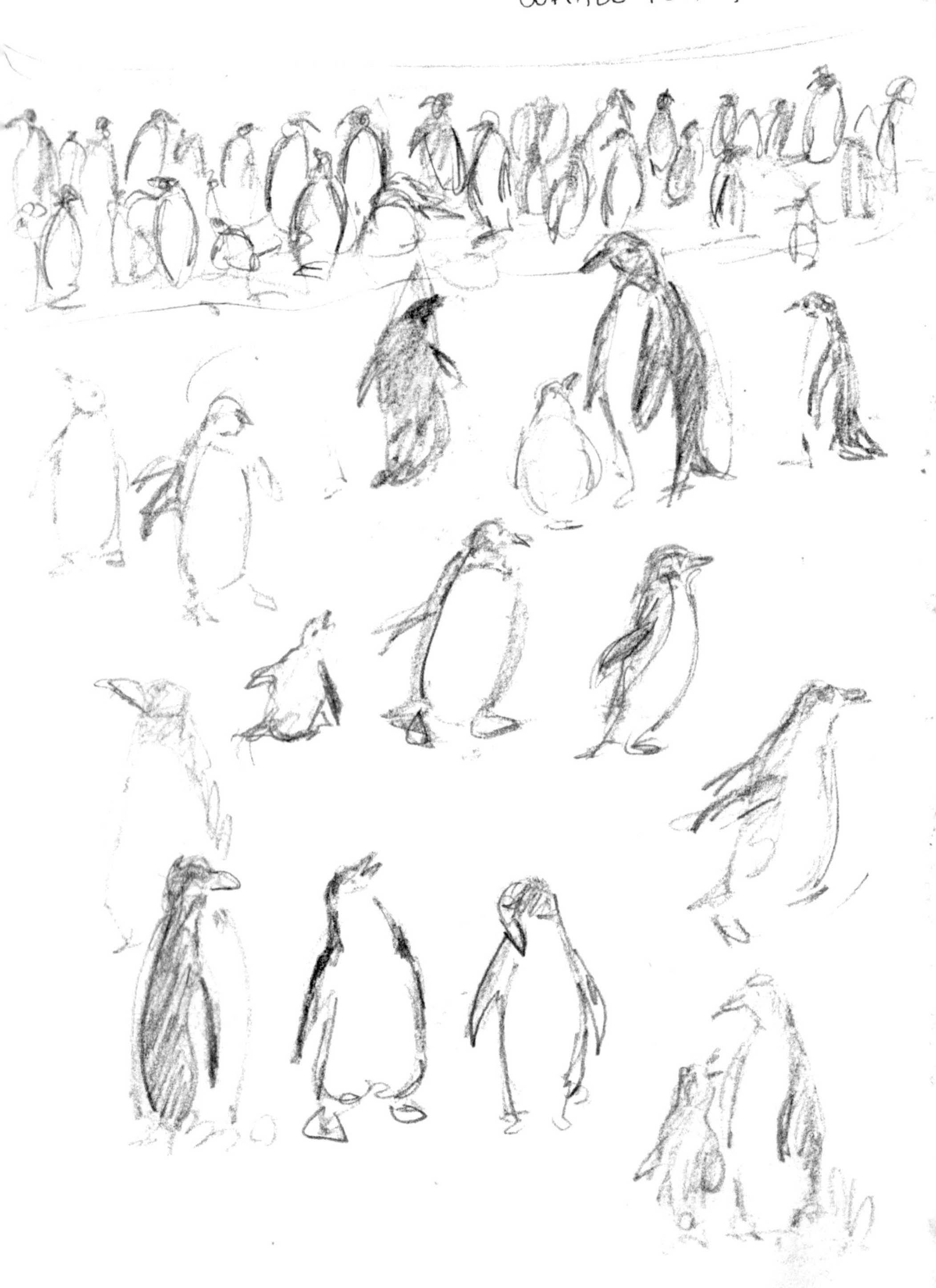

wideopen spaces, white sandy bay & big skies.
whalebones litter the shoreline, sheep graze and a
    large colony of gentoo penguins chatter, squabble, tend
                their chicks.

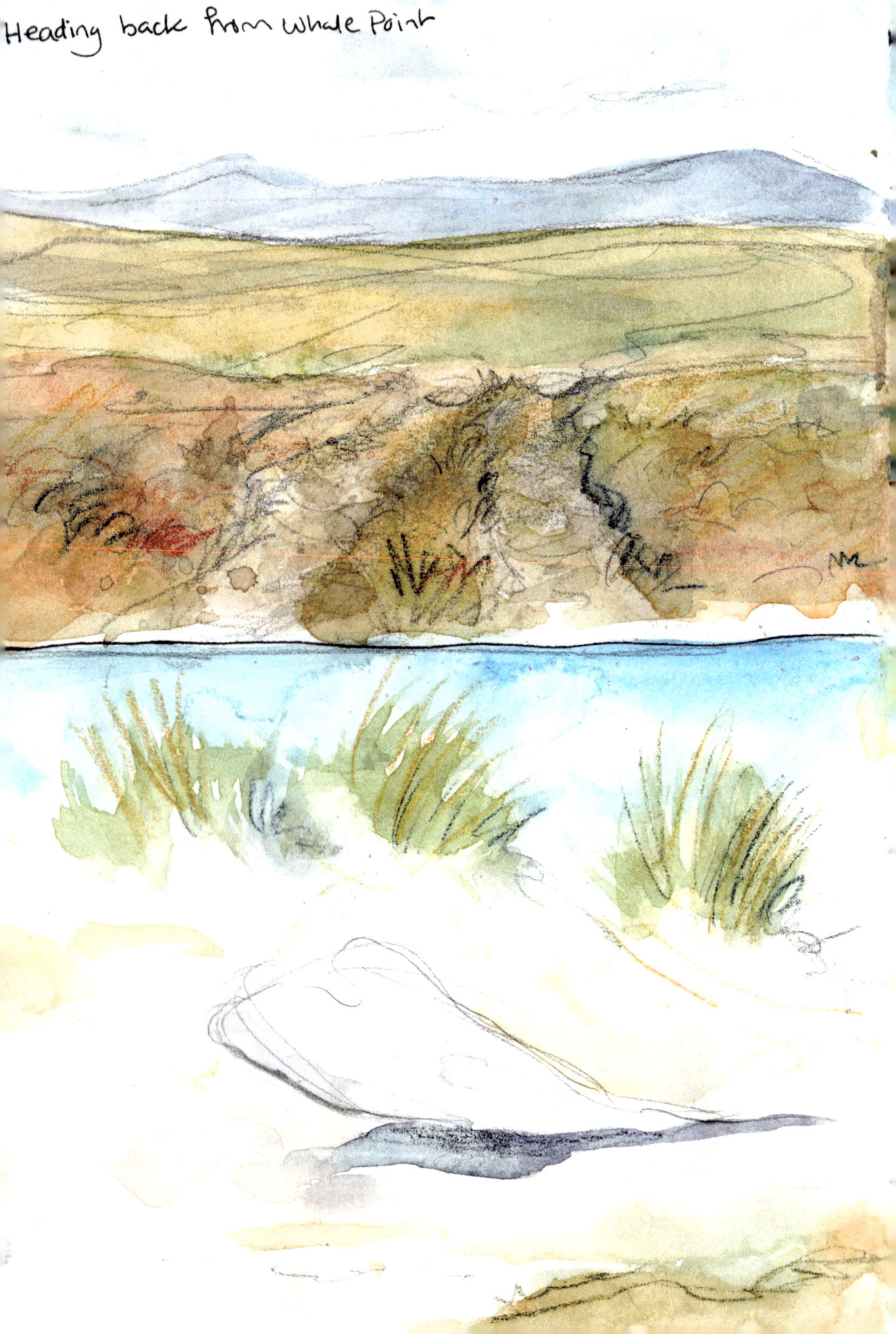
Heading back from Whale Point

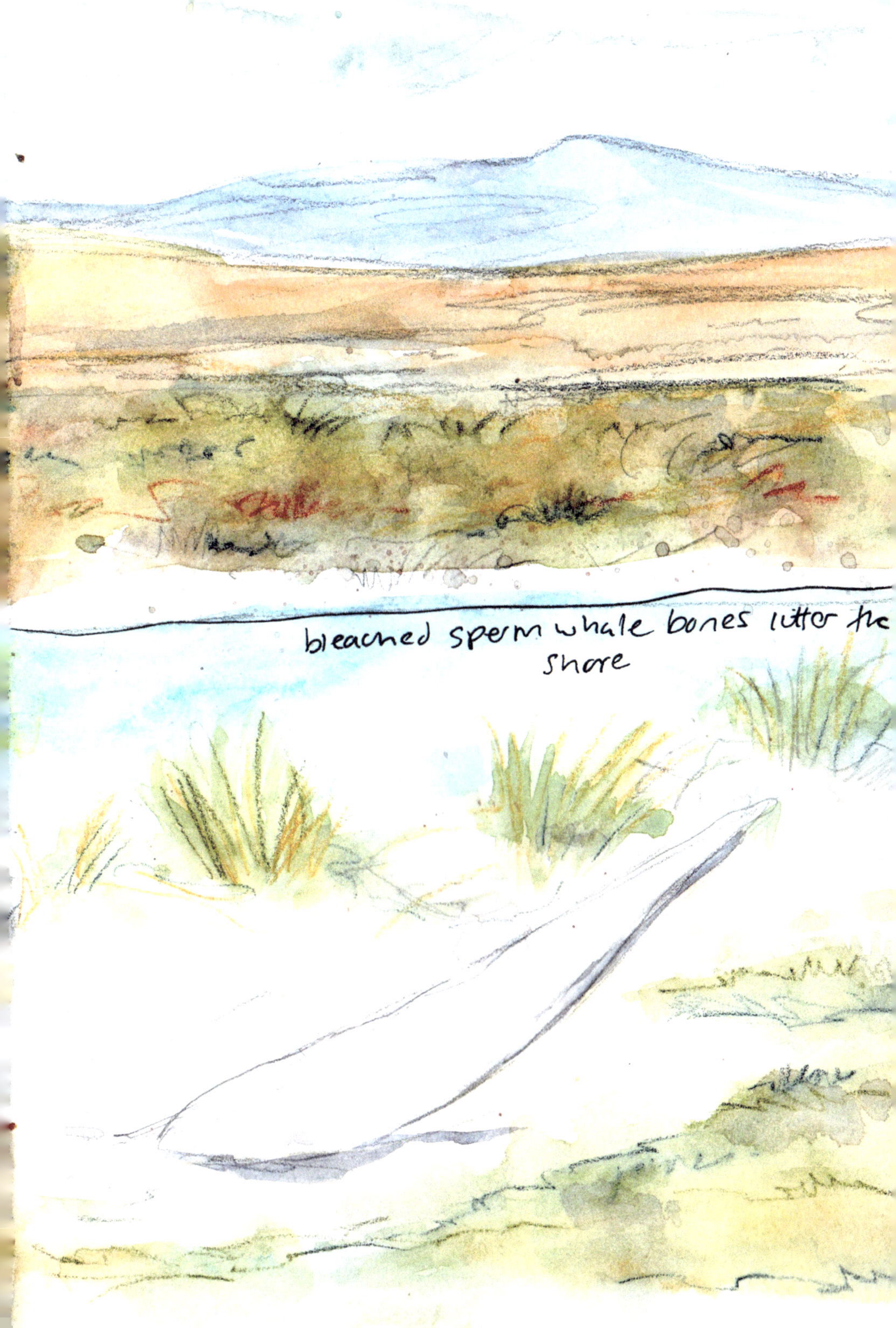
bleached sperm whale bones litter the shore

wednesday 8th January

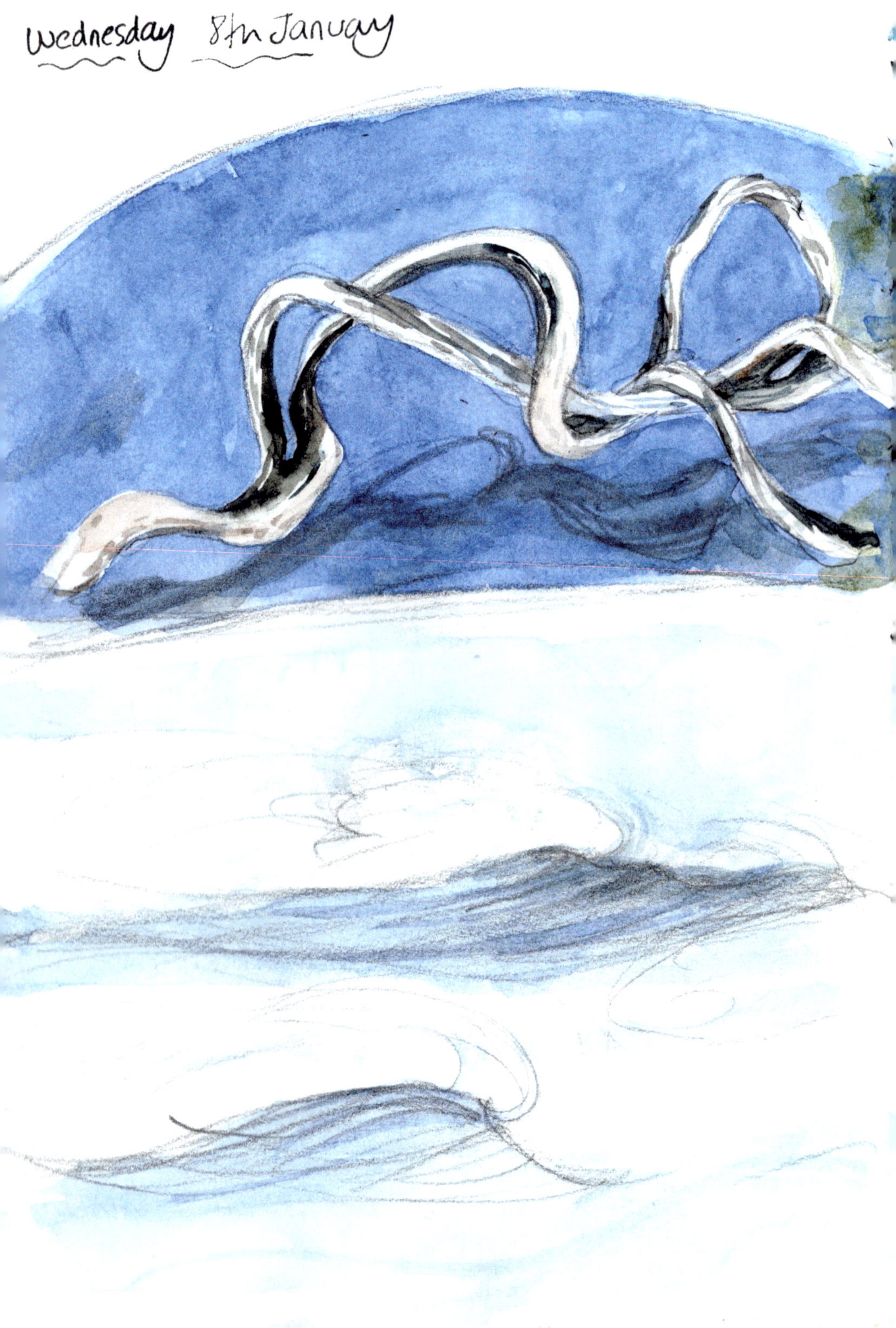

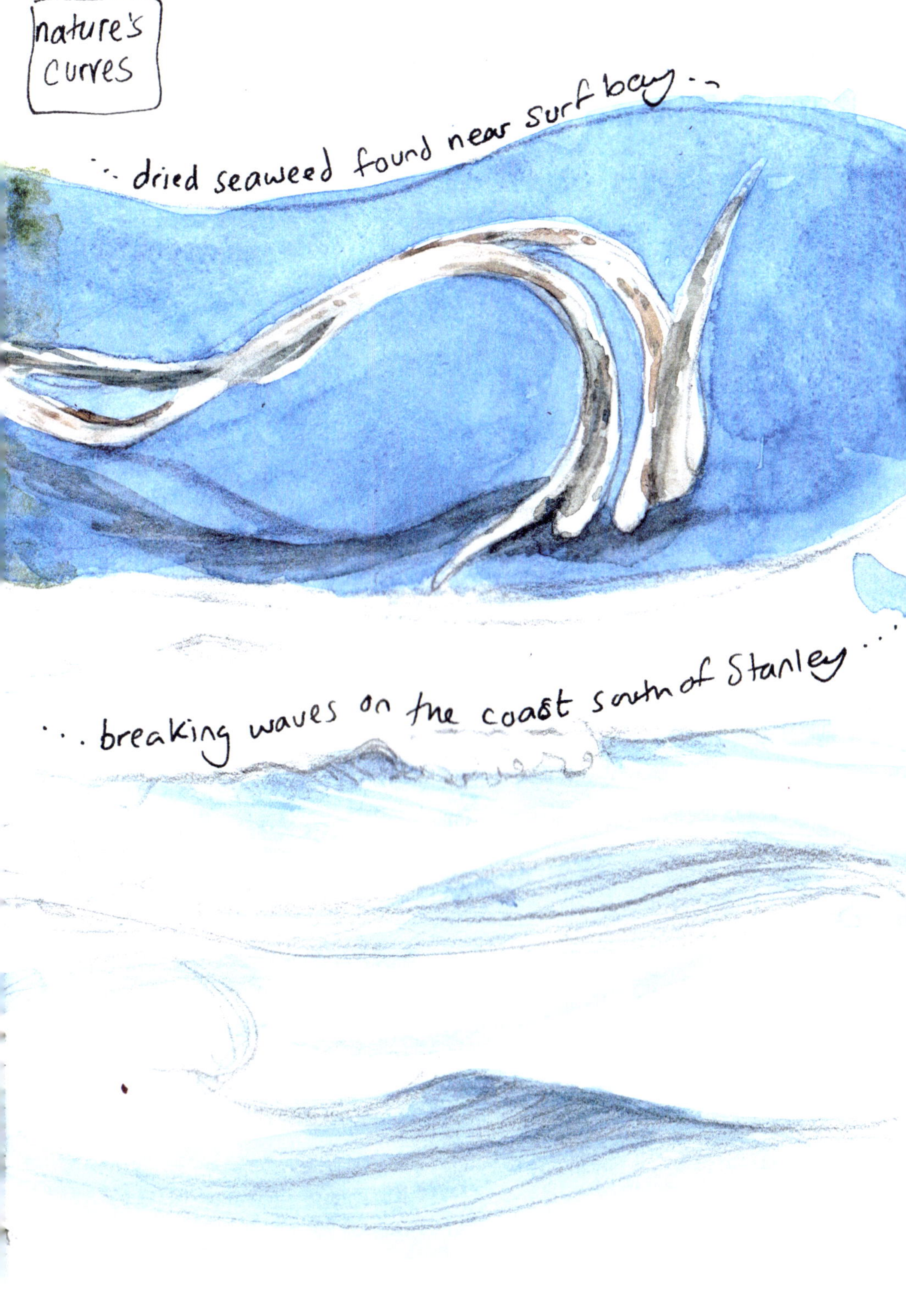

nature's
curves
... dried seaweed found near Surf bay ...
... breaking waves on the coast south of Stanley ...

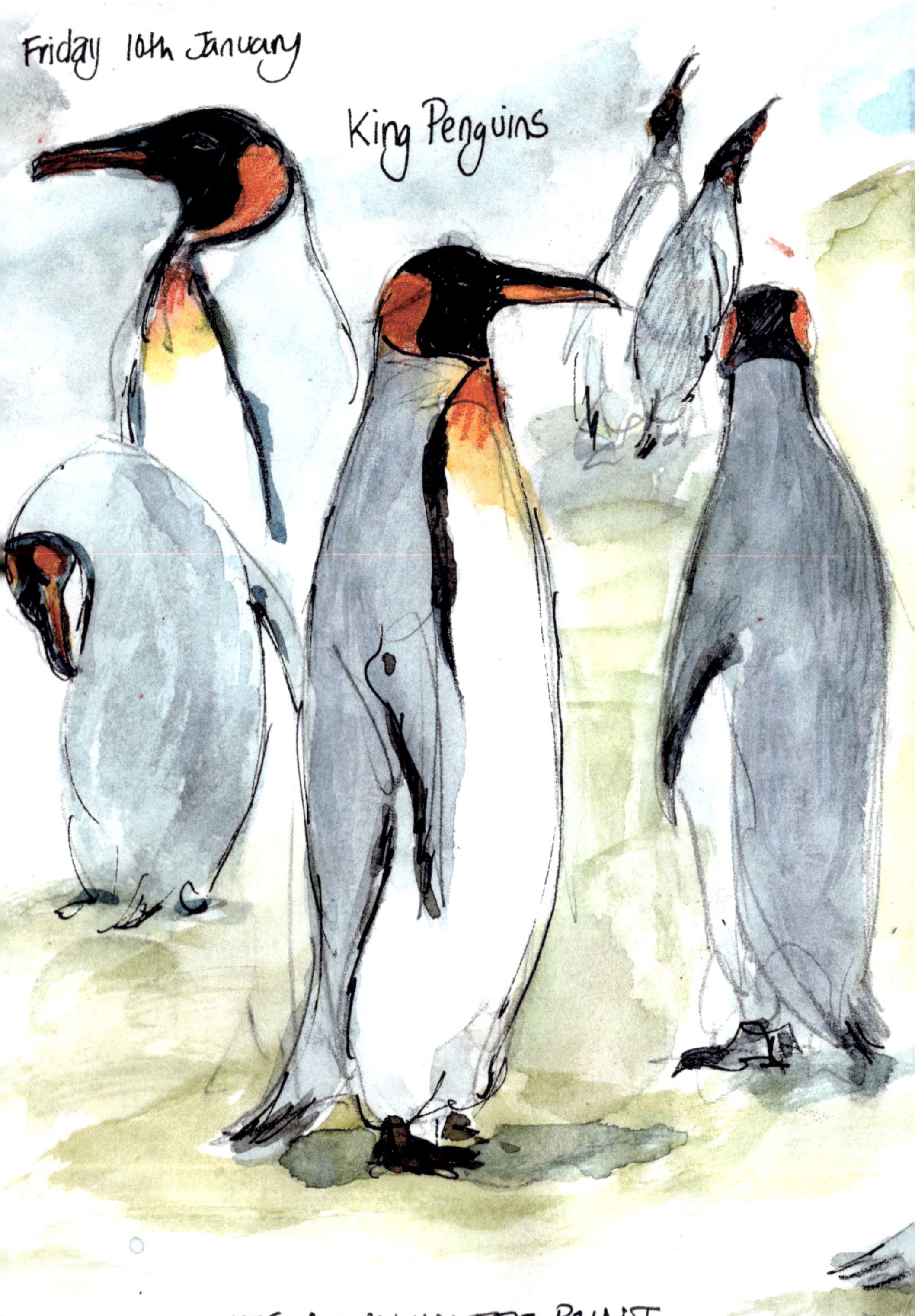

Friday 10th January
King Penguins
PENGUIN COLONIES AT VOLUNTEER POINT

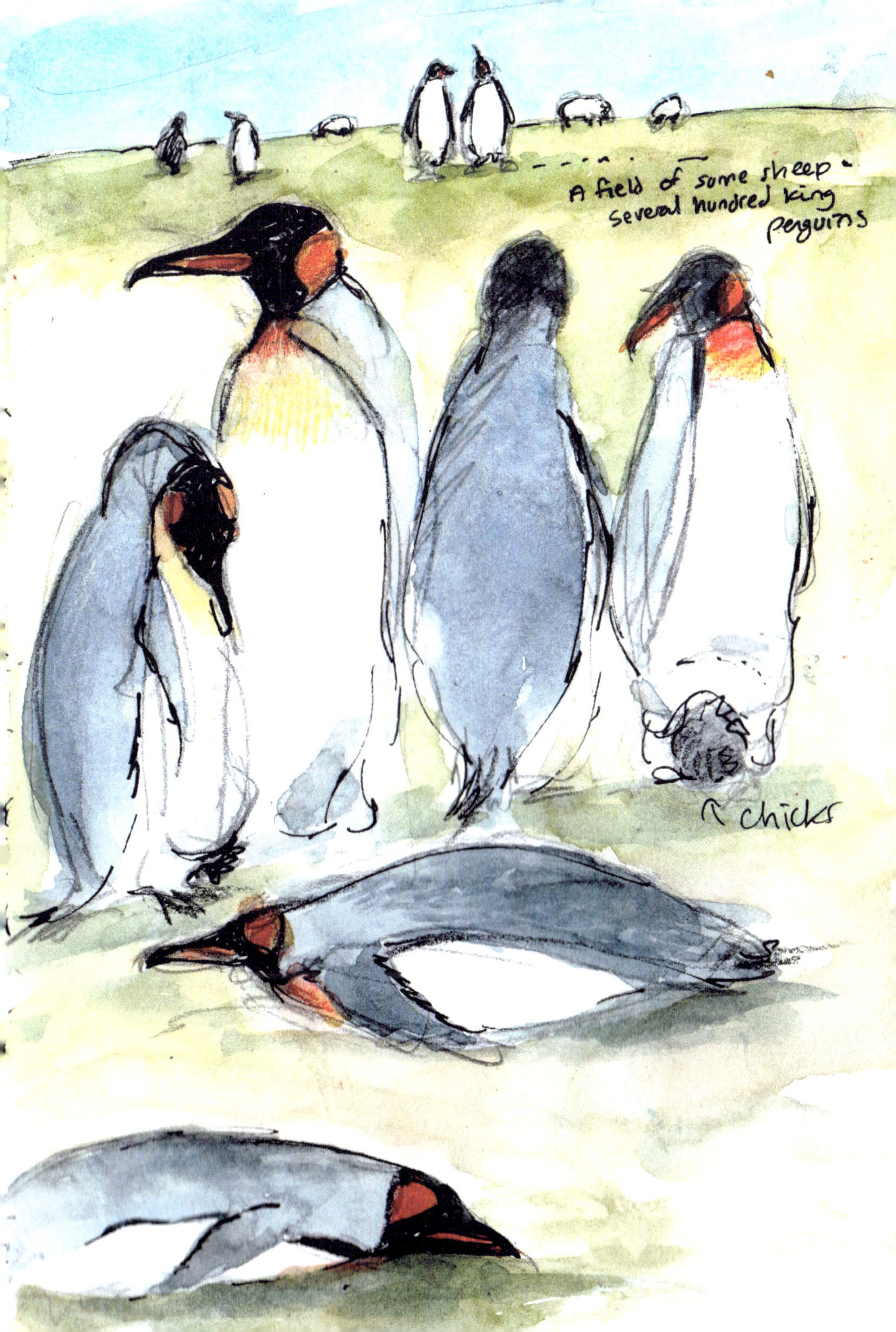

A field of some sheep -
several hundred king
penguins
chicks

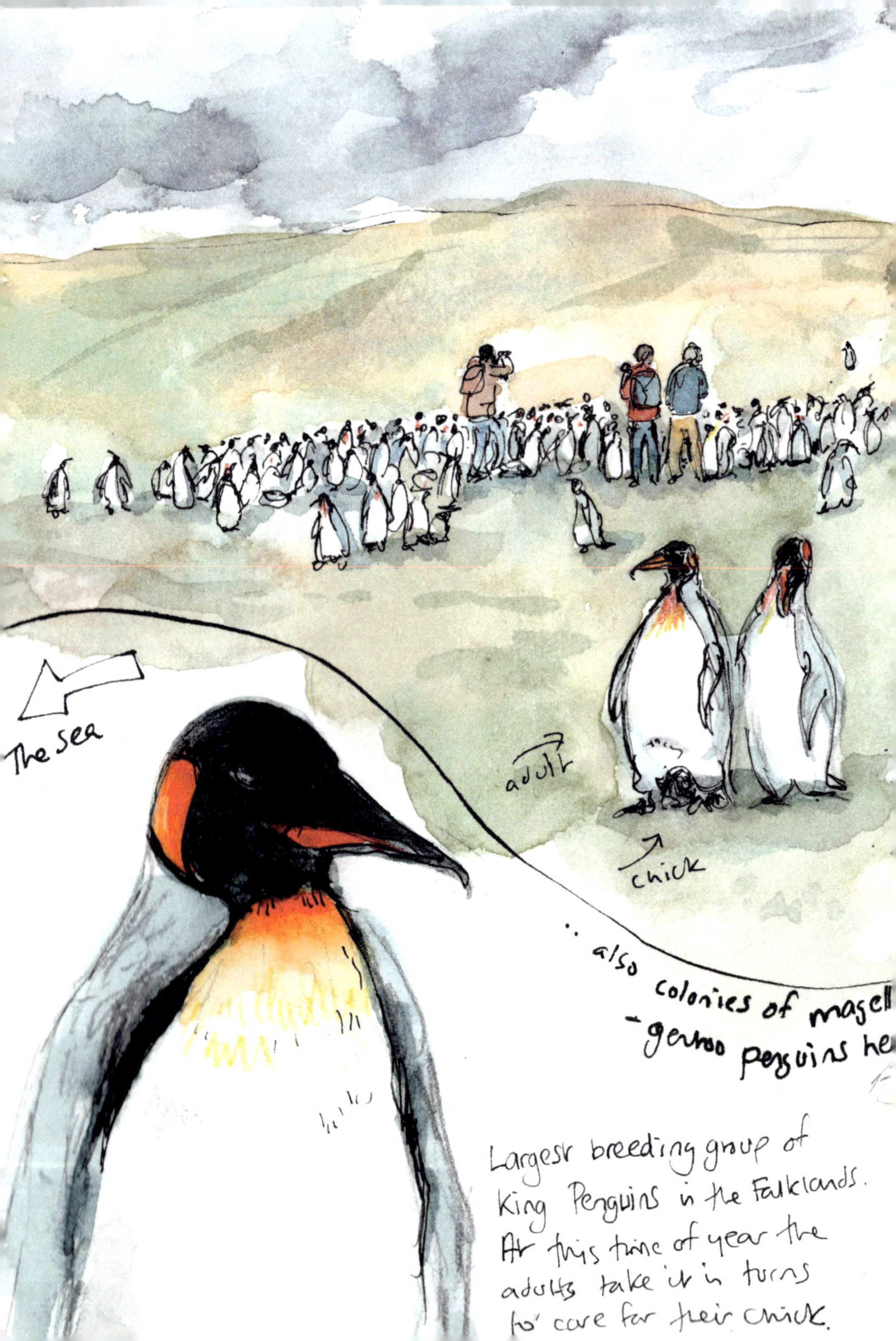

The sea
adult
chick
.. also colonies of magell
- gentoo penguins he
Largest breeding group of
King Penguins in the Falklands.
At this time of year the
adults take it in turns
to care for their chick.

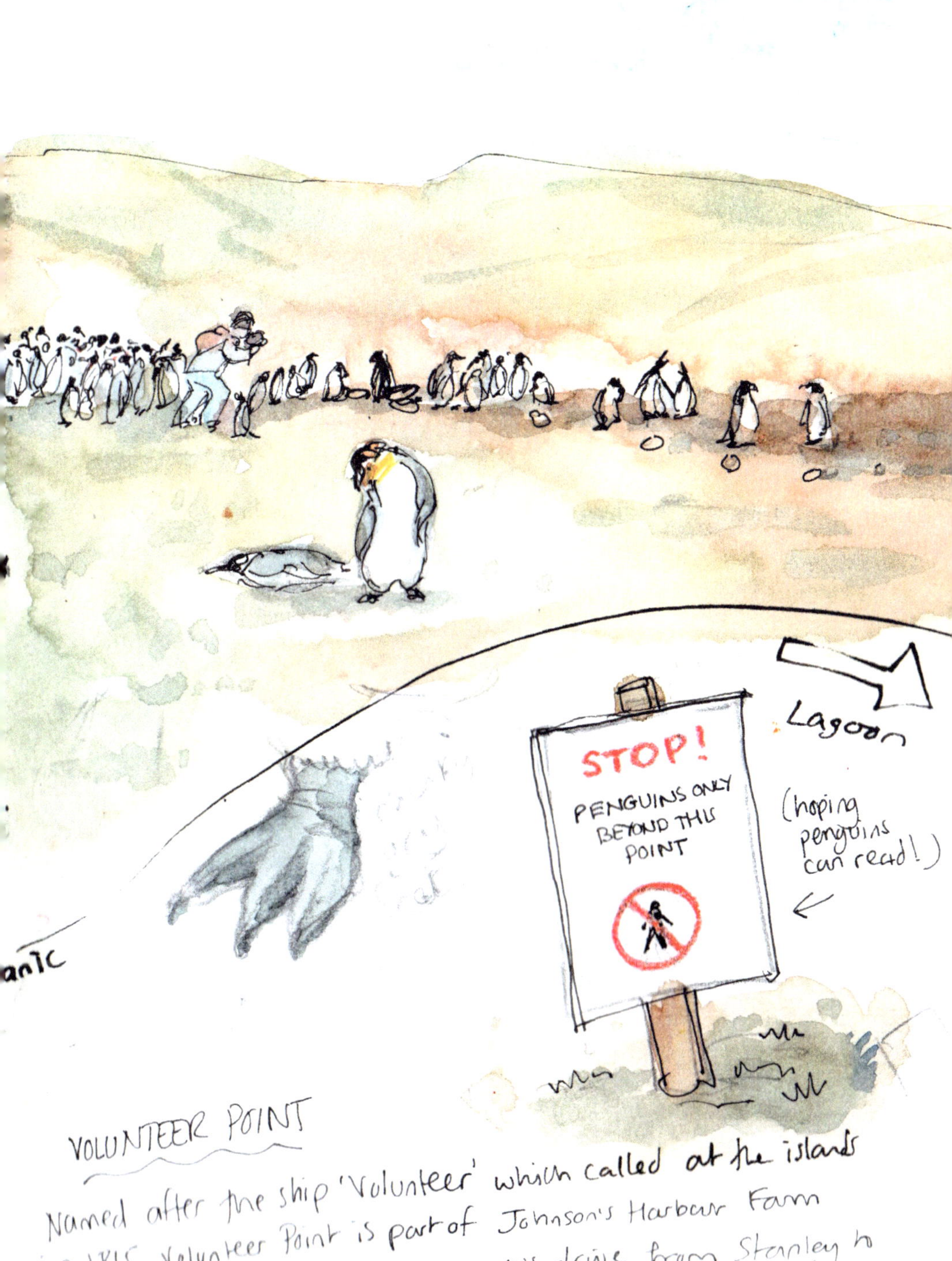

VOLUNTEER POINT

Named after the ship 'Volunteer' which called at the islands in 1815, Volunteer Point is part of Johnson's Harbour Farm (52,000 acres, 10,000 sheep). An hour's drive from Stanley to the settlement, then two hours off-road.

By 1870 the colony had
been almost wiped out
for their oil & skins.
Today there are about
1,500 breeding adults here.

King penguins ignore
the humans wandering
amongst them. It's
possible to get close &
observe in
detail.

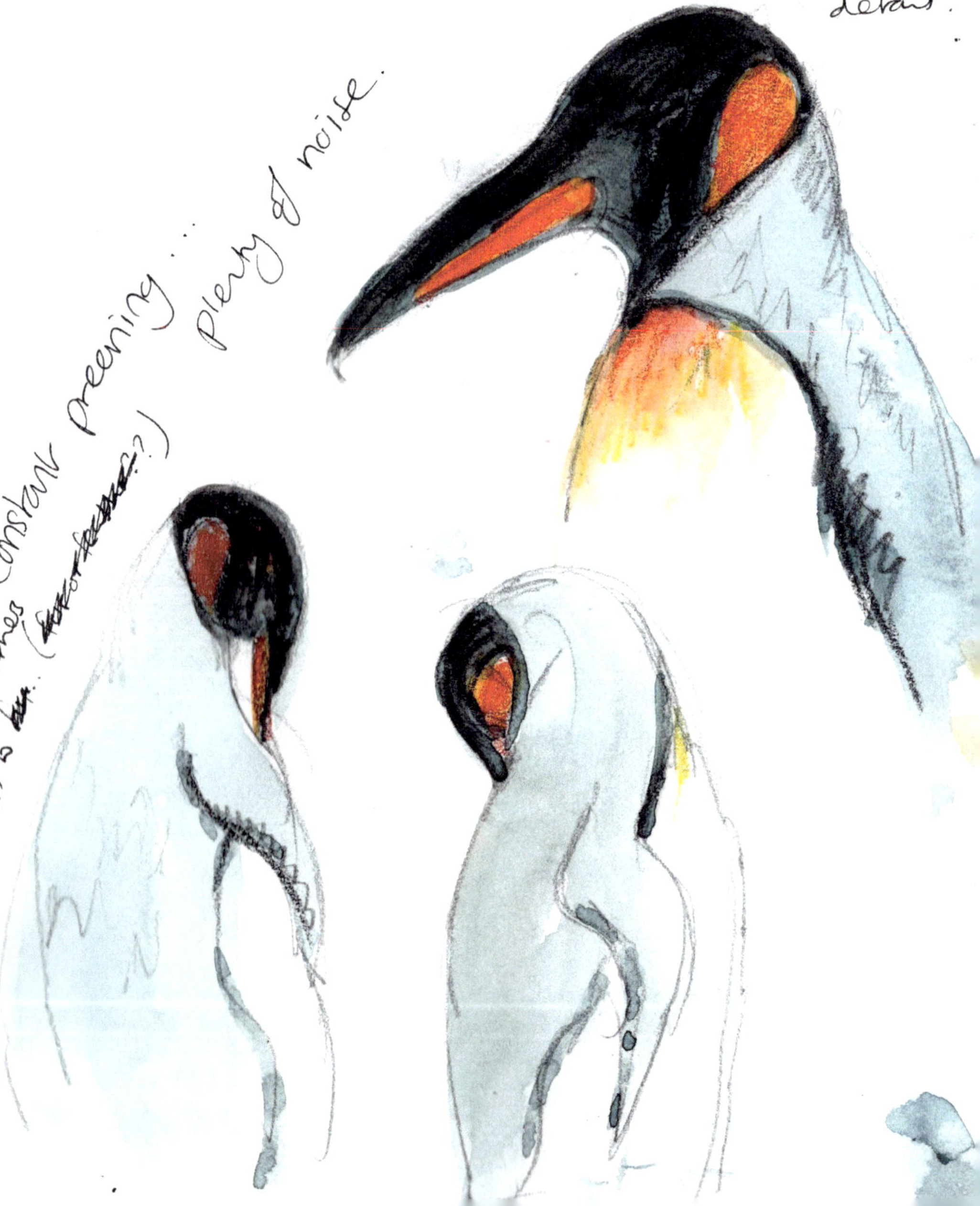

velvet-sheen to feathers. Constant preening... Plenty of noise.

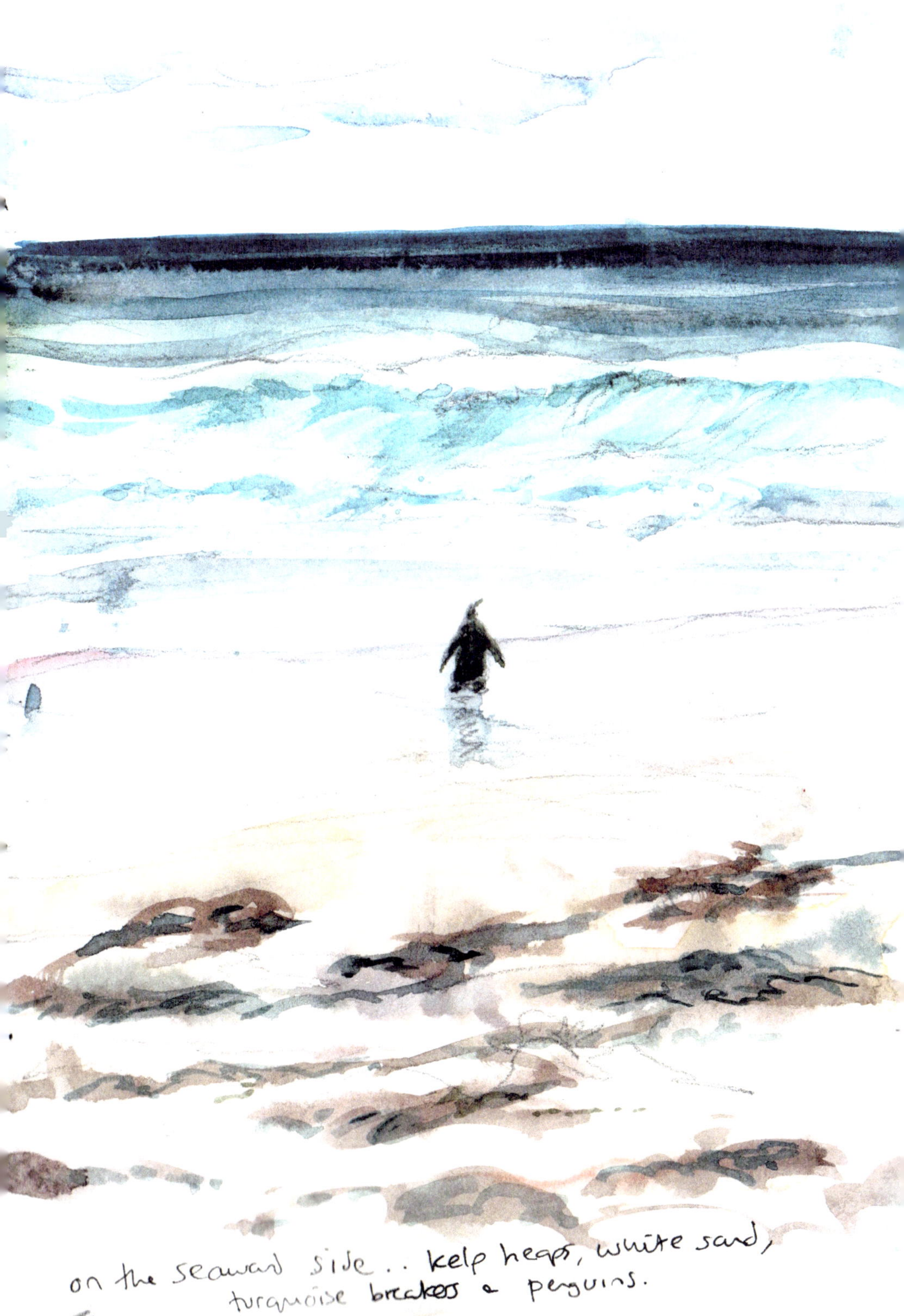

on the seaward side .. kelp heaps, white sand,
turquoise breakers & penguins.

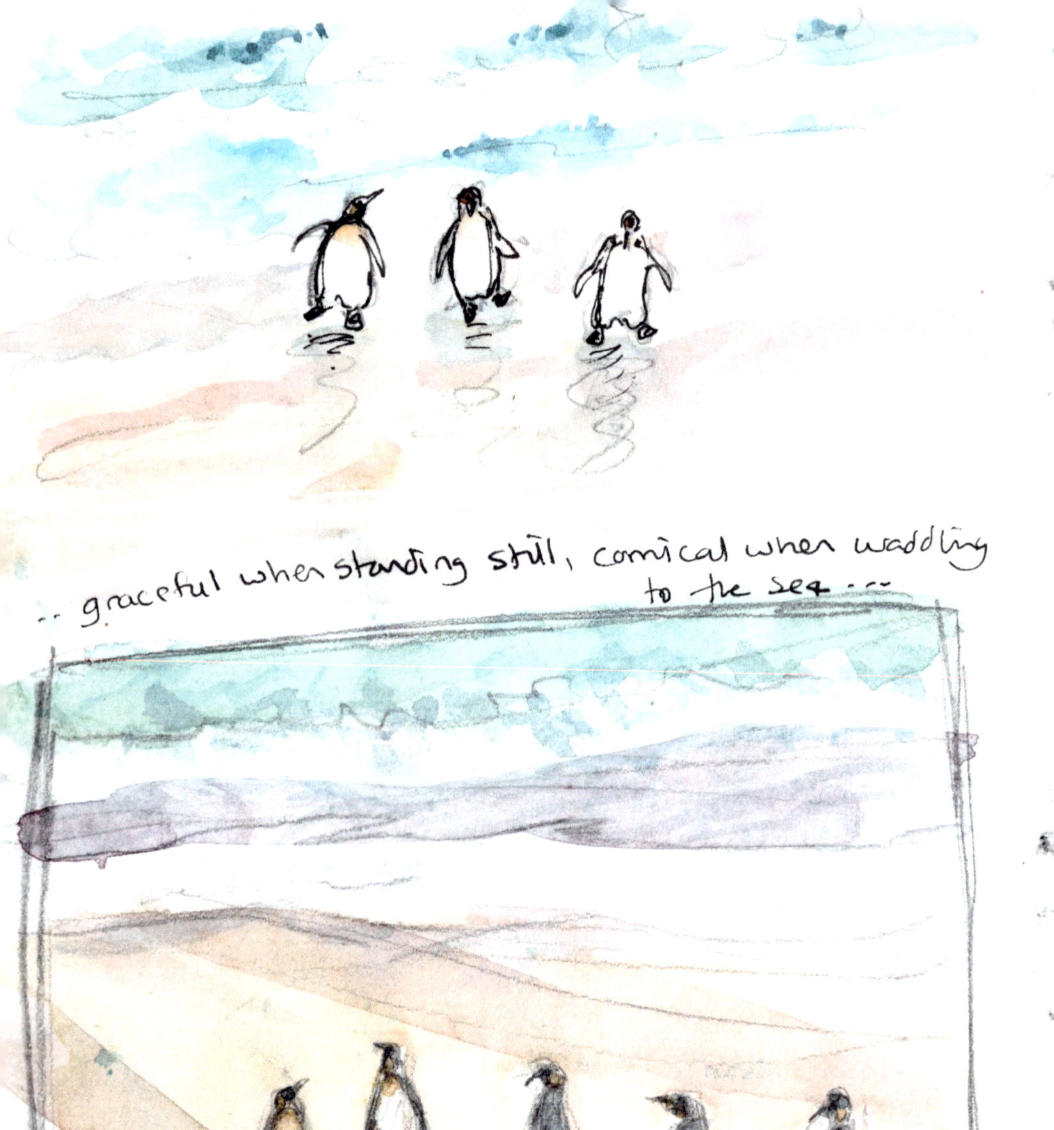

.. graceful when standing still, comical when waddling
to the sea ...

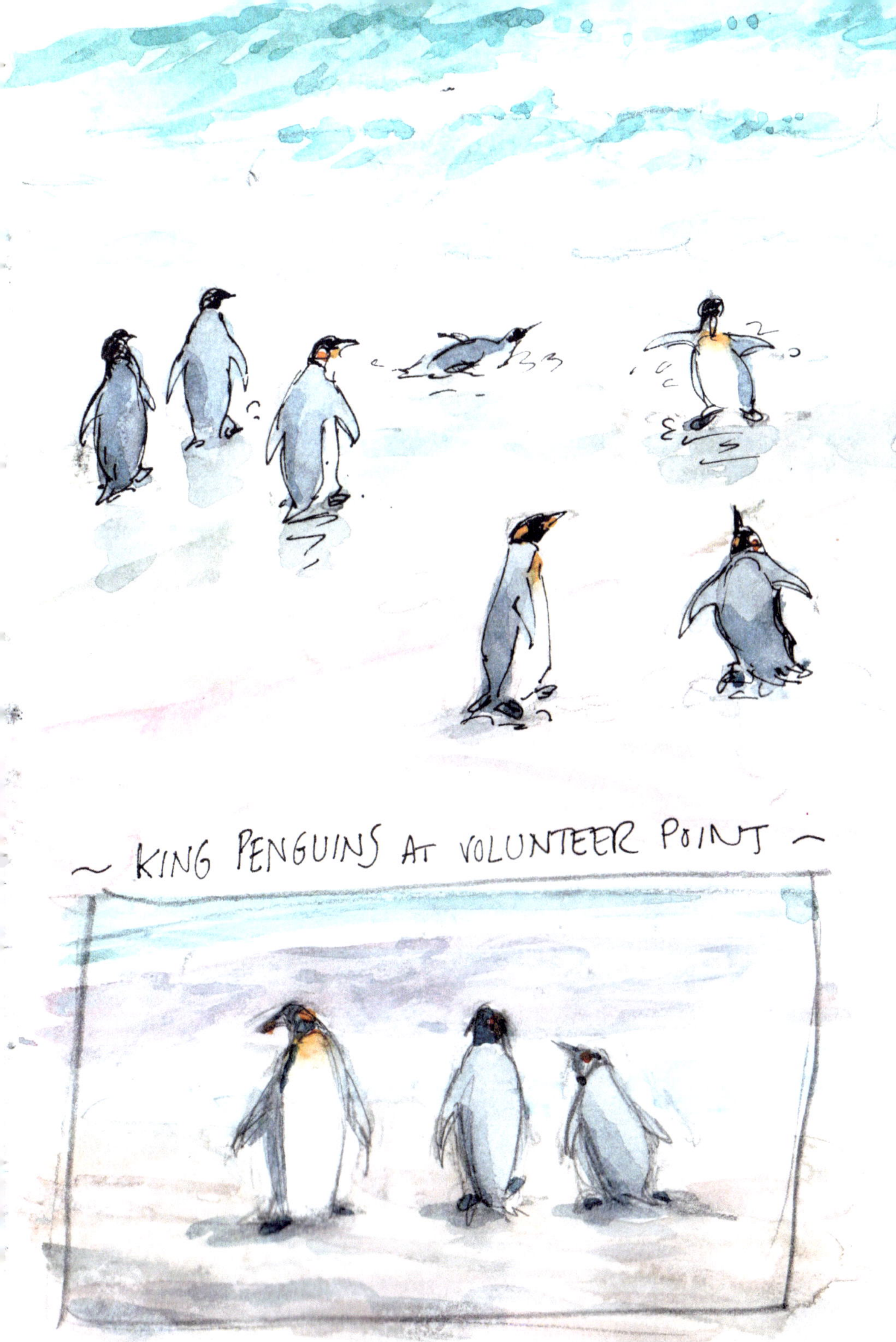
~ KING PENGUINS AT VOLUNTEER POINT ~

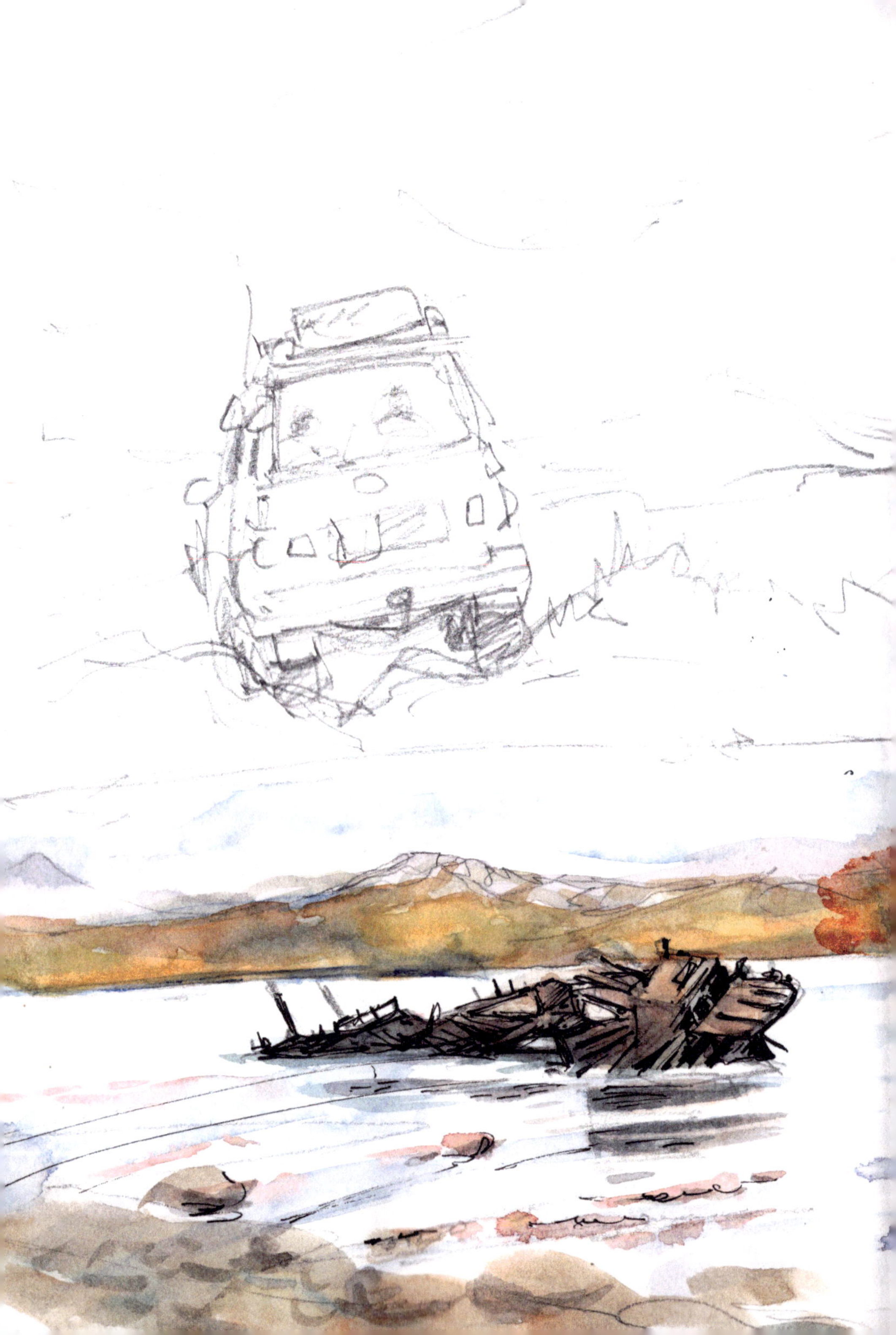

Homeward bound ... the convoy bounces its way
back across the moorland

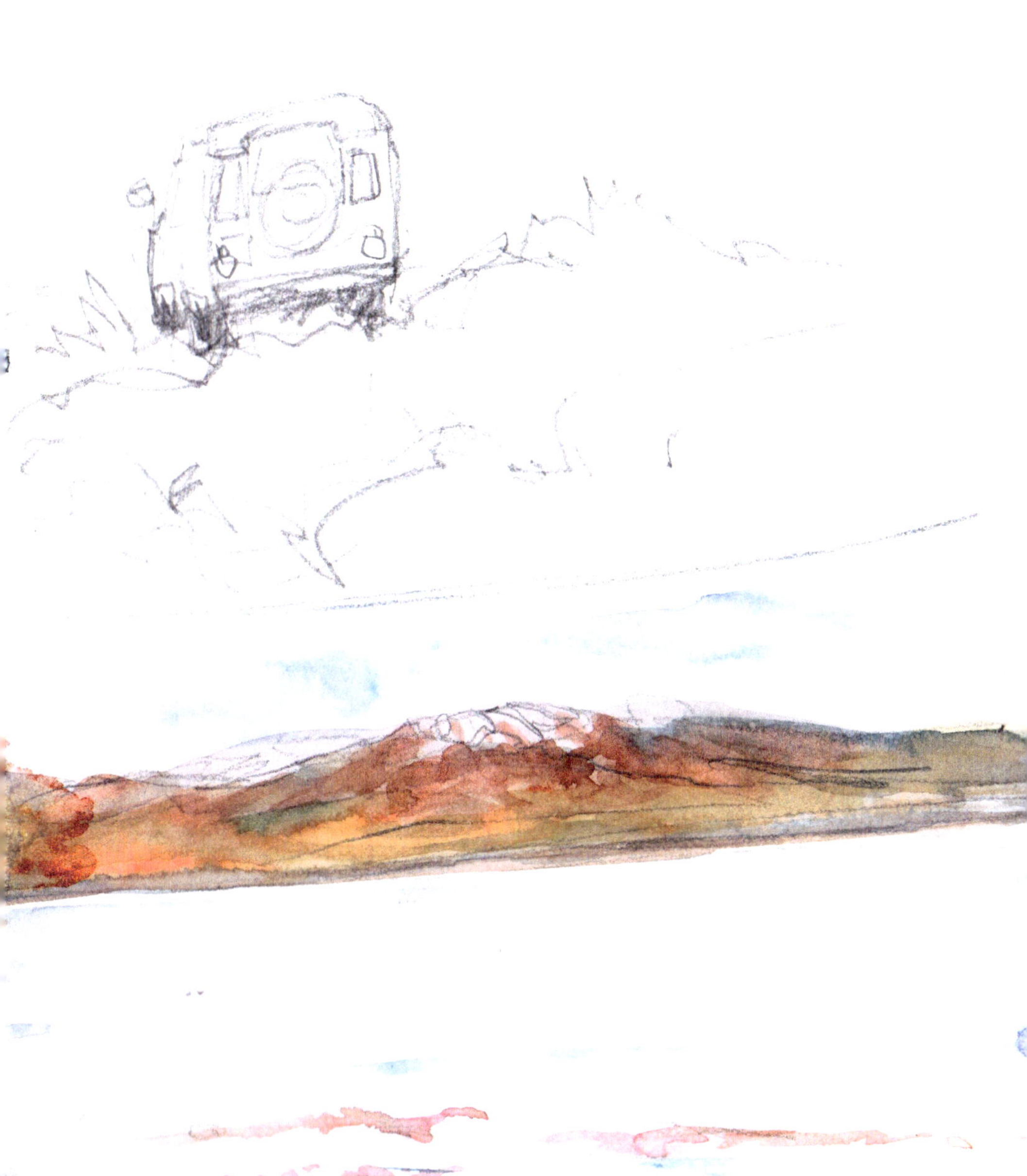

Wreck of the JHELUM (Liverpool)
1849 – 1871

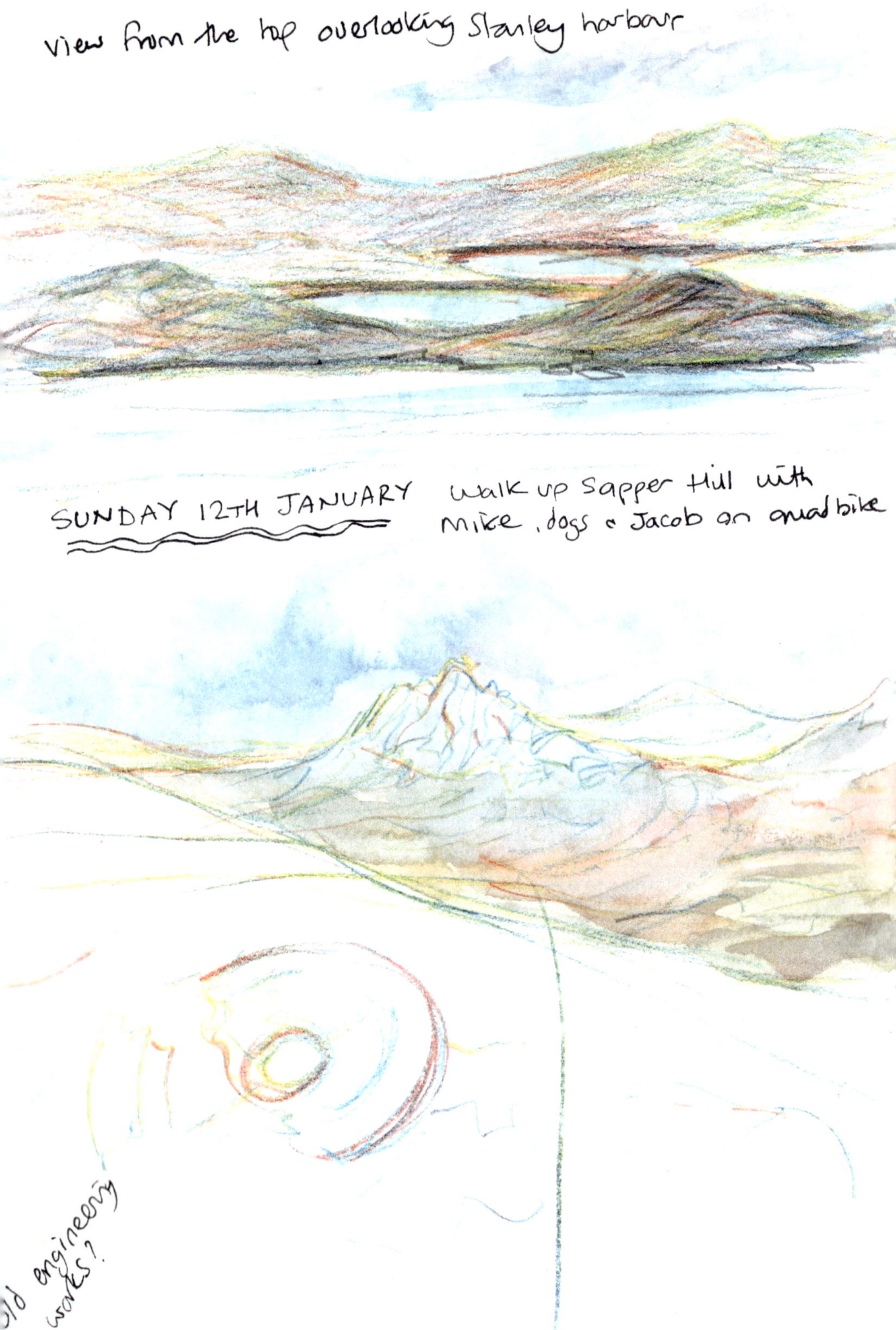

View from the top overlooking Stanley harbour

SUNDAY 12TH JANUARY

walk up Sapper Hill with
Mike, dogs & Jacob on quad bike

old engineering
works?

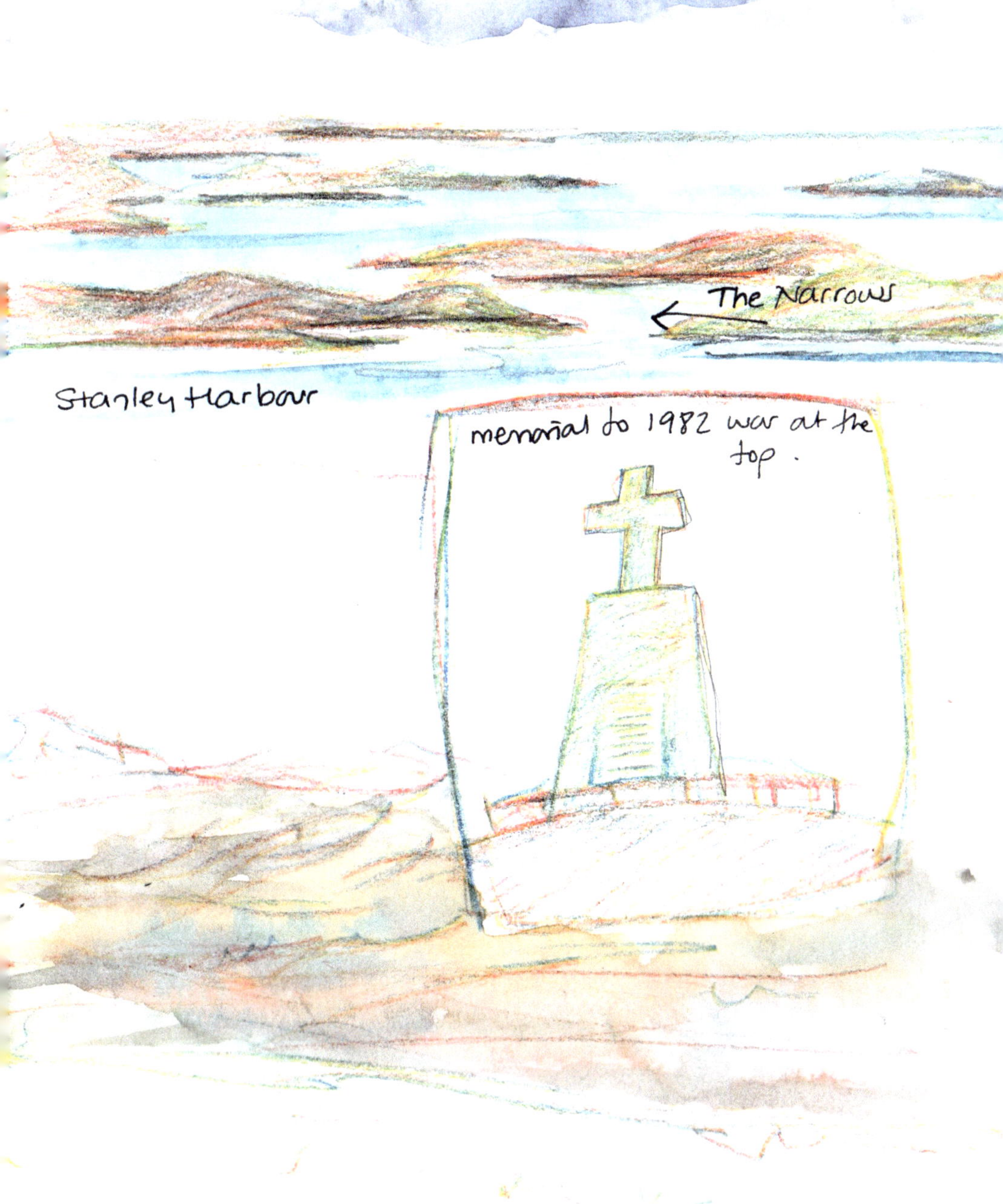

Reminders of the war litter the hill — makeshift Argentinian rock hideouts & shelters, mortar holes, now looking like small round ponds in the peat.

mike + Jacob on Sapper Hill
12/1/20

said farewell to the lovely Ford family after lunch and went back to the Docky and museum.

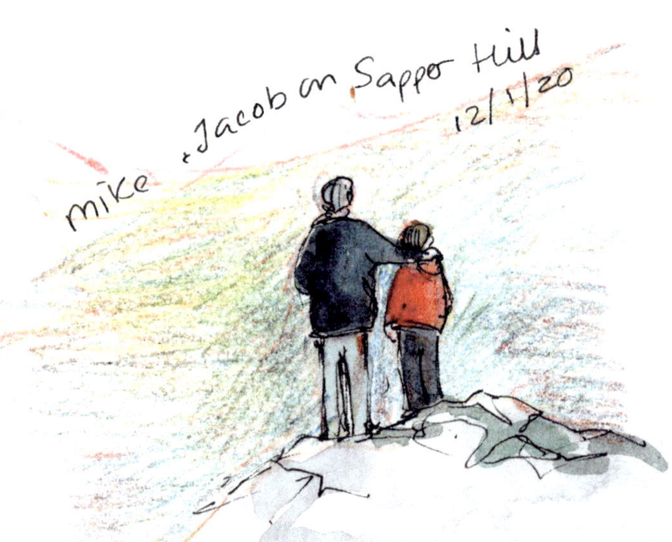

Model schooner in a display box - several of these is the museum. These boats were the only means of transport to the remote settlements & islands before air travel.

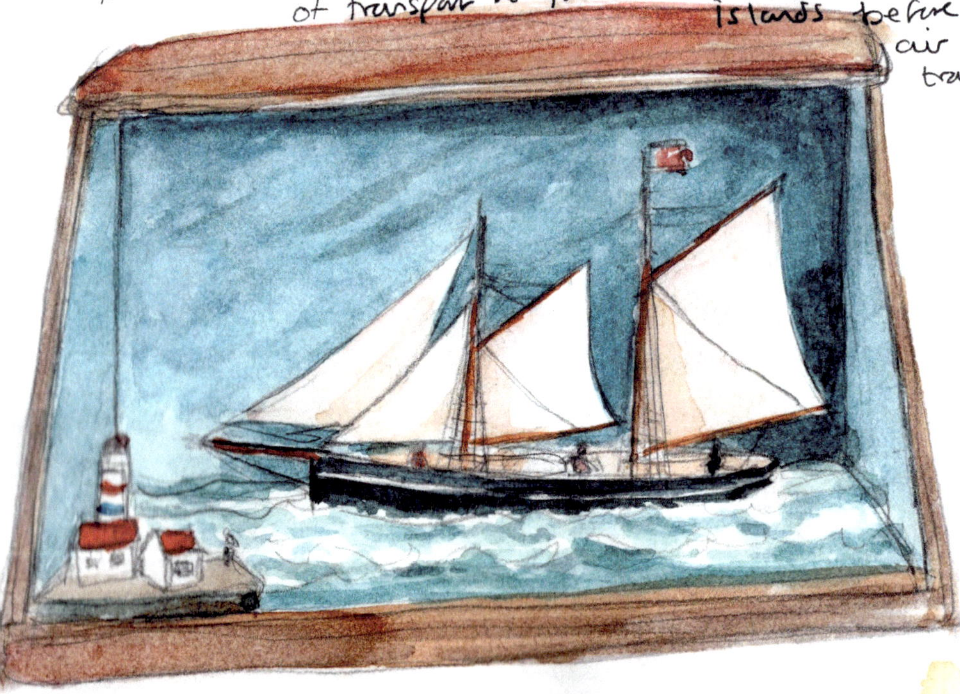

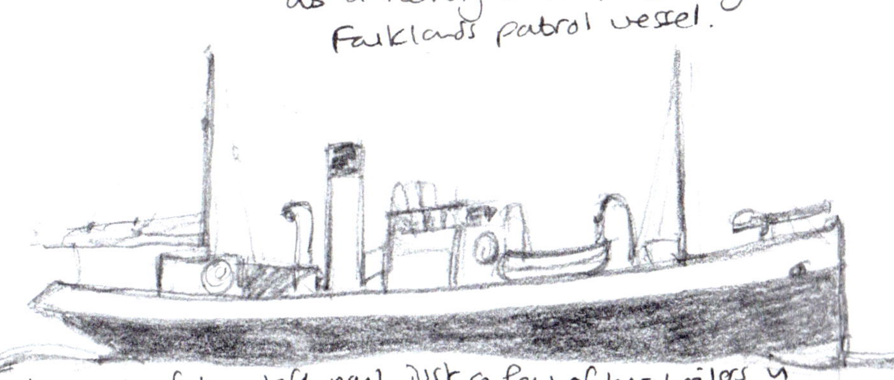

'AFTERGLOW' - one of many ships to end their days
in Stanley harbour. Built in Lowestoft 1915
as a herring drifter. 95' long. Became a
Falklands patrol vessel.
not much of her left now, just a few of her boilers in
Stanley harbour.

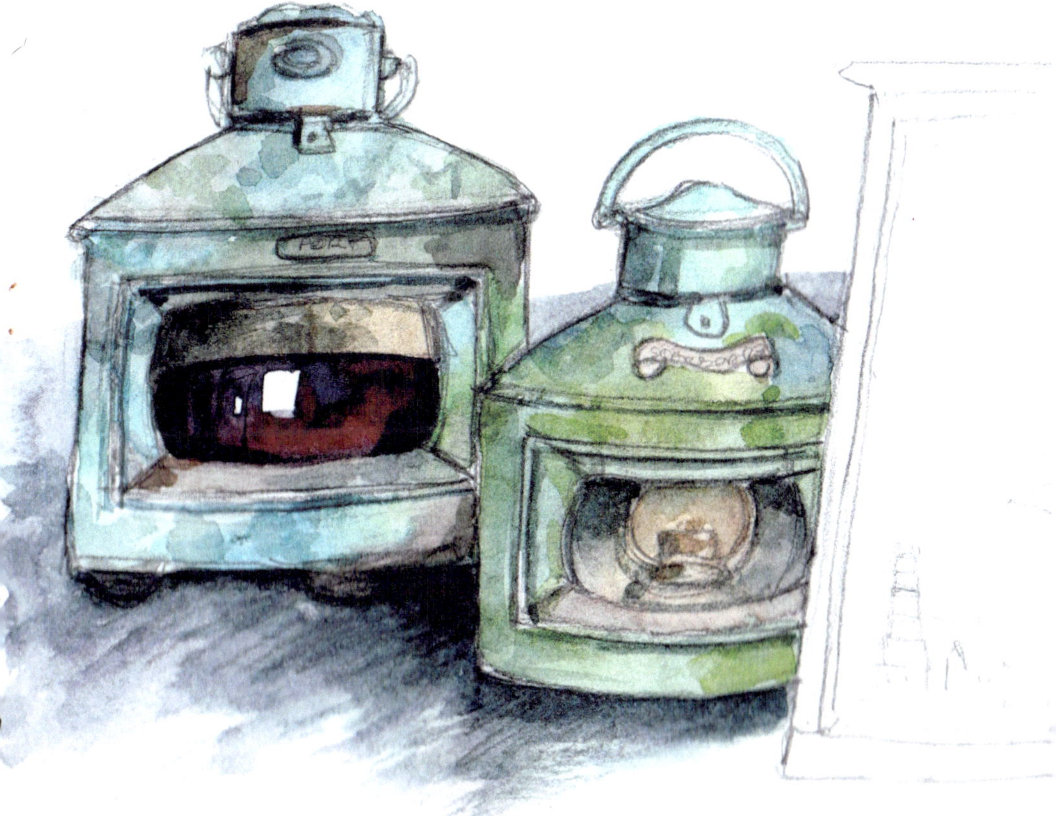

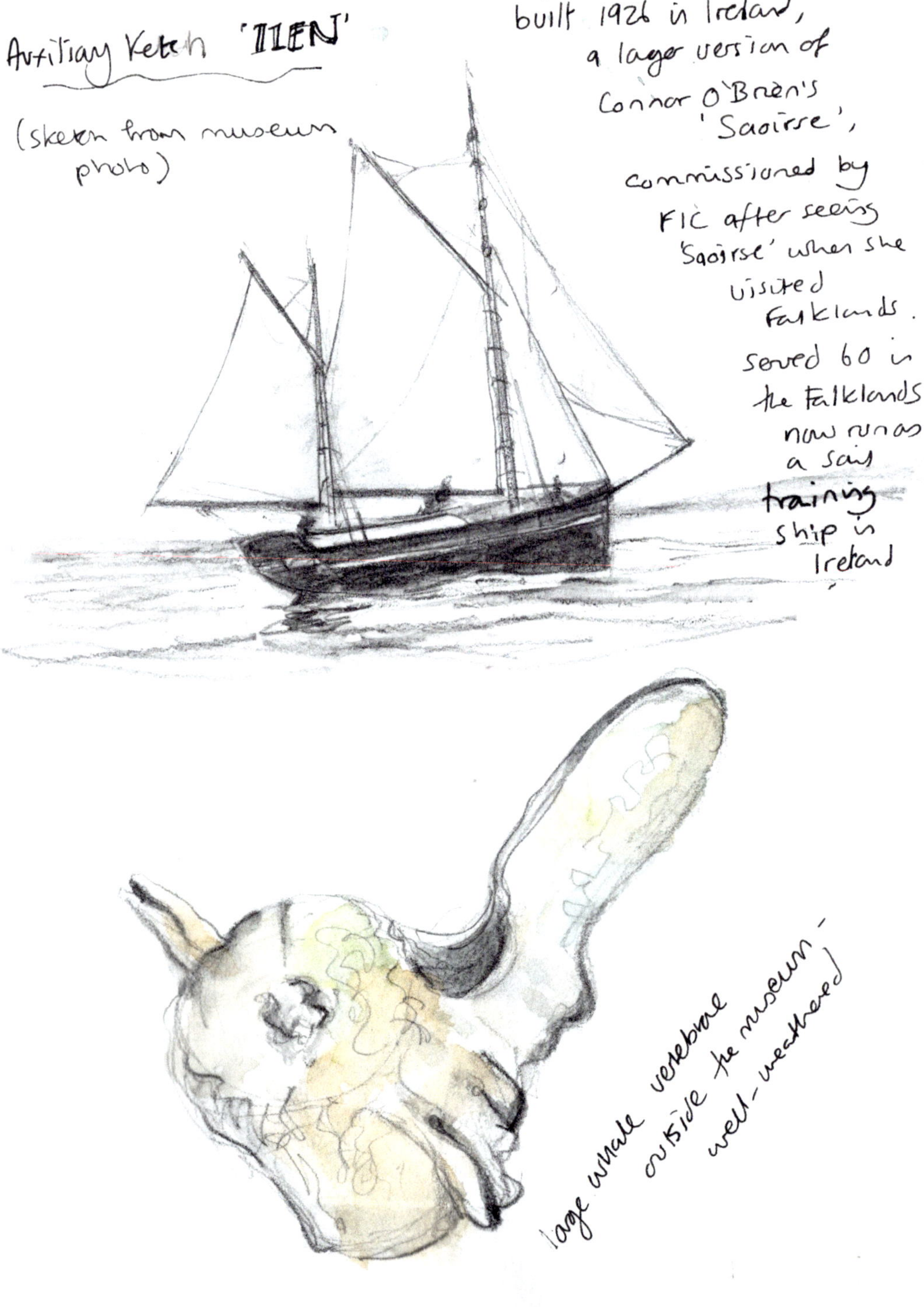

Auxiliary Ketch 'ILEN'

(sketch from museum photo)

built 1926 in Ireland, a larger version of Connor O'Brien's 'Saoirse', commissioned by FIC after seeing 'Saoirse' when she visited Falklands. served 60 in the Falklands now runs as a sail training ship in Ireland

large whale vertebrae outside the museum - well-weathered)

Monday 13th January

Hot, sunny day. A walk along the
coast to the east of Stanley,
wreck - sketching.

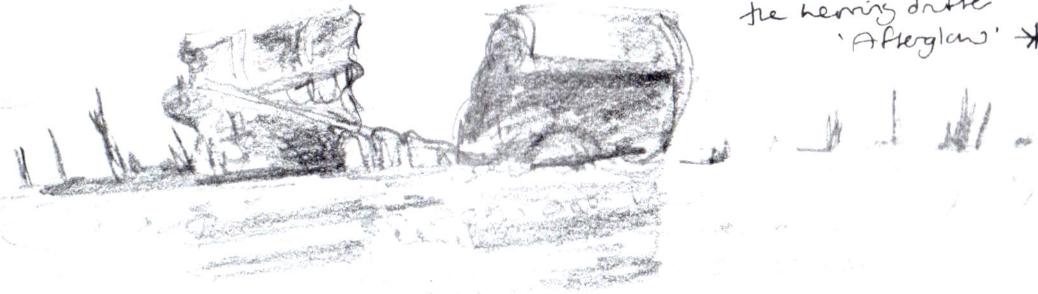

All that's left of
the herring drifter
'Afterglow' *

One of several old boats at the boatyard
by Boxer Bridge

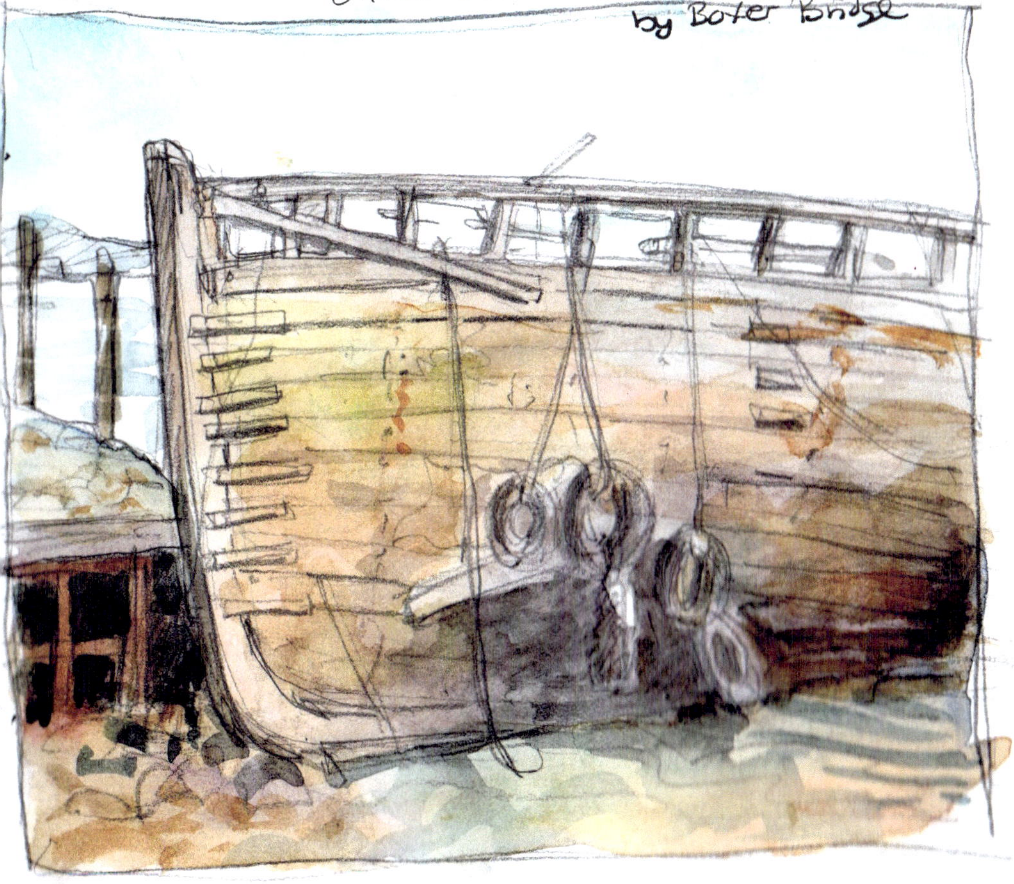

Two more old boats ending their days by
Boxer Bridge. The first another Lowestoft herring
drifter built in 1914 'Golden Chance'

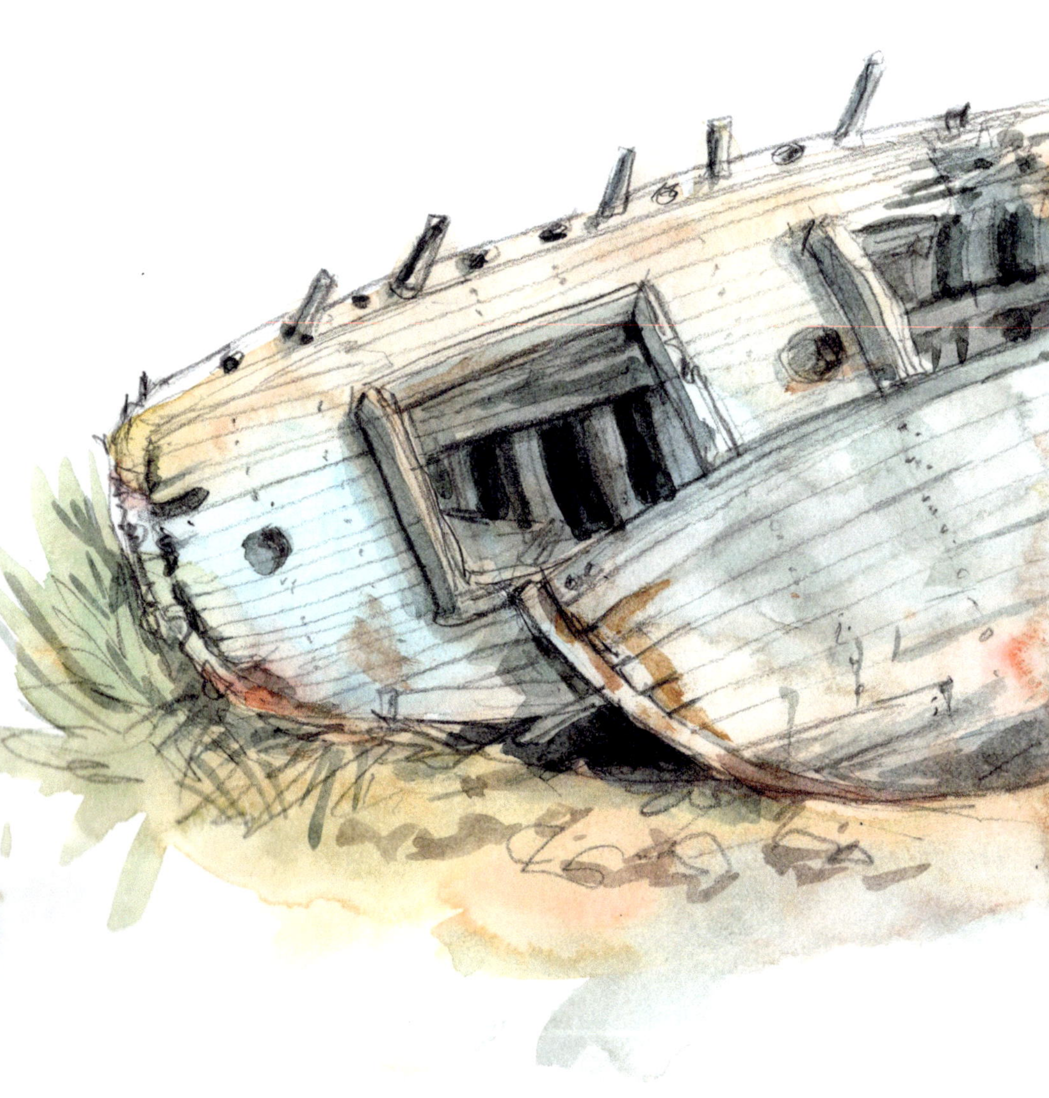

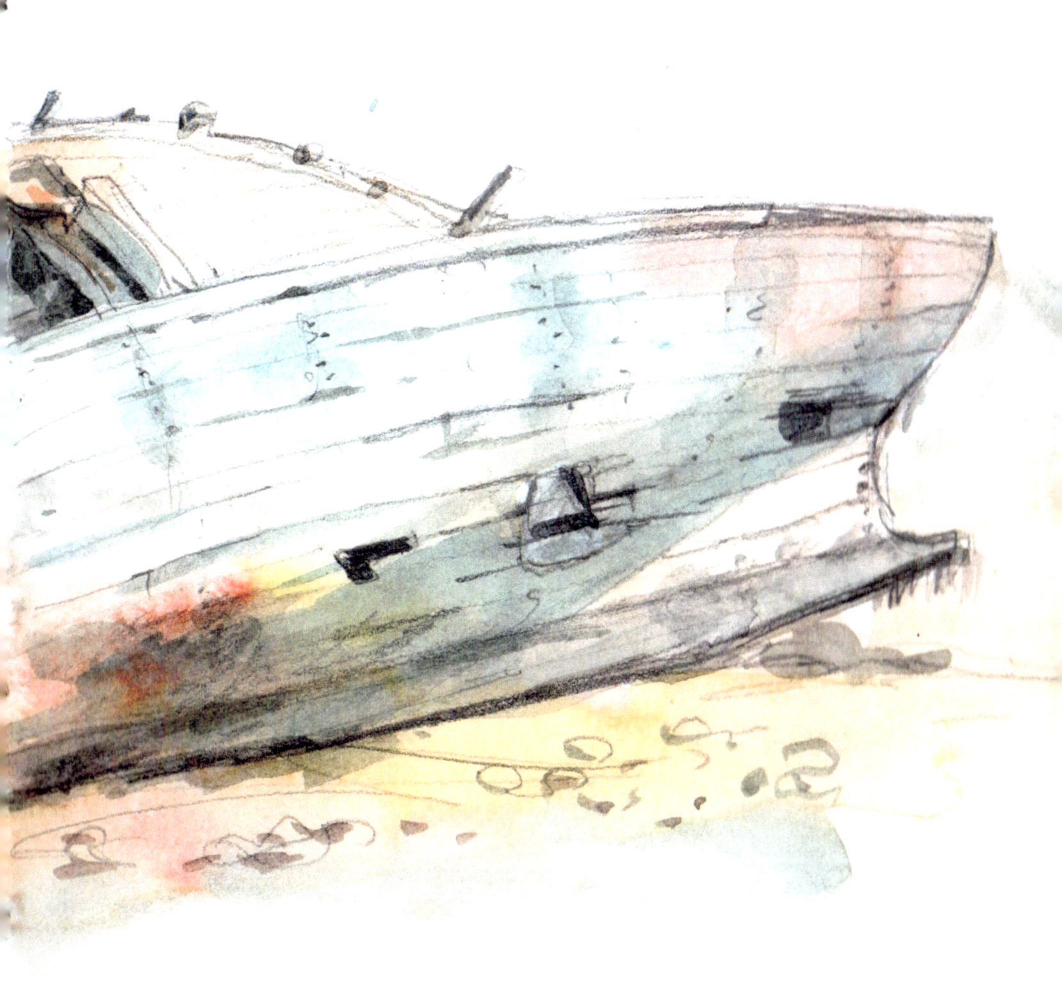

Enjoyable walk to Bever Bridge

Hot day, the smell of sea & wide open
spaces, moorland shrubs & flowers

MONDAY 13TH JANUARY

Home

After 12 days on friendly and fascinating East Falkland it was time to leave. I had booked a seat on the RAF Airbridge direct to Brize Norton, but the wind hadn't finished with me yet and strong winds delayed the flight. I was kept in touch by messages from the shuttle bus and there was the real possibility of another few days on the islands. Luckily I was in my room when the hotel staff knocked on the door to say the flight was on after all, only 12 hours later than planned, taking advantage of a short lull in the wind. The flight was straightforward and good friends were there to meet me when we landed 19 hours later. The adventure was over.

I sat at my desk in the studio on the first day back at work feeling odd and displaced, as if I had stepped into someone else's life and didn't know what to do with it. The memories of the intense light and clean air of the Southern Ocean, the image of an albatross gliding behind us, a wing tip clipping the wave sometimes during their long, graceful glide – these things were there whenever I shut my eyes, and seemed still to be more real than the familiar objects around me.

Then, two months after my return, I'd settled into my 'normal' busy life and my diary was filling up with work and play when the Covid-19 pandemic made a mockery of our expectations, challenging our concept of 'normal life'. As this book goes to press, the pandemic is not yet over. Whatever altered ways of living emerge from it, I feel privileged to have had the chance to see and appreciate the quiet places of the world, remote but sadly not free from our influences and greed. I hope the sketchbook pages give some flavour of what this voyage was like, and help you to imagine the splash of the waves and the rolling swell of the oceans that are so crucial to our lives.

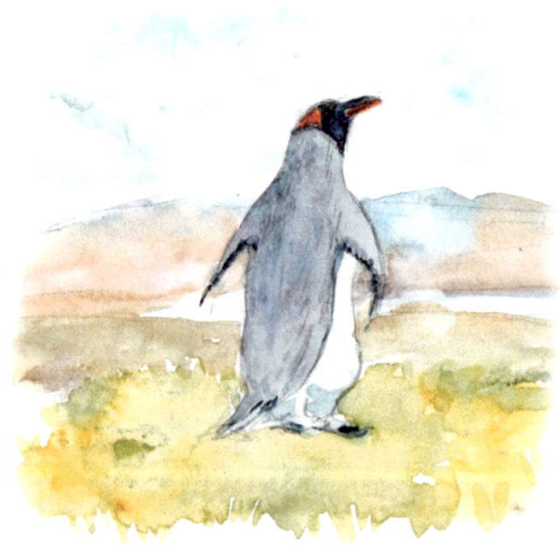

SKETCHING ON THE MOVE

Sketching at sea

I used an A4 'Moleskine' watercolour sketchbook at sea as a 'Carnet du Voyage', an illustrated daily log book. I had no idea how I would manage to sketch every day on a ship that was sailing into some of the wildest waters on the planet, but I did keep it up every day once I got into the habit. Some pages were harder to fill than others, when seasickness made me lethargic or because the motion of the waves made drawing and painting difficult. My admiration for the early sea captains who kept meticulous illustrated navigation log books increased enormously as I tried to stop my watercolours sliding onto the deck, or found my pencil lines wandering off track as we fell off a wave. Once I got my sea legs and could sit at the cabin table without feeling queasy, I could start a sketch on deck, then finish it off and add colour down below where it was warmer.

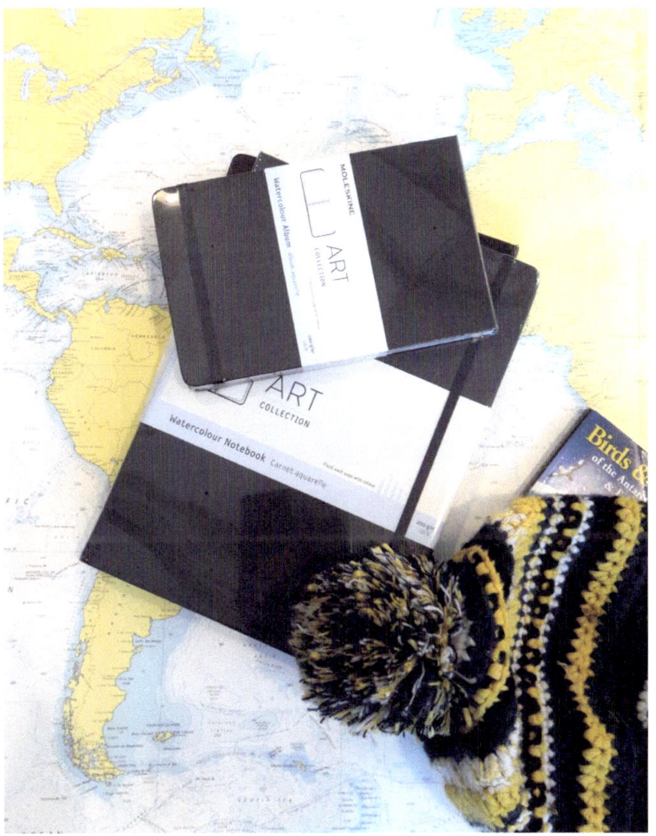

Sketching ashore

I used an A5 hand bound sketchbook for my time on shore. The book was made by Janet Watson from Old School Printworks in Suffolk and given as a present from an artist friend just before I set off. I like to have sketchbooks that open flat and stay open, so that I can work across both pages when needed. Outdoors in windy conditions I use bulldog clips to hold the pages and stop them flapping around.

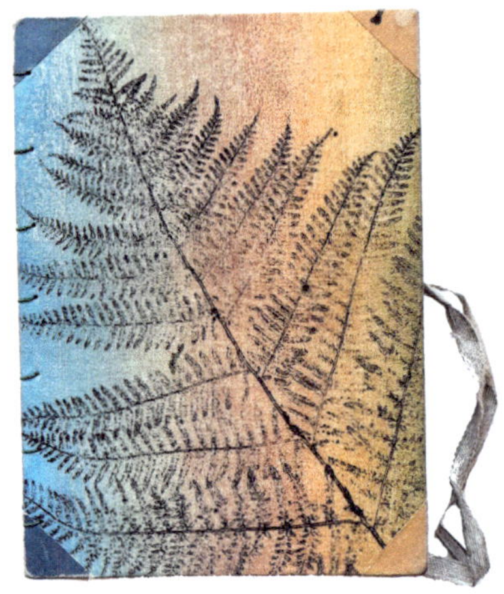

Sketching on land can seem much easier than sketching at sea, given that you're on solid ground rather than on a moving boat, but there is still the need to find shade and somewhere to sit. Sketching in the rain or bright sunlight is challenging, so is having enough time to draw when you're on a guided walk and everyone else is taking photos.

I discovered on this trip how much it helps having a table to work at. It sounds obvious, but if there's nowhere to set out paint and pencils when I come back in the evening, then the finishing off tends not to get done. The most comprehensive part of the island sketchbooks was done in the Falklands where I had a desk in my room and no distractions in the evenings.

Looking through both sketchbooks it's clear that the later pages are far more fluent, colourful and confident that the early ones. Even though I've been drawing and painting regularly for many years this still happens when I start something new. I think you have to warm up, relax into it, like a musician or dancer would do. With sketching, as with other creative acts, the more you do, the easier it gets.

Art materials

I'm used to travelling with only a few art materials as I focus on observation sketching rather than finished paintings, so I've no need for drawing boards, easels, large sheets of paper or canvas. But I do manage to fit a good range of bits and pieces into a small zip up bag:

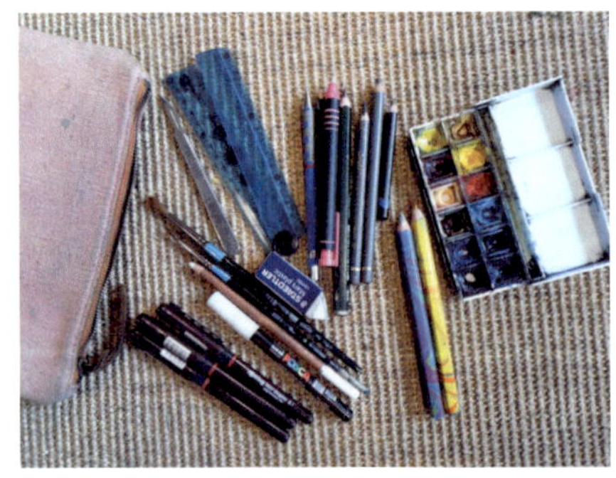

Here's my kit list:

- Assorted pencils, mostly 2B
- A pencil-style eraser, easy to carry alongside a pencil and for erasing detail
- Scalpel for sharpening
- Assorted sketching pens, different nib sizes
- Two watercolour brushes, no 3 and no 6
- A couple of multi-coloured Koh-i-Nor magic pencils
- Folding ruler
- White pen and white pencil
- Watercolour box
- Glue stick
- Derwent 'Inktense' watercolour pencils

I also took tracing paper and some old Admiralty Charts of Pacific and South Atlantic that I had bought online before leaving. These I tore up or cut out and used to create my title page for each stage of the voyage.

Colour choices

I use a small, lightweight, Winsor & Newton paintbox with my own choice of colours that I squeeze into the pans from the tubes in my studio. These are the colours I filled up with before setting off:

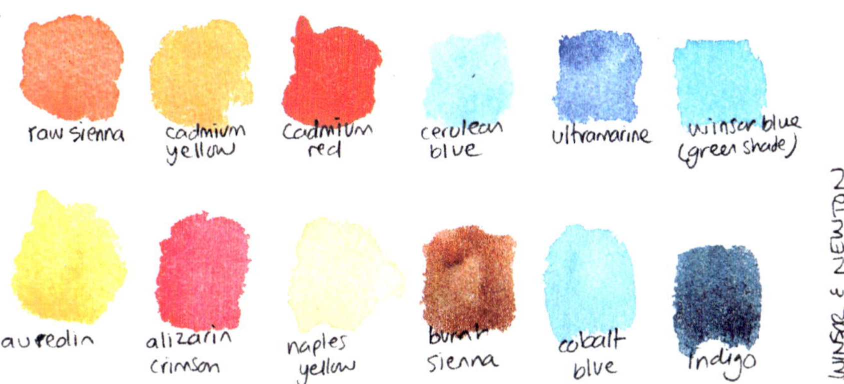

- Reds – alizarin crimson, cadmium red, burnt sienna

- Yellows – aureolin, cadmium yellow, raw sienna, naples yellow

- Blues – cobalt, ultramarine, indigo, cerulean, winsor blue (green shade)

On the first part of the trip I took viridian (a bright turquoise green) instead of burnt sienna as I thought it would be useful for sea colours, but didn't use it much. In the Falklands I swapped it for the burnt sienna which is useful to mix greys, browns and blacks..

I used burnt sienna and indigo for these seals—it's a quick way to create a range of light brown, dark brown and black quickly.

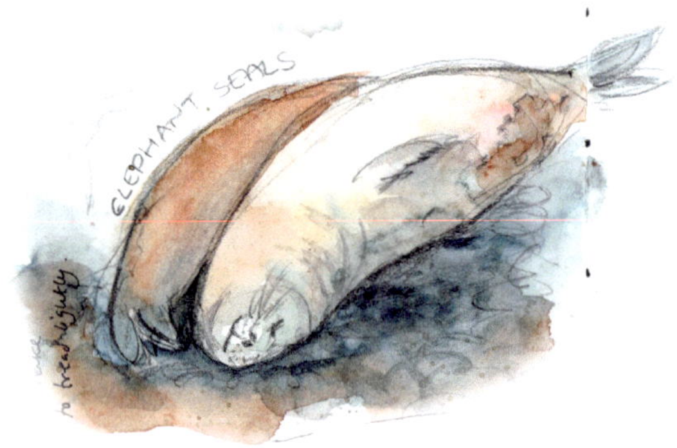

Sketching tips

I'm not going to go into detail here about how to keep a sketchbook. It's never been easier to find out how, with plenty of art courses, websites, groups and books on the subject including my own (*Keeping a Sketchbook Diary* and *One Line at a Time*, both from Golden Duck Publishing). For now I'll simply offer a few tips for sketching on the move.

1. Travel light

The more gear you carry, the less likely you are to use it. If you are walking any distance at all, being loaded down with gear limits your options. I use a small rucksack to keep my hands free and keep all my pencils, pens and paintbox in a small zip up bag.

2. Prepare for weather

Bulldog clips stop your pages flapping about on windy days. I also carry a folding pad to sit on damp grass or rocks, and of course a waterproof jacket. A hat with a brim is useful to help stop glare.

3. Mix words and pictures

I use my sketchbook as a diary, noting down impressions in words as well as images. It's a good way of filling in the gaps. If you're worried about passers by peering at your sketches, start writing instead of drawing and they will back off—drawing is seen as public but writing is private!

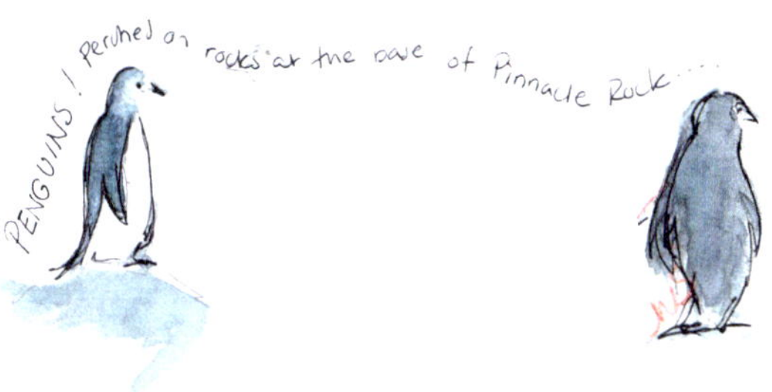

4. Choose your colours to suit the landscape

You'll need different colours in different parts of the world – earth colours for inland, bright colours for tropical gardens, plenty of blues for islands and coast. My challenge on this trip was taking colours to suit a wide variety of landscapes, but it helps that I take mainly primaries so that I can mix any colour I need. I top them up from tubes before I go rather than fiddling around getting the little half pans in and out.

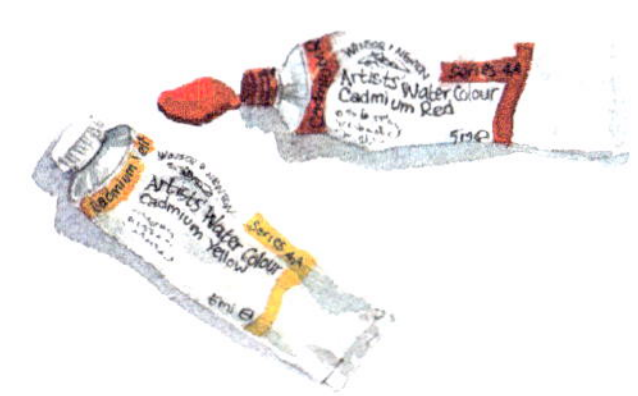

5. Keep water safe

Use a water pot with a lid so that you can stow it quickly if you need to move on. Another option is to use a water brush (which has a reservoir of water) – especially handy if you have to paint standing up and have nowhere to put a water pot.

6. Use a firm support

I use a hardback sketchbook so the covers give a firm support to work on (I prefer stitch bound to spiral bound as I often go across two pages). Another option is to have sheets of paper clipped to a small drawing board.

7. Start anywhere – don't wait!

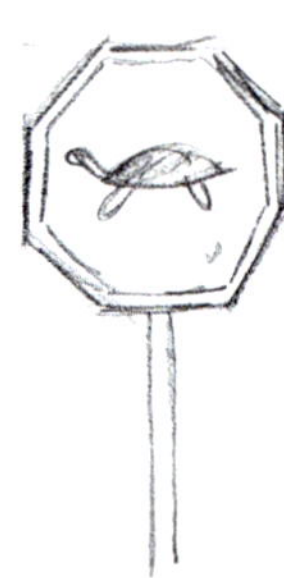

Don't wait until you are in front of a pretty scene to start sketching – drawing can make the ordinary extraordinary. Everything that you see, talk about or think about can be worth noting. Taxis, buses, stopping at a cafe, meals, cakes, signposts, snatches of conversation, anything that catches your eye. Sketchbooks are your personal view on the world.

8. Add a map

If you love maps as much as I do, add them, either drawn freehand, traced or cut out from a brochure and stuck into your book. Then you can illustrate them, write on them, add your journey, or just use them as decoration. You'll notice I stick travel tickets in my book as well, and anything else that catches my eye. Sticking something in your sketchbook is a good way to cover up mistakes, too!

9. Draw on the move

If there is a chance of a wildlife sighting, or I'm with a group and can't stop when I see something I like, I walk with sketchbook in hand and pencil strapped to the book. If the object is moving, don't worry about making a mess, just grab a few lines. All movements tend to repeat so as long as the subject is in sight, wait, then draw again when the pose is repeated. Draw on top of drawings, just keep looking at the object more than at the paper, keep the pencil moving and you'll capture something of what you are seeing.

10. Finish off later

If it's difficult to get paints out on location, get some pencil lines down and add colour as soon as you get back to somewhere with a table. Your colour memory will improve dramatically the more you do it (a quick photo with your phone can be useful, but you'll be surprised at how much you can remember without it). I also add notes later, sketch any bits and pieces I've picked up during the day (leaves, pebbles, feathers, shells) and fill out the page. There is a sense that completing the page is helping to complete the day.

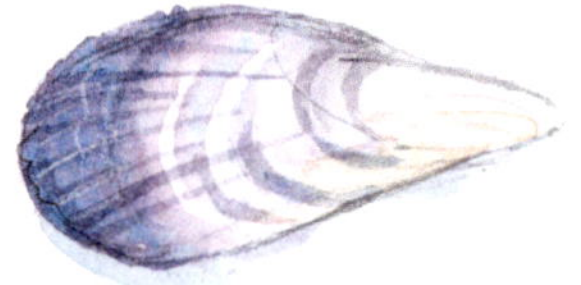 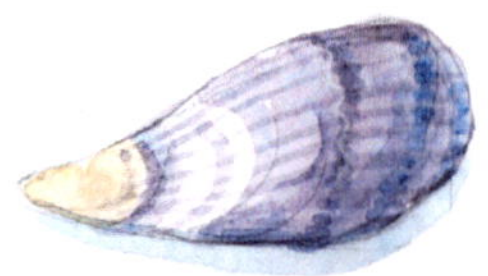

ACKNOWLEDGEMENTS

Firstly, to Jet and Gijs Sluik and their mum Jannette, who have the experience and courage to sail their fine little ship to some of the most extraordinary places on our watery planet. Also to Debbie Purser at *Classic Sailing* who encouraged me to overcome my fears and book the Cape Horn voyage.

To my shipmates on both stages of the voyage. They varied hugely in background, age and nationality but were all unfailingly good natured and interesting company both afloat and ashore. Thanks also to Mike Ford and family for going out of their way to show me the best of East Falkland.

A big thank you to Julia Jones of Golden Duck Publishing, a sailor, wordsmith, editor, book-midwife and much more besides.

Finally, to a French artist by the name of Gildas Chasseboeuf who introduced me to the idea of keeping a sketchbook as a journal. I need to tell you a story if you have the time:

In 2012 I 'hitched a ride' as crew on board a Welsh schooner (thank you Scott Metcalf and the lovely *Vilma*) to the French festival of sail in Brest harbour. The festival takes place every four years; it's the biggest in Europe and a feast of colour, music, culture and watery chaos. I had budgeted ten euros a day for meals ashore and with plenty of quayside food stalls available this worked fine. I don't eat seafood but there were always frites or crepes to be had and enough cash left for some wine. Gildas Chasseboeuf was showing his artwork as one of the shoreside exhibits. He didn't speak much English and my French was not up to telling him how much I liked the colourful sketches he was working on, but he was selling a beautiful hardback book called 'Carnet du Port', full of his humorous, surprising and personal sketches each day of the harbour where he lived.

I knew I had to have this book, but it was 30 euros. I bought it, of course, and had to go the next three evenings without supper. It was worth it and gradually became more of an influence as my interests turned from 'painting pictures' to the wider world of artistic possibilities that grow from using a sketchbook.

I didn't get too hungry, as when you go for a meal with fellow crew members and they notice you are not eating, there's always someone who says 'have a chip - I've got too many here!' Or 'would you like my bread roll? I don't want it...' Always good to know if travelling on a budget!

The phrase 'Carnet du Port' is a variation on 'Carnet du Voyage' - a travel diary. It's traditionally done as a way of making a visual and written record of places visited and sights seen. But you don't have to be a traveller to keep a sketchbook journal. Gildas stayed where he was and sketched the boats, people and events passing through his world. Some of the most beautiful sketchbooks I've seen record the gardening year, and others the life of a town, village or island. The possibilities are as wide as your imagination.

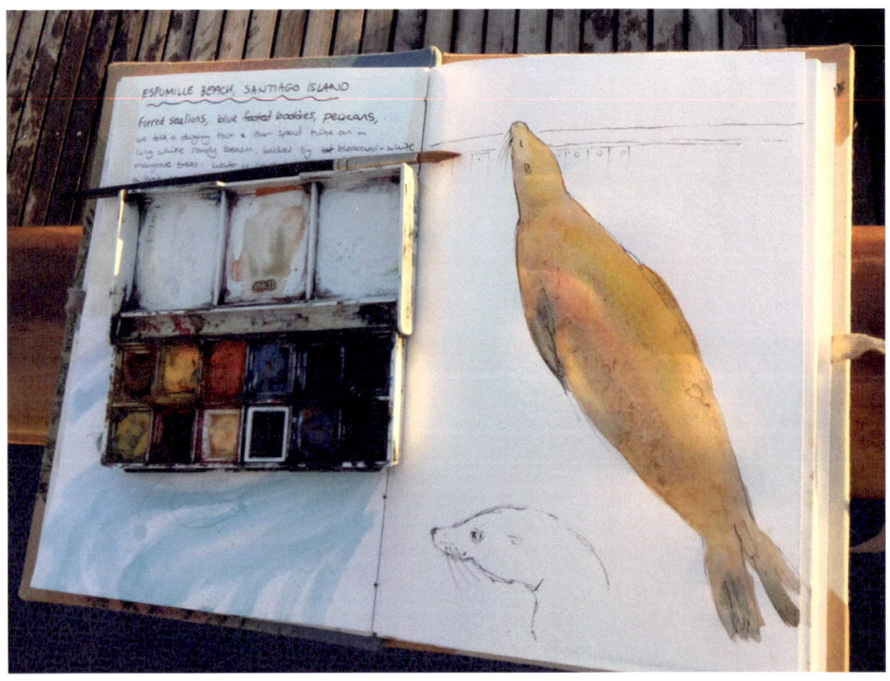